D0226129

KEY CONCEPTS IN COMMUNICATION AND CULTURAL STUDIES

Second Edition

STUDIES IN CULTURE AND COMMUNICATION
General Editor: John Fiske

KEY CONCEPTS IN COMMUNICATION AND CULTURAL STUDIES

Second Edition

Tim O'Sullivan, John Hartley, Danny Saunders, Martin Montgomery and John Fiske

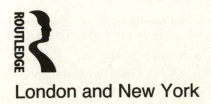

London and New York

First published 1994
by Routledge
11 New Fetter Lane, London EC4P 4EE

Simultaneously published in the USA and Canada
by Routledge
29 West 35th Street, New York, NY 10001

Typeset in Bembo 10/12 Linotron by Florencetype Ltd, Kewstoke
Printed and bound in Great Britain by Clays, St Ives plc

British Library Cataloguing in Publication Data
A catalogue record for this book is available from the British Library

Library of Congress Cataloging in Publication Data
Applied for

ISBN 0–415–06173–3

CONTENTS

GENERAL EDITOR'S PREFACE

This series of books on different aspects of communication is designed to meet the needs of the growing number of students coming to study this subject for the first time. The authors are experienced teachers or lecturers who are committed to bridging the gap between the huge body of research available to the more advanced student, and what new students actually need to get them started on their studies.

Probably the most characteristic feature of communication is its diversity: it ranges from the mass media and popular culture, through language to individual and social behaviour. But it identifies links and a coherence within this diversity. The series will reflect the structure of its subject. Some books will be general, basic works that seek to establish theories and methods of study applicable to a wide range of material; others will apply these theories and methods to the study of one particular topic. But even these topic-centred books will relate to each other, as well as to the more general ones. One particular topic, such as advertising or news or language, can only be understood as an example of communication when it is related to, and differentiated from, all the other topics that go to make up this diverse subject.

The series, then, has two main aims, both closely connected. The first is to introduce readers to the most important results of contemporary research into communication together with the theories that seek to explain it. The second is to equip them with appropriate methods of study and investigation which they will be able to apply directly to their everyday experience of communication.

If readers can write better essays, produce better projects and pass more exams as a result of reading these books I shall be very satisfied; but if they gain a new insight into how communication shapes and informs our social life, how it articulates and creates our experience of industrial society, then I shall be delighted. Communication is too often taken for granted when it should be taken to pieces.

John Fiske

PREFACE TO
THE SECOND EDITION

In this edition we have added one new author and 60 new entries. The book is 90 pages longer, the references are expanded from 13 to 21 pages, and we've added 'cultural studies' to the 'communication studies' of the original title. Meanwhile, 14 of the original entries have been deleted altogether, and a few others entirely rewritten. Minor editorial changes have been throughout as necessary.

Now we are five, we have decided to identify who wrote what by 'signing' each entry with the initials of its author. We think this will assist readers by making clear that the concepts are written from differing disciplinary and personal perspectives. Such differences are an inevitable consequence of the increasing diversity of cultural and communication studies, not to mention our own geographical dispersal across three continents (to Australia, England, Scotland, the USA and Wales), since the first edition was published.

In the ten years since then, communication and cultural studies have changed and developed as fields of intellectual inquiry, and they have also become much more institutionalized in universities around the world, both in undergraduate programmes and as recognized research areas. We hope that *Key Concepts in Communication and Cultural Studies* will continue to prove useful and stimulating for those who want to know more.

INTRODUCTION

Fort Knox is reputed to be full of ingots of gold. These ingots are almost uniform blocks, virtually indistinguishable from one another. Although they seem to be intrinsically valuable they are in fact useless in themselves. Their value lies in their potential – what you can get for them in exchange, or what you can make them into by the application of your own resources and skills. So it is with this book. The entries are cast in a uniform shape but they are in fact fairly useless in themselves. It won't pay you to leave them just as you find them – their value too lies in their potential, in what you do with them.

What this amounts to is the difference between treating concepts as ingots of *information* with a given content and a known value on the one hand, and, on the other hand, treating them in terms of their possible *meanings*. Concepts don't 'contain' little nuggets of meaning, however widespread their currency. And their value or meaning need not depend at all on their given or 'obvious' contents – as everyone knows, links can be forged by rhyme as well as reason, and sense can be made by metaphor (transferring meanings across different words) much more readily than it can by stores of information.

In communication and cultural studies it is as important to be alert to potential meanings (even when they are at cross-purposes) as it is to search for exact information. This is because the object of study is the social world that we ourselves inhabit – we are not dealing with an 'exact science'. One of the basic tenets of this book (taken from structuralism) is that without *difference* there is no meaning. That is, signs (like words in general and the following concepts in particular) can be understood only by reference to others in the same system. 'Their most precise characteristic is in being what the others are not' (Saussure 1974, p. 117). So it is with these concepts. Each of them is significant only to the extent that it relates to others, both within and beyond this book. They have no intrinsic but only established and relational meanings, and most of them have more than one.

If you use the book simply to supply yourself with ready-made and self-contained bits of information you may well be able to use them in essays, but by themselves they won't mean very much. In order to make full use of them you need to be alive to their relations and their potential for multiple and sometimes changing and contradictory meanings. Often this can be revealing in unexpected ways. You will find that some entries don't seem to agree with others, and in the unstated differences between them there may be quite important issues at stake. As a result, we hope you will find that the entries as a whole add up to more than the sum of their parts: they mean more than they say. But what they mean depends in the end on what *you* make of them. The 'key' in *Key Concepts in Communication and Cultural Studies* is designed to open things up so that you can take them away and work on them.

As relatively new areas of study, communication and cultural studies have been characterized by fast-moving and innovative research work; by the attempt to say new things in new ways. At the same time, they have borrowed widely from a variety of established academic disciplines and discourses. As a result, there is often an uneasy period of disorientation for the newcomer to communication and cultural studies; a distinct lack of communication between researcher and newcomer. All spheres of intellectual work are of course characterized by their specialist terms and concerns, but in many cases these have become familiar over the years, or else the subject area is served by introductory books and courses designed to make them familiar. Communication and cultural studies are diverse subjects and do not have unified and 'orthodox' contents and terminologies. Whilst that is unsettling, it is also one of the most attractive features of the field of study. For communication and cultural studies have elaborated new discourses, theories, methods of study and even new focal points ('problematics') of research, debate and analysis. In the process, some of our most ingrained assumptions and beliefs have been called into question, including the assumption that what is 'obvious' and 'common sense' is quite as simple and uncontroversial as it appears.

Our experience of teaching in and around communication and cultural studies has led directly to this book. We think that it has a lot to offer once you're familiar with it, but at the same time the day-to-day context of our own work has made it clear that the early period of not being able to see the wood for the trees can be offputting for even the most enthusiastic newcomer. So what follows is a fieldguide to help you identify some of the trees and their position in the wood. It is designed to put together in an accessible form some of the most important concepts that you will encounter, and to show some of the ways in which these concepts have been (or might be) used. Since communication and cultural studies are interdisciplinary and international, we have tried to explain the origin and range of the terms that have been coined or have gained currency in the field. Many terms have been borrowed directly from established disciplines, like sociology, psychology, linguistics, literary theory, etc., though the way they are taken up in communication and cultural studies may have reshaped them somewhat. Other terms are more foreign still, coming from work originally published in French, Russian, German or Italian, or from work that is still 'foreign' to many academic disciplines (for example, Marxism and feminism). And there are quite a number of terms in communication and cultural studies that are also commonplace in 'ordinary language', but which have been tested almost to destruction in a theoretical process that makes them hardly recognizable as the familiar terms we're used to (two such words being communication and culture themselves).

A book like this is risky for both writers and readers. It is risky for the writers because of the need to offer short, introductory entries for each concept that will be widely applicable without 'solidifying' into prescriptive definitions. The risk is that an abstract account won't do justice to the full potential of a given concept, since isolating (abstracting) a concept from the context of its use in particular circumstances necessarily removes it from the social and political relations it is determined by and may itself determine. Thus though it may be helpful to isolate individual concepts for the purposes of explanation, it is certain that each one of them could have been written up in a different way, with different emphases and different assumptions in mind.

It follows that books like this are not without risks for readers too. The entries are not definitions (the book is not a dictionary), which means that we are not claiming privileged access to what each concept 'really' means. They are not destinations but starting points for further intellectual and practical work. We've framed the issues involved, and indicated how you might follow up particular lines of thought through the further reading and the cross-references.* And we'd be glad to hear from you (via the publishers) if you have suggestions for other concepts or different ways of putting things. Meanwhile, having made our introductions, we leave the most interesting part to you: the continuing encounters with cultural, social and political practices that are conducted by means of the discourses and languages we all have to use to make sense of communication and culture in the late twentieth century.

Tim O'Sullivan
John Hartley
Danny Saunders
Martin Montgomery
John Fiske
May 1992

* Each concept is introduced by an explanatory, contextualizing or cautionary sentence enclosed between asterisks. Words in **bold type** indicate concepts with discussion of their own. Almost all of these have their own main alphabetical entries.

aberrant decoding ⋆ This is a term used by Eco (1965) to describe what happens when a message that has been encoded according to one code is decoded by means of another. ⋆ The received **meaning** will therefore differ from the intended one, and the theory of aberrant decoding casts doubt upon the role of intentionality and upon the idea that the meaning is contained in the **message**.

Eco lists a number of kinds of aberrant decoding which range from the ignorance of the original **codes** (as when the Achaean conquerors misinterpreted Cretan symbols) to the overlay or imposition of later codes upon a message (as when early Christians overlaid a Christian meaning upon a pagan symbol or **ritual**, or when post-romantic scholars find erotic images in what an earlier poet conceived of as philosophical allegories).

But the key application of the concept is to the contemporary mass media. The variety of **cultures** and **subcultures** that receive a typical mass mediated message means that it must inevitably be subject to a variety of aberrant decodings if it is to make sense to the variety of cultures receiving it. A news item on the economy will be decoded differently by a Surrey stockbroker, a South Wales steelworker and an aerospace engineer. This brings a new dimension to the term for, as Eco says, 'the aberrant decoding is the rule in the mass media', which leads to the idea that the main influence upon the meaning are the codes available to the reader

1

or **receiver**. As a result, Eco suggests, mass media **texts** tend to be closed. That is they prefer one particular reading over other possible ones: his theory of aberrant decodings suggests that this **closure** is more likely to be effective for those who decode the text according to the dominant codes used in the encoding.

JF

See **closure, discourse, meaning systems, preferred reading, text**
Further reading Eco (1965); Morley (1980, 1986); Gray (1987)

absence ⋆ A concept from **semiotics** and **structuralism** referring to the significant exclusion of a **sign** or element from a position in a **syntagm** that it might potentially occupy. ⋆ The result is that the elements which are selected (present) mean what they do only in contrast to the absent possibilities from which they have been selected. Hence absence is a major determinant of meaning at all levels of **signification**.

JH

See **closure, commutation test, ex-nomination, paradigm, preferred reading**

accent ⋆ Distinctive ways of pronouncing the sounds of a language associated with membership of a particular social **group** defined by reference to either region or social **class**. ⋆ Most **languages** are subject to some kind of regional variation in pronunciation and the more widely dispersed the language the greater is the likelihood of accent variation. Thus, the French of Quebec sounds to a native speaker quite different from the French of Paris; and Portuguese as spoken in Brazil sounds quite different to a native speaker from Portuguese as spoken in Portugal. English is something of an extreme example in this respect since it has a range of different accents which are associated with a distinctive national affiliation: hence, for example, Irish, Indian, American, Nigerian and Australian accents of English. But accent variation does not, of course, stop at this level of differentiation. In the case of British English, for example, there is a whole spectrum of internal variation ranging from regionally marked rural and urban accents (such as Somerset, Scouse or Geordie), through to that pattern referred to as *Received Pronunciation (RP)*, commonly heard on the BBC's World Service, amongst the judiciary, in public schools and so on. In this sense, all speakers have 'an accent', including habitual users of Received Pronunciation. And although this latter accent is now primarily a class-based accent, it is important to note that historically it once had strong regional affiliations with the area south-east from the English Midlands. Its specific promotion through, for example, the English public schools in the nineteenth century, and the BBC in the early phases of sound **broadcasting** helps to explain its social ascendancy today in the UK, where it now seems to be the neutral or unmarked accent of English to such an extent that it becomes identified with the 'natural' and 'right' way of speaking the language. It is probably now the most widely understood and spoken accent within the UK and until recently the accent most commonly adopted for teaching English as a foreign language.

This does not, however, make RP more correct as an accent of English than other patterns of pronunciation. It may command more prestige but it is worth remembering that all accents attract social stigma and approval in varying measure from varying quarters. And, whilst experimental studies of reactions to accents within the UK have shown that RP speakers are rated more highly than regionally accented speakers in terms of general competence, these same studies have also shown that RP speakers emerge less favourably than regionally accented speakers on scales of personal integrity and social attractiveness. Such judgements ultimately have a social rather than a linguistic basis. Judgements of the correctness and aesthetic appeal of particular patterns of pronunciation are similarly difficult to justify by reference to intrinsic properties of the sounds themselves. They are strongly motivated – if unconsciously – by social factors.

MM

See **attitude, dialect, stereotype, variety**
Further reading Hughes and Trudgill (1979); Wells (1982)

accessing ⋆ The practice of including verbal quotations and film/tape interviews or statements (in news/current affairs coverage) which originate from people or groups not directly employed by the media organization itself. ⋆ Accessing is a curious term in use, since it surfaces as a significant issue only when it is absent. So you'll come across demands for access much more frequently than analyses of accessing.

Demands for access are based on a **reflection theory** of the media – that is, that the media ought to reflect the plurality of different **groups**, politics or **lifestyles** that can be identified outside the media in social life. Many groups argue that their access to television is blocked and that as a result they are unable to establish their point of view in the public mind. The assumption often is that the blockage is caused by a more or less deliberate **conspiracy** by the media to exclude them.

Even when access is achieved, 'minority groups' are often disappointed with the coverage they get. This is because the media, as industrial organizations with an extensive division of labour and an **occupational ideology** of **professionalism**, won't let you simply appear on television or radio and state your case or tell your story. What you say is **mediated** by the professionals, and whether you get as far as the studio at all may depend on your own professional or representative **status**.

But the professional **mediation** of accessed voices goes even further than this. It extends to the message itself. Even when you have your say on television, you won't speak for yourself. What you say becomes what television says, and television discourse has its own peculiarities. When a newsreader quotes you or an interviewer questions you, your utterance becomes a discursive element which is subordinate to the **narrative** flow and visual **codes** of the item as a whole. Its meaning is not self-contained, but depends on what is said and seen before and afterwards. You become, in effect, one actor in a drama, and even if you're lucky enough to be playing the lead it is still the case that what you say is significant only in the context of what all the others say, and of what the drama is about. Further, one aspect of your **role** is entirely at odds with your own purposes. For simply by accessing you, the institutional **discourse** is able to claim authenticity and credibility for itself. You become the means through which the *legitimacy* of media representations can be established – whatever it is that you actually say.

There is, then, a conflict of interest between professional media discourses and the demands for access that various groups express. The way this has been handled in practice takes two forms. First, news and current affairs subscribe to the principle of **impartiality**, thereby ensuring that a (narrow and 'balanced') range of voices is accessed on any one topic. Second, specialist 'access programmes' have been established on many networks. In these off-peak slots media professionals may relinquish control of the programme content, but retain control of the production process. Unfortunately, both these well-intentioned practices have negative consequences. Impartiality legitimates the mainstream bipartisan form of politics at the expense of the various single-issue groups (environmental campaigns and so on), ethnic 'minority' groups, socialist or feminist groups, and community groups that tend to end up having to make do with the marginal access slots. For such groups, the very fact of winning access results in **representations** that seem 'naturally' to confirm their marginal status.

JH

See **alternative media, bardic function**
Further reading Hartley (1982, 1992); Glasgow Media Group (1982), Willis and Wollen (1990)

actuality ⋆ Professional term for film/tape footage used in news and current affairs broadcasts, which records events as they happen. ⋆ Contrasted with studio presentation (talking heads) and with archive (stock) footage.

In **semiotic** analysis, actuality is seen as a key device in producing ideological **closure**, by **anchoring** the **preferred reading** on the apparently unarguable 'facts' of the event-as-filmed. Actuality is presented as self-evident; the production processes are rarely shown, so that viewers are encouraged to make sense of the footage in terms of the event, and not of the way it is represented. However, actuality rarely appears on the screen without an accompanying commentary – and considerable professional skill is expended on contextualizing it for the 'benefit' of viewers. As Peter Sissons, a British news presenter has put it:

> Let's remember that although a picture can tell the story, only a word can put it into its historical perspective, can caution against gullibility, can weigh the true significance of the event.
>
> (*Independent Broadcasting*, 1982)

In short, actuality is a device for **naturalizing** meaning (it proposes the cultural as natural); it provides an excuse for commentary.

JH

See **closure, naturalizing, realism**

aesthetics ∗ A concept inherited from idealist philosophy, referring to principles of taste, especially good taste, and hence of beauty. ∗ Popularized as a concept in the late nineteenth century, aesthetics was captured by the discourse of 'art for art's sake', becoming associated with the 'refined' appreciation of beauty in the arts. Its idealist connotations remain, however, in the attempt to elaborate the said principles of taste as transcendent, that is, going beyond any one period, culture or medium, and going beyond any one person's **subjective** responses. The object of study for aesthetics is the art–object itself, taken out of its historical, **cultural** and means–of–production context. It is studied in relation to other art objects and in relation to the already-established **discourse** of aesthetics, with the purpose of isolating those textual properties which can be said to render it beautiful. The difficulty with such an approach, of course, is that it completely fails to 'place' the criteria for taste and beauty within the context of their own production – they are assumed to be somehow 'there' in art objects. This has rightly attracted the criticism of Marxist critics and others who see aesthetics as an **ideological** discourse which attempts to 'objectify' (reify) the interests of one particular **class** faction and pose them as universal abstractions with a claim on all.

However, once recognized as an ideological discourse, bourgeois–idealist aesthetics itself becomes an interesting object of study, raising questions about the relations between particular social formations and their more elaborate forms of **cultural production**. The main question, of course, is can there be a materialist, 'Marxist' or feminist aesthetics, and how would it differ from what exists already?

The term *aesthetic* has gained some currency in **semiotics**, especially in the notion of an *aesthetic code*. This is taken to be a **code** in which the production of meaning within the terms of recognized (conventional) expression is not the aim but the starting point of a given message. It prioritizes the **signifier** over the **signified**, and seeks to exploit rather than confirm the limits and constraints of the form, **genre** or convention within which it operates. Hence aesthetic codes put a premium on innovation, **entropy**, experimentation with the raw materials of **signification**, and are deemed to evoke pleasurable responses for that reason. Semiotics may perhaps claim to have broken ranks with idealist aesthetics in its attempt to find a **value**-free and culturally specific description of aesthetic codes, and thence to find such codes operating in discourses not usually associated with the category 'art': advertising copy, political slogans, graffiti and the output of mass commodity and mass media production, for example.

JH

See **code**

Further reading Bennett (1979); Lovell (1981); Wolff (1981); Bourdieu (1984); Felski (1989)

after image ⋆ The visual or auditory after effect of a **stimulus** as perceived by the viewer or listener. ⋆ Such after effects are typically short-lived but may well interfere with and/or complement other information presented within the same or similar contexts.

Exactly how long the after image lasts for depends on many factors: for example, speed of presentation, **attention** of perceiver, and type of perceptual field within which the original

image, now part of history, was located. Usually, however, we refer to a period of, at most, half a minute following the actual image. You might consider whether the image constitutes **sensation** whereas the after image refers to **perception**.

DS

See **image, perception, subliminal**

agenda setting ★ A term used to describe the ways in which the **media** wittingly or unwittingly structure public debate and awareness. ★ A committee usually has an agenda; a list of topics to be discussed in descending order of importance. Anything not on the agenda is not normally discussed. Media agenda setting refers to the way that the media, particularly in news, current affairs and documentary output, have the power to focus public attention on a defined and limited set of selected issues, while ignoring others. One result is that some topics are widely debated, beyond the media in the public sphere, while others are ignored.

In the first instance agenda setting refers to the question of *what* topics the media present to the **audience**, and second *how* information on those topics is presented. This relates to the dynamics of coverage; for example, *what* spectrum of viewpoints, symbols, questions and so on are selected to construct a particular news item or documentary programme, and crucially *how* they are ranked, or accorded legitimacy and priority. The consequences of this process lie in the ways that the agenda is internalized by the audience, and this relates to the general issue of the role of the media in defining social reality, and their role as agencies of ideological **power**.

TO

See **amplification, frame, moral panic, news values, primary definers**
Further reading Cohen and Young (eds) (1981); McQuail and Windahl (1981); Philo (1990)

alienation ★ A term developed particularly in the work of Marx, to refer to that process whereby individuals become progressively estranged from central aspects of their social existence, which they experience as being controlled by ungovernable 'alien' forces. ⋆ Marx identified alienation as an inevitable feature of the social and economic organization of productive activity in capitalist societies, its causes rooted in the ways that social relations are determined by and responsive to economic forces. These forces, such as wages, profits, demand, supply, and so on, seem to have an independent existence, operating to oppress and control individuals.

The activities of labour and work within such forces and relations of capitalist production, are the main site of alienation. Marx identified four main dimensions of alienation:

First, the *act* and *process of production* itself is fragmented and forced upon the worker, becoming unfulfilling and hence unrewarding. Active and creative production and labour, ideally ends in themselves, become meaningless, serving rather as means to ends.

Second, under capitalism workers become alienated from the *products* of their labour. These are commodities, produced not for themselves but for the market, for consumption and for profit. Workers therefore produce for others, thereby directly contributing to the unequal **class** relations of wealth and property that ensure their continuing subordination.

Third, people become alienated from *others*, as social relations become determined and conditioned by economic forces. Hence the potentially co-operative basis of social life is replaced by exploitative, contradictory and antagonistic relations between **groups** of workers, employers, and owners. Competition and self-interest eclipse communality and co-operation.

Fourth, as a consequence, **individuals** become alienated from *themselves* and their unique potentials, from what Marx called their 'species being', their distinctive capacities to produce creatively, in both conceptual and practical terms. Capitalist forms of production alienate individuals by dividing the unity of production into mental and manual **roles**, serving to suppress individual creativity and fulfilment.

While alienation is often used to describe a **subjective** state of boredom and disorientation, especially in the face of machinery and technology, it is more correctly viewed as an analytic concept referring to an **objective** condition of social life in advanced capitalist societies. It underscores the need to recognize the importance of economic relations as determinants of particular social and cultural forms of **interaction** and communication.

TO

See **base, class, hegemony, ideology**
Further reading Cuff *et al.* (eds) (1979); Worsley (ed.) (1977); Bilton *et al.* (1981); Lukes (1969)

alternative media ⋆ Those forms of mass communication that avowedly reject or challenge established and institutionalized politics, in the sense that they all advocate change in society, or at least a critical reassessment of traditional values. ⋆ They are also referred to as 'radical' or 'underground' media and stand in opposition to mainstream productions by representing political and social doctrines that lie outside the defined limits of parliamentary **consensus** and debate. Community media may also sometimes be classed as alternative in that they frequently represent groups who feel that their viewpoints and concerns are not sufficiently represented within existing local and national media. Often founded to **campaign** on one particular issue, alternative media face considerable problems of survival, given their tendency to be under-financed, and unattractive to advertisers and the mass commercial market.

TO

See **accessing, concentration, independence, representation**
Further reading Minority Press Group (1980) vols 1 and 2; Royal Commission on the Press (1977); Noyce (1976); Fountain (1988)

amplification of deviance ⋆ The process whereby initial activity, labelled as deviant, is increased or 'amplified' as a result of social reaction which is largely co-ordinated and articulated by the mass media. ⋆ The concept has been developed particularly by Wilkins (1964) who argued that under certain conditions when a society receives simplified, **stereotypical** and often misleading information about groups and activities **labelled** as **deviant**, it reacts in such a way as to produce more deviance. Initial information generates an agitated **response**, which in turn uncovers and may promote even greater deviant activity. This cycle is usually presented in the form of a spiral:

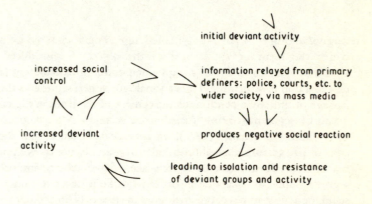

This underscores the role of the mass media in providing information, particularly their provision of labels and definitions of deviancy. Young (1981) suggests that they are 'guardians of the consensus' and in his work in the context of illicit drug use (1971) he provides a comprehensive account of variations on this spiral theme. Rock (1973) offers an alternative interpretation of this self-fulfilling cycle, involving the following stages:

(1) An apparent 'crime wave' appears, orchestrated by mass media, which generates increased public concern.
(2) Public concern, expressed and represented by mass media, pressure groups and political demands focuses the attention of police and control agencies on the deviant activity.
(3) This increase of attention boosts arrest rates apparently uncovering greater or increasing deviance.
(4) This accelerates the crime wave and further mobilizes public sentiment and concern (go back to stage 1).

The concept offers a useful way both to think through and to analyse specific examples.

TO

See **agenda setting, deviance, labelling, moral panic, primary definers**

Further reading Young (1971); Cohen and Young (eds) (1981); Rock (1973); Hall *et al.* (1978)

analogue/analogy ⋆ An unsegmented representation or code in which the form or appearance of the object is reproduced. ⋆ Often opposed to *digital* (a segmented **code**) or **homology** (a reproduction of structure). Thus an analogue watch represents the passage of time by a continuous movement of the hand, a digital watch by segments of time (usually one second). A photograph is, according to Barthes (1977), an analogue of reality, and the code of **proxemics** an analogue code. In practice, just as we put marks for each minute on a watch-face, so we need to impose segments upon an analogue in order to make it easier to understand, or at least to **perceive** analogues in segments (in proxemics we perceive 18 inches to 3 feet approximately as an intimate distance, 3 feet to 8 feet as private or personal, and over 8 feet as public). In 'reading' a photograph, the segmentation occurs in both the first and second orders of **signification**. Thus on the first order, a photograph of a familiar object from an unfamiliar angle or distance cannot be 'read' until we know which marks on the **signifier** are categorized with others to enable us to form a **signified**. We have to categorize the analogic, unsegmented marks on the (temporarily) meaningless signifier in order to understand what the photograph is of. In more conventional photographs, of course, this process is non-conscious and apparently unproblematic, but it still occurs. In the second order we need to categorize parts of the photograph in order to understand them according to the **codes** and **conventions** of our cultural position (which is the only way that we can understand them). A photograph of political demonstrators, for one instance, may be decoded by one reader as a mob of long-haired layabouts, while another may decode them as being representative of all ages, both sexes and of a range of classes and races. The second reader is segmenting the photograph differently and is thus negotiating a different set of meanings for it. Most photographs have captions (words are not analogues) to guide the reader in this process. Barthes calls this **anchorage**.

JF

See **anchorage, code, preferred reading**

anchorage ⋆ A term used by Barthes (1977) to describe the main way in which words work upon visual images – usually advertisements or news photographs. ⋆ Photographs are potentially *open texts* and words are used to direct the reader towards a particular **preferred reading** of the image. Words 'fix the floating chain of signifieds' and Barthes illustrates his theory by referring to an advertisement showing a few fruits scattered round a ladder. This could mean the paucity of the harvest, the damage done by winds, or freshness. The words 'as if from your own garden' close off the unwanted readings, and strongly prefer the one of 'freshness'. Written or spoken words usually operate to close down the potential range of meanings suggested by advertising images, and in recent years they have often done this in a reflexive or joking fashion. News photographs and imagery are also conventionally anchored by means of a caption, a commentary or voice-over. This serves to reduce the potential 'openness' of the image, and, in seeking to interpret and naturalize its significance, may act as a guide for readers or viewers. Barthes explains however that words identify the *desired* connotation of the image: 'The (verbal) text loads the image, burdening it with a culture, a moral, an imagination.' He concludes that the final function of anchorage is ideological.

JF

See **closure, preferred reading**

anomie ⋆ A concept originating in the work of Durkheim (1858–1917) referring to the state of **individuals** and **groups** when they are deprived of, or lose, secure and meaningful **norms** to regulate their expectations and conduct. ⋆ Anomie is the consequence of an absence of appropriate social and moral regulation, and may result in depression, deviance, and in extreme cases suicide or homicide. It suggests that what are apparently individual 'states of mind' should in fact be understood as products and responses to their wider social and cultural conditions (see, for example, Durkheim's study of suicide).

In many senses the term is used to describe the social experience of powerlessness, and disorientation. It was extended in the work of Merton (1957) to explain **deviance**. He suggested that anomie characterized certain groups who experienced a conflict between the goals defined by the wider society (that is, material success) and their likelihood or means of achieving such goals. Deviance (for example, robbing a bank) is therefore viewed as a result of anomic tension or 'strain'.

Durkheim saw anomie as an increasingly characteristic feature of modern life, because of the nature of social relationships in rapidly changing and unstable conditions.

TO

See **alienation, norm**
Further reading Lukes (1969); Giddens (1978); Worsley (ed.) (1977); Bilton *et al.* (1981); Thompson (1982); Mestrovic (1991)

anti-language ⋆ A term used to describe those languages that are more or less consciously generated and sustained to express opposition to a dominant linguistic order. ⋆ As such they represent forms of resistance in the linguistic sphere. As Halliday (1978) has noted, they are rooted within 'anti-societies' such as **deviant** or criminal subcultures, their function being to express opposition to the dominant order, and to maintain and increase the solidarity of their members. In this way they operate to keep out outsiders, and as a means of expressing the tensions and antagonisms between the realities of subordinate **groups** and the wider, **hegemonic** order.

Examples of anti-languages would include Elizabethan 'pelting speech' and its Victorian counterpart 'gobbledygook', both languages of vagabonds and criminals; 'Grypserka' the anti-language of Polish prison inmates; and cockney rhyming slang which served to express a particular local identity and system of values, in the same way that the language of Rastafarian **subcultures** operates to articulate the oppositional identity and values of some black West Indian youth. The language of Rap music and culture provides a recent example.

TO

See **deviance, language, subculture**
Further reading Halliday (1978)

archetype ⋆ An underlying process which determines the form of imagery and symbolism although not necessarily its content. ⋆ This concept was especially emphasized by Jung (for many years Freud's closest student and colleague), and occupies a central position within the subsequent school of analytical psychology. Archetypes are to be inferred from a vast range of **symbols** and **images** which appear to have some common property, or shared characteristics, which allow them to be traced back to simpler yet stronger **signs**. As such, an archetypal image possesses powerful appeal, is highly motivated, and may transcend cultural and historical boundaries. Jung (1969) takes the reader on a journey through **nations**, religions and eras whilst all the time comparing and contrasting symbolic **representations** that have been highly valued by societies. He suggests that much cultural content should be followed back to its earliest primordial beginnings: the resulting archetypal roots include 'the shadow' (a moral problem, revealing the darker side of personality); the 'anima' (the inner, and possibly the most repressed, face of man which is best represented by femininity); the 'animus' (the inner, and possibly the most repressed, face of woman which is best represented by masculinity). There are other archetypes – such as 'the persona', 'the old wise man', 'mother', and 'trickster', but from the very mention of these words you can see the ambition to classify images for all people in all societies. To illustrate, if we return to the anima/animus, Jung (1969) simply states: 'A very feminine woman has a masculine soul, and a very masculine man has a feminine soul'. The problem with the concept of archetype is that it deals in such generalities that a close definition according to content is impossible: the content is too varied to be scientifically pinned down. Instead, and as emphasized by Storr (1983), archetypes manifest themselves through an ability to organize images and ideas at an unconscious level which might be occasionally detected at a later date. Jung's own favourite **analogy** was with the axial system of crystal: ions and molecules aggregate according to a given system, but the resulting crystalline masses can be of different sizes and shapes – all that remains constant is the geometric proportions of each crystalline cell.

Jung's search for underlying patterns within symbolic worlds thus complements a science of signs, in as much as he attempts to identify large-scale paradigms for cultural imagery. It is therefore somewhat ironic that so little reference is made to Saussure or **semiology** in Jung's writing – or that later **structuralist** and semiotic theorists have not recognized Jung's interpretations. This may be because of certain psychodynamic assumptions which determine much Jungian literature: for example, that there may be a collective of inherited **unconscious** for various social groups, that this might imply a genetic blueprint for consciousness and unconsciousness (especially when Jung discusses the concept of **race**, as noted by Billig (1976)). At times discussions of archetypes become positively speculative as with the possibility of an underlying form which determines a link between an imagined and real event – for example, dreaming about a long-forgotten friend and then actually hearing about that person soon afterwards. For Jung this is meaningful coincidence; where the simultaneous occurrence of symbols within the lives of separate individuals (notwithstanding the intervention of mass communication) underlines the importance of shared coincidence associated with a collective unconscious. This type of argument borders on a world of spirituality and psychic phenomena: in so doing, Jung's work has often been marginalized within the discipline of psychology.

We might also be suspicious of such an ambitious project which examines **signifier/signified** relations in so many cultures and eras: is it possible to achieve this when historical evidence can be so patchy and when such different languages, religions and art forms have to be familiarized? Even so, analysis of 'clustered' images has been aided by the archetype concept, which emphasizes a world of symbolism that goes way beyond the popular imagery of television screens or newspaper advertisements, and that extends to dream worlds and **memories**.

DS

See **condensation, image, psychoanalytical theory, subconscious, symbol, unconscious**

Further reading   Samuels (1985); Storr (1983); Jung (1969)

articulation   ∗ In cultural studies, articulation doesn't carry its most familiar sense of 'uttering clearly'. It is used in the sense you may recognize from 'articulated lorry' – where articulation denotes the joining of two things together. In **cultural studies**, what may be articulated are not two components of a truck but large-scale social forces (especially *modes of production*), in a particular configuration or *formation* at a particular time, called a *conjuncture*, to produce the structural determinants of any given practice, text or event.   ∗   Just as an articulated lorry has a prime mover and a trailer (where the prime mover, though smaller and lighter, determines the movement of the trailer – it provides motive force *to* the trailer), so articulation describes not simply a combination of forces but a hierarchical relationship between them. Forces aren't simply joined or jointed, they are '*structured in dominance*'.

The term comes from Marxist analysis, where it refers to the articulation of different *modes of production*. The economic and social relations of a society during a given epoch will display an articulation of different modes of production – capitalist, feudal and even communal, all at once – but one of these modes of production is *structured in dominance* over the others or '*overdetermines*' them and obliges them to adapt to its needs, or integrates them to the mechanisms of its **reproduction**. Hence the *feudal* monarchy survives into the *capitalist* epoch, but is adapted to its purposes; or an industry like publishing retains feudal relations between **author** and publisher within the overall capitalist mode of production of books; or a social **institution** like the family allows for communal modes of production to be exploited by a capitalist economy. These are classic articulations.

Lately, however, the term has been extended in use to include articulations of other social forces. You might read, for instance, of the articulation of **race** and **class** in an analysis of **subcultural** music; or of the articulation of **gender** and **nation** in an analysis of sport.

The term peppers the writings of analysts who are not only Marxist but also connected with the Birmingham Centre for Contemporary Cultural Studies in Britain. Elsewhere it has been used to account for certain problems in cultural anthropology, especially the specific forms of, say, Asian or pre-conquest American modes of production within a Marxist (i.e. Eurocentric and modernist) framework of analysis.

JH

See **cultural reproduction, ideological state apparatuses, interpellation**

attitude ⋆ An opinion, belief or **value** judgement which is based on experience or shared knowledge. ⋆ These dispositions either develop through direct **experience** or are learned from others through **socialization**. The study of attitudes is particularly important when assessing **stereotypes**, **bias**, **prejudice**, **persuasion**, and survey material. With particular reference to attitudes about people, it is important to recognize how often we display attitudes towards new **groups** with which we have had little or no contact. For example, we may form stereotypes about journalists, thinking of them as ambitious, well-travelled, tough and cynical, without ever having met one. In this sense the process of generalization occurs, where an attitude extends from specific instances within a category to include all members of that category.

Attitudes can be said to have three main components: the **cognitive** or intellectual (the information that is at hand about the target); the emotional or affective (the 'gut reaction' to such information); and the behavioural (the degree to which we act out that which we know and feel). In this way a football supporter can have an extensive knowledge of his or her team's history, a liking of the game, and will have attended some fixtures. It is difficult to describe intellectual and affective qualities because they can usually be inferred only from the behavioural component. When faced with **questionnaires** people often give replies which they think **conform** to others' expectations of them, and which are therefore socially acceptable. In this way respondents to attitude tests may well provide contrived answers. Because of this possibility many questionnaires ask seemingly indirect questions, in the hope that people will not realize the actual purposes of the test, and will therefore provide 'real' and spontaneous answers.

Attitude measurement is thus considered to be a highly problematic area in terms of the reliability and validity of replies and in the ethics of deceiving participants. These are important considerations to bear in mind when reading data gleaned from studies of attitude measurement (particularly opinion polls and market research surveys).

DS

See **bias, methodology, persuasion, prejudice, questionnaire**

Further reading Tajfel and Fraser (1978); McCroskey and Wheeless (1976); Eiser (1986)

audience ⋆ The unknown **individuals** and **groups** towards whom mass communications are addressed. ⋆ In its original sense the term refers to that relatively restricted, but public, group of listeners who can be encompassed within hearing of a performance. Goffman (1974) and others working in the **dramaturgical** tradition have utilized the term in the analysis of everyday interaction, breaking **encounters** down into actors, actresses and audiences. It is employed, by extension of its original use, to describe all members of advanced industrial societies, whose **consumption** of and interaction with media products constitutes 'at least a mark, and possibly even a requirement of membership of modern society' (McQuail 1969, p. 3).

Not surprisingly the audience has traditionally formed a prime, if not the, overwhelming focus for **mass communication** research, although overriding concerns have tended to be framed within the analysis of direct unmediated **effects**. Early research images of the mass media audience claimed that it was fragmented, passive and impersonal, thus underscoring the vulnerability of the individual within the mass to powerful media stimuli. This view has now been variously supplanted by more complex and productive sets of perspectives on the socially structured nature of the audience, particularly the consequences of social context for the interpretative relationships established between members of different social groups in society, and mass media **texts**.

TO

See **discourse, effects, meaning systems, preferred reading**
Further reading Ang (1991); Morley (1992); Seiter *et al.* (eds) (1989); Moores (1992); Fiske (1989a, 1989b)

author/ship ⋆ A **common sense** concept which accounts for meaning by ascribing it to a creative, individual source. ⋆ Commonsensically, an author's intentions govern and warrant a particular reading for **texts**, whose **meanings** are taken to be a form of private property, belonging to the author (even though the text itself, in the form of a book, may belong to the reader). Meaning is deemed to be a creation of individual genius or **experience**, which is then transferred in a linear way directly to the brain of the reader. The activity of reading is reduced to that of a receiver, more or less finely tuned to pick up the already-finished meanings sent down the **channel** by the author. This **common sense** approach to authorship has become controversial in recent textual criticism, because it takes the obvious fact that texts are written or scripted by a human agent (or agents) and uses this fact to underpin the highly ideological theory of meaning outlined above.

An author is not 'one who writes'. Only some writers and writings 'count' for the purposes of authorship. For instance, private, ephemeral and functional writings usually don't count as authored; letters, diaries, shopping lists, school exercises, notes in the margins of books, telephone messages and even 'creative writing' – most things that most people actually write. In the public domain the same applies. It would be hard to find an author for labels, advertisements, news, posters, street and shop signs, graffiti, junk mail, technical instructions, etc. – perhaps most of the reading matter we encounter from day to day.

Nor is authorship found any more readily in creative and fictional writing. Much of the fiction circulating in modern societies comes in the form of television and movies, where the concept of authorship is very hard to sustain, given the input of so many people in the production process. Other creative works circulate orally and aurally – stories, jokes, songs. These too escape the traditional definition of authorship, even when they can be traced to an individual writer.

Authorship is a creation of literary culture and the marketplace; it is one of the great markers of 'high' as opposed to **'popular' culture**, and it is invoked to ascribe not just meaning but value – **aesthetic** or moral as well as monetary – to works and authors identified by literary criticism (and marketing managers) as 'significant'. Once an author's name has been established, then potentially any writing under that name counts as authored – even down to shopping lists, if any were to turn up that had been penned by, say, Shakespeare. Such are the ironies of 'significance'.

Authorship is, then, a social system imposed on the domain of writing; it is not the act or trade of writing. It is a system for producing hierarchies within that domain. Authors are a product of a social division of labour, and authorship is an **ideological** notion which functions to privilege not only certain kinds of writing and writers, but also, more importantly, certain ways of thinking about the meaning of texts.

The ideology of authorship locates the source of literary quality not in aspects of writing itself – the exploitation of **genre**, **convention**, **rhetoric**, **intertextuality** and so on – but in the bodies of writers. Creativity, inspiration, experience, the ability to 'express' thought, emotion and truth: these personal attributes are supposed to emanate from a free-floating individual consciousness which is assumed to the source of meaning, with writing merely a transparent medium through which the great

21

thoughts can flow to the reader's equally free-floating consciousness.

The ideology of authorship leads, for example, to the fruitless search for 'what Shakespeare *really* meant' – an impossible quest which leads inexorably to the imposition of authoritarian meanings on a given work by a critic who seeks to establish *one* reading as the only or *true* reading. In other words, any appeal to 'the author's intentions' is coercive – it seeks to impose **ideological closure** on a text, to minimize its **polysemic** potential. It's dishonest too, imputing to the author meanings which are necessarily the creation of the critic. 'Intentionalist' criticism is reduced to second-guessing an author who's conveniently absent, often dead, so it's impossible to verify what his or her intentions were.

Moreover, an author's intentions do not account for the meanings of a text. Even if the author can be interrogated, as, for example, in an interview, what results from this process is not a direct account of his or her intentions, but merely *another text*. Authors always work within the domain of writing, which is an autonomous domain with its own history, modes of production, genres, conventions and established practices. Writers are to a large extent at the mercy of the discursive resources available to them, and creativity comes not from abstract 'genius' but from an ability to exploit these resources. Once written, a text takes on a life of its own, and what it means depends on the conditions of its circulation and the uses to which it is put in different places and times. Its meanings are always plural, and always exceed what the writer thought was going on, intentionally or otherwise.

However, so established has the concept of authorship become that it has achieved a kind of **hegemony**. It seems to represent a pathological desire for an ultimate origin, a god who will finally limit the infinite potentiality of meaning.

The desire for a singular origin for meaning has proved strong enough to infiltrate areas of culture hitherto regarded as too lowbrow to warrant authors, especially cinema, where the 'auteur' approach seeks to account for certain films by conferring author-status on their director. Naturally, 'auteur' directors are credited with 'significance', which may be traced across a number of films, and their 'genius' is seen as an individual 'vision'.

However, the source of meaning in cinema is notoriously hard to pin down, that is to say, there is no one source, even at the point of production, let alone once a film is released into the cultural sphere at large. But 'auteur' theory fixes upon just one person to represent the creative input of the whole cast and crew – often hundreds of people working on and off for months or even years, all of whom may change for that director's next project. And in the history of cinema it has never been clear who out of all these people should be treated authorially – the screenwriter has never enjoyed this status, but it has been conferred not only on directors but also on stars and, more recently, even on producers.

It seems in cinema, as in literature itself, that authorship is more a way of organizing marketing strategies, and conferring value on intellectual property, than a way of accounting for meaning.

The general reader or viewer approaches authors not as persons at all but *textually*; either solely by engagement with a text, or additionally by knowledge gained *intertextually* about the author. The author is 'implied' in the writing itself. Hence, for readers, authors are not persons but an ensemble of **rhetorical** and **narrative** ploys, dedicated to hooking and drawing them into the writing. Throughout any discursive text or fictional story there are devices which 'guide' the reader as to its **preferred reading** and direction. Such devices may also be more intrusive or coercive – an authorial introduction telling readers how to read what follows, or a cover blurb which seeks to sell the writing on the basis of the author's name, institutional clout or biographical credibility.

JH

See **cultural production, difference, individualism, sender/receiver, subjectivity, text**
Further reading Wolff (1981); Barthes (1977)

autonomy/relative autonomy ⋆ The degree to which **individuals** (agents) and **institutions** (agencies) while determined by wider socio-historical structures and processes are nevertheless self-controlling, self-determining and able to act independently of those external forces. ⋆ The term serves to raise a general problem in the study of societies, culture and communication, which is posed on three analytically distinct levels.

(1)   The *structural*: where the problem concerns the inter-relationships between elements or 'parts' of social structures, the ways in which they may combine or relate historically, especially with regard to issues of social change or transformation. A persistent focus for debate, for example, has been the degree to which ideas, **ideologies**, or cultural movements can be seen as autonomous from, as opposed to produced and shaped by, other structural forces, such as the economic, the political, the technological and so on.

(2)   The *institutional*: here the concern is with the power relations between and within institutions and processes of social organization. The degree to which **broadcasting** institutions and their personnel are able to act autonomously of state and commercial control forms a useful example of the problem at this level.

(3)   The *interactive*: here the focus is on the extent to which individual identities, biographies and actions can be seen as products determined by wider social, psychological and historical processes and structures as opposed to the view that they are autonomous, spontaneous, and innovative.

In all of these cases, and the debates surrounding the questions they raise, the central problem rarely concerns absolute autonomy or unbounded freedom, as against total determinism. Rather the major issue at stake is the degree of *relative autonomy* of particular phenomena, whereby autonomy is redefined *within* certain limits or structures.

TO

See   **determination, determinism, ideology**

B

bardic function ★ A comparative concept, proposing a similarity between the social role of television and that of the bardic order in traditional Celtic societies. ★ The concept was suggested by Fiske and Hartley (1978) to emphasize the active and productive **signifying** work of television. The idea is that like the original bards in medieval Celtic societies, the media are a distinct and identifiable social institution, whose role is to mediate between the rulers and patrons who license and pay them, and the society at large, whose doings and sayings they render into a specialized **rhetorical** language which they then play back to the society. The concept seemed necessary to supersede previous conceptualizations of the media, which had concentrated on the way they were/are supposed to reflect their society. The notion of the bardic function goes beyond this, first in its insistence on their role as manipulators of language, and then in its emphasis on the way they take their **mediating** role as an active one, simply reproducing neither the opinions of their owners, nor the '**experience**' of their viewers. Instead, the 'bardic' media take up signifying 'raw materials' from the societies they represent, and rework them into characteristic forms which appear as 'authentic' and 'true to life' not because they are but because of the **professional** prestige of the bard and the familiarity and **pleasure** we have learnt to associate with bardic offerings.

One implication of this notion is that once established, bardic television can play an important role in dealing with social conflict and cultural change. Dealing as it does in signification – **representations** and **myths** – the ideological work it performs is largely a matter of rendering the unfamiliar into the already known, or into '**common sense**'. It will strive to make sense of both conflict and change according to these familiar strategies. Hence bardic television is a strongly reactionary or *socio-central* force for its 'home' culture. It uses **metaphor** to render new and unfamiliar occurrences into familiar forms and meanings. It uses **binary oppositions** to represent oppositional or marginal groups as deviant or 'foreign'. As a result, it strives to encompass all social and cultural action within a **consensual** framework. Where it fails, as it must, to 'claw back' any group or occurrence into a consensual and familiar form, its only option is to represent them as literally outlandish and senseless. Bardic television, then, not only makes sense of the world, but also marks out the limits of sense, and offers us everything beyond that limit as nonsense.

JH

Further reading   Fiske and Hartley (1978); Hartley (1982, 1992); see also Williams (1981); Turner (1990)

base   ⋆ Derived from Marx's analysis of societies and social change, this concept **metaphorically** refers to the fundamental economic structure or 'material foundations' of a given society.   ⋆   Its usage also denotes the more or less determining relationship that Marx distinguished between these 'foundations', and other parts of a society, which he termed the *superstructure*:

> the economic structure of society [is] the real foundation on which arises a legal and political superstructure and to which correspond definite forms of social consciousness. The mode of production of material life conditions the general processes of social, political and intellectual life.
>
> (Marx 1971, pp. 20–1)

Marx argued for a materialist view of history, whereby changes in societies, and certain key dimensions of their social structure, such as **class** divisions, are seen to stem from, and be initiated by, changing relations in the economic base. The Marxist concept for a particular social organization of economic **production** is *mode of production*, and Marx argued that history could be divided into different periods, each of which was characterized by a different mode of production. He called these primitive communism (for example, tribal societies); ancient slaveholding (for example, ancient Rome); the feudal (for example, medieval Europe); capitalism and communism. A particular mode of production is distinctive in its combination of specific forces of production, with specific social relations of production.

By *forces of production* Marx directed attention towards the complex of material and social factors that shape any society's ability to produce. These would include raw materials, labour, and technical knowledge and machineries as they are organized in the production process. The *relations of production* refer to the social distribution of the ownership of the forces and means of production within any society, and as a consequence the way in which the economic product is distributed. He argued that in capitalist societies these relations are structured by the private ownership of the means and forces of production, which determine social class relations between those groups and individuals who do and do not own property and the means to create wealth.

A crucial point to note here is that the superstructure, which includes the spheres of politics, education, the family, and culture, is in effect shaped and conditioned by the economic base. As Williams (1977) has noted:

> Any modern approach to a Marxist theory of culture must begin by considering the proposition of a *determining* base and a *determined* superstructure. (p. 75)

The economic base is therefore an integral concept in Marxist theory, capable of uniting and giving direction to the study of communication, culture and society. It should be handled with care.

TO

See **class, determination, hegemony, ideology, power, production**
Further reading   Cuff *et al.* (eds) (1979); Williams (1977); Worsley (1982); McLellan (1975); Turner (1990)

behaviourism ⋆ A philosophy in social science – and especially in psychology – which stresses the importance of empirically observing 'behaviour' (as opposed to invisible mental processes – such as thoughts, feelings and memories). ⋆ Authors such as Skinner (1974) emphasize the importance of studying environmental influence, which is understood in terms of *stimuli* that cause people's and animals' behavioural 'responses'. The major feature of behaviourist theories is their continual reference to the **individual**, and to controlled observation – often involving **experimentation** in laboratories. Because the strict emulation of science is the basis for such research, the desire for experimental control and for replicable data has led not only to the isolation of the individual, but also to the generalization from the behaviour of rats or pigeons to that of human beings. Out of behaviourist research, it is claimed that general laws have been established for behaviour. Indeed the behaviourist stimulus response model has underpinned a great deal of research on **persuasion**, and the effects of mass media on **audiences**.

Behaviourist criticisms of other methods as value laden, non-scientific, and open to **bias** have attracted the critical attention of those researchers who emphasize the *importance* of **subjectivity** and who question the scientific study of the individual. Assumptions about the relevance of laboratory-based research to 'real life' have been seriously questioned. Furthermore, any general emulation of the scientific method by researchers of society and social relationships leads to a questioning of the basic tenets of behaviourism. Can the complexities of social phenomena ever be analysed in the same way, and with the same degrees of confidence, as the study of rats in mazes?

Despite such queries, behaviourist-oriented approaches have continued to draw much research funding in the study of communication – not least because of their ability to offer tangible advice about social influence and social control. One of the key words in behaviourist literature is 'shaping' – where responses are gradually moulded by someone else who selectively rewards the 'right' action and punishes the 'wrong' behaviour. Shaping principles have been applied to the school, the mental hospital, the prison, and in some cases television or cinema audiences.

DS

See **empiricism, methodology, objectivity, positivism, response**

Further reading Skinner (1974); McQuail and Windahl (1981); Hall (1983)

bias ＊ A **common sense** term for the presumed distortions in media representations that result from (i) deliberate **prejudice** against or (ii) unwitting neglect of an aspect of a story or a party to a dispute. ＊ The notion of bias is extraordinarily influential in public debates about the media, especially news. But it is not in fact a very useful metaphor for the way media **representations** work. It assumes that these representations simply 'reflect' a pre-given 'real' ('natural') world; and it assumes that this world is endowed with an essential truth that can be rendered without bias. Neither of these assumptions stands up to close inspection. Events are very different from representations of events, so these cannot simply reflect events; and the idea that there is just one truth inherent in an event or a representation is usually a sure sign of special pleading – where one's own point of view is imputed to the event itself.

The problem with the concept of bias is not that the media are free from particular interests or **ideologies**, nor that they can escape the charge of representing certain points of view more often and more systematically than others. The problem with the concept of bias is that it is too simplistic to account for the very real characteristics of media output that it is supposed to describe. If you imagine the media as rolling forward in a line that would be straight but for some 'inbuilt bias' (the metaphor comes from the game of bowls), you'll end up misunderstanding the media. Further, discussions about bias lead more or less inevitably to questions about the identity of those towards or against whom the media are biased – so you then have to beware you don't fall into **conspiracy theory** as well.

It might be more helpful for the purposes of analysis if the term were avoided altogether – it is more appropriate as an object of study in itself; 'bias' as a *part* of media **discourses**, not an explanation of them. Alternative analytical approaches and terms can be found under the following entries.

JH
See **consciousness industry, cultural reproduction, discourse, hegemony, ideology, impartiality, news values**
Further reading   Philo (1990)

binary opposition   * An analytic category from **structuralism**, used to show how meanings can be generated out of two-term systems.   *   Basic propositions are as follows:

(1) *Meaning is generated by opposition* This is a tenet of Saussurian linguistics, which holds that **signs** or words mean what they do only in opposition to others – their most precise characteristic is in being what the others are not. The *binary* opposition is the most extreme form of significant difference possible. In a binary system, there are only two signs or words. Thus, in the opposition LAND:SEA the terms are mutually exclusive, and yet together they form a complete system – the earth's surface. Similarly, the opposition CHILD:ADULT is a binary system. The terms are mutually exclusive, but taken together they include everyone on earth (everyone can be understood as either child or adult). Of course, everyone can be understood by means of other binaries as well, as for instance in the binary US:THEM – everyone is either in or not in 'our **nation**'.

Such binaries are a feature of **culture** not **nature**; they are products of signifying systems, and function to structure our perceptions of the natural and social world into order and meaning. You may find binaries underlying the stories of newspaper and television news, where they separate out, for example, the parties involved in a conflict or dispute, and render them into meaningful oppositions.

(2) *Ambiguities are produced by binary logic and are an offence to it* Consider the binaries mentioned so far:

LAND:SEA
CHILD:ADULT
US:THEM

These stark oppositions actively suppress ambiguities or overlaps between the opposed categories. In between land and sea is an *ambiguous category*, the beach – sometimes land, sometimes sea. It is simultaneously both one and the other and neither one nor the other. Similarly, in between child and adult there is another ambiguous category: youth. And in between us and them there are **deviants**, dissidents, and so on.

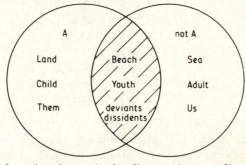

The area of overlap shown in the diagram is, according to binary logic, impossible. It is literally a scandalous category that ought not to exist. In anthropological terms, the ambiguous boundary between two recognized categories is where taboo can be expected. That is, any activity or state that does not fit the binary opposition will be subjected to repression or **ritual**. For example, as the anthropologist Edmund Leach suggests, the married and single states are binarily opposed. They are normal, time-bound, central to **experience** and secular. But the transition from one state to the other (getting married/divorced) is a *rite of passage* between categories. It is abnormal, out of time (the 'moment of a lifetime'), at the edge of experience and, in anthropological terms, *sacred*. The structural ambiguity of youth is one reason why it is treated in the media as a scandalous category – it too is a rite of passage and is subjected to both repression and ritual.

News often structures the world into binarily opposed categories (US:THEM). But it then faces the problem of dealing with people and events that don't fit neatly into the categories. The structural ambiguity of home-grown oppositional groups and people offends the consensual category of 'us', but cannot always be identified with foreigners or 'THEM'. In such cases, they are often represented as folk-devils, or as sick, deviant or mad – they are tabooed.

(3) Binary oppositions are structurally related to one another Binaries function to *order* meanings, and you may find *transformations* of one underlying binary running through a story. For instance, the binary MASCULINITY:FEMININITY may be transformed within a story into a number of other terms:

MASCULINITY:FEMININITY
OUTDOORS:INDOORS
PUBLIC:PRIVATE
SOCIAL:PERSONAL
PRODUCTION:CONSUMPTION
MEN:WOMEN

First, masculinity and femininity are proposed as opposites, mutually exclusive. This immediately constructs an ambiguous or 'scandalous' category of overlap that will be tabooed. Then, the binaries can be read downwards as well as across, which proposes, for instance, that men are to women as production is to consumption, or MEN:WOMEN::PRODUCTION:CONSUMPTION. Each of the terms on one side is invested with the qualities of the others on that side. As you can see, this feature of binaries is highly productive of **ideological** meanings – there's nothing natural about them, but the logic of the binary is hard to escape.

The ideological productivity of binaries is further enhanced by the assignation of positive:negative *values* to opposed terms. Thus, in an industrial dispute in the National Health Service in 1979 the television news structured the parties to the dispute into binaries which were assigned positive and negative values. This was done by the simple device of identifying one side in the dispute with the hospital patients, and by showing children rather than other kinds of patients. This assignation of value to opposed parties then structured the entire story, so that everyone was implicated:

POSITIVE:NEGATIVE
NURSES/CHILDREN/PATIENTS:STRIKERS
GOVERNMENT:UNIONS
MANAGEMENT:PUBLIC SERVICE WORKERS
'ANY DECENT TRADE UNIONIST':'IRRESPONSIBLE MINORITY'
US:THEM

JH

See **bardic function, orientalism**
Further reading Hartley (1982, 1992); Leach (1976, 1982); Leymore (1975)

bricolage ⋆ A cultural process of improvisation or adaption whereby objects, **signs** or practices are appropriated into different **meaning** systems and cultural settings and, as a result, are re-signified. ⋆ The concept originates in the work of French structural anthropologists, but has been used in the more recent study of **subcultures** and **lifestyles**. In this context, Hebdige provides a useful range of examples including the changing symbolic fortunes of the Italian motor scooter, the safety pin and the Union Jack as they have been adapted and given altered significance as emblems of different youth groups in British postwar culture. In these and other cases, there has been a tendency to emphasize the subversive functions of bricolage, whereby elements of dominant or taken-for-granted culture are given new critical meanings, often by ironic or surreal juxtaposition. The concept usefully directs attention to the objects, **rituals** and meanings which constitute **styles**. Furthermore, it requires that we regard these as elements within *dynamic* historical and cultural process.

TO

See **lifestyle, style, subculture**
Further reading Hebdige (1979, 1988)

broadcasting ⋆ The sending of messages via the media of television or radio with no technical control over who receives them.
⋆ Anyone who has the appropriate receiver and is within range

33

of the transmitter can receive them. (Contrast with **narrowcasting**.) By extension it means sending messages via the airwaves to a mass **audience**, and thus involves the use of broadcast **codes** and **conventions** designed to appeal to that mass audience.

JF

See **audience, elaborated and restricted codes, mass communication, narrowcasting**

campaign ⋆ An organized and co-ordinated process of **persuasion**, usually conducted and orchestrated by means of mass media, directed towards public opinion and behaviour in the attempt to achieve a defined set of objectives. ⋆ Campaigns may be initiated by a wide variety of **institutions**, **groups** and **individuals** in pursuit of their particular interests. Perhaps the best and most obvious examples are political campaigns, where the goals may include election to political office, or the rejection or adoption of some principle or policy. Advertising campaigns are equally obvious examples. Here the goals of the campaign generally concern sales of either products or services, or at least the maintenance of a climate of positive consumer opinion.

In both of these cases regulations usually govern the methods, timing or costs of campaigning. Campaigns and campaigners are preoccupied with, and judged largely in terms of, their **effects**. The measurement and analysis of such effects have constituted both an important problem and a source of sponsorship for **mass communications** research. In methodological terms direct media effects upon patterns of sales or votes has proved an elusive, inconclusive area, extremely difficult to isolate from the wider social and political context.

Under certain circumstances the media themselves may initiate and amplify campaigns. Professing to voice 'public opinion', to

35

speak on behalf of 'the people', their readers or viewers, the media campaign is always a part of wider social and political conflicts and processes.

TO

See **agenda setting, amplification, moral panic, persuasion, propaganda**
Further reading Hall *et al.* (1978); Dyer (1982); Seymour-Ure (1974); Negrine (1989)

case study ⋆ The detailed observation of a particular person, process or social event characterized by in-depth analysis, interviewing, and detailed empirical research. ⋆ The case study provides detailed and specific information about one situation or event, and then suggests general links between this material and wider issues. Case studies can therefore provide both illustrative and comparative material. For example, a case study of the 1981 riots in Toxteth, UK (Tumber 1982) provides a way of understanding those specific riots plus guidelines for understanding other riots in other cities and possibly in other societies (but see Herridge 1983).

Case studies sometimes attempt the integration of a variety of perspectives and concerns. More often they present one particular viewpoint. They should usually acknowledge any serious limitations. For example, in the study above, it was only rarely possible to interview participating youths. In general, making such limitations explicit prevents the author from misrepresenting material because of self-interest or **methodological** shortcomings. As with **participant observation**, the case study offers great potential but care must be taken in its completion. Good examples of the case study approach are Festinger *et al.* (1956) and Elliott (1972).

DS

See **methodology**
Further reading Tumber (1982); Elliott (1972); Festinger *et al.* (1956); McKeown (1982); Stempel and Westley (eds) (1981)

catharsis ✶ The elimination of desire, fear and emotion through vicarious experience. ✶ Catharsis commonly refers to a symbolic purging of the **audience**, originally within the theatre, where the acting out of a tragic situation allows for symbolic expression and resolution of our own melancholy. It is assumed that such purging actually rids the audience of sad or painful association although explanation for how or why this happens often remains vague.

Some studies of **violence** on television have concluded that catharsis may act as a 'safety valve' and thus serve to reduce violence in society. These are commonly called 'cathartic studies', but the evidence in their favour is not very convincing (Howitt and Cumberbatch 1975).

In **psychoanalytical theory** catharsis refers more to the releasing of repressed **memory** into **consciousness**, often through means of hypnosis or free association. This may be therapeutic: once conscious and out in the open such memory and desire can be easily recognized and discussed – a process that has even been described as moral fumigation. Catharsis thus involves a discharge of emotion, a process labelled by Freud as abreaction.

DS

See **audience, psychoanalytical theory, violence**
Further reading Stafford–Clarke (1967); Mortensen (ed.) (1979); DeFleur and Ball–Rokeach (1975); Howitt and Cumberbatch (1975)

censorship ✶ A process involving the blocking, regulation and manipulation of all or part of some original message. ✶ Censorship operates **consciously** or **unconsciously** at a variety of social and psychological levels. Perhaps the most obvious institutional and organized process of censorship takes place with reference to the mass media. Here the term generally refers to the regulation of information, normally by the state. It implies a process of control and selection according to certain, often implicit, criteria and **values**. This results in the deliberate exclusion or withholding of information from either the public in general, or certain specified **groups** within that population. Here censorship, and the legal codes and practices that achieve such control ('D' notices, Official Secrets Acts, libel and obscenity laws) are open to a variety of interpretations. It is commonly presented in terms of a necessary safeguard, a means of protecting the 'national interest', or the moral and social welfare of groups defined as vulnerable. Alternatively censorship is inextricably linked to **power** and **authority**. The ability to censor implies the legitimate capacity to define what is appropriate, to manipulate and control directly public information. The tensions between these two views have been well evidenced in debates about sexuality and **violence** on television and in the cinema. The issue of censorship is also fundamental to the analysis of formal and informal relations between the state, politics and the mass media.

In **psychoanalytical theory** Freud initially proposed a powerful mental agency called the censor, which is responsible for repression and dream distortion resulting from socially unacceptable or painful associations of memory fixed in the unconscious. It is difficult to repress continually or even to destroy such information, and hence the censor translates it into a more distanced and less aversive form.

Unconscious censorship holds for contexts where we may be shocked by the unexpected, threatening or unpleasant. We may refuse to admit that we ever witnessed the event, or that we did but refuse to recognize its significance. It is often unclear as to whether such reluctance is attributable to some kind of personal conviction, or to a realization about the inappropriateness of public admission because of reactions from **others**.

DS

See **agenda setting, propaganda, psychoanalytical theory**
Further reading (media) May and Rowan (eds) (1983); Schlesinger (1987)

channel ⋆ A term from **communication theory** for the physical means of carrying a **signal**. ⋆ Light waves carry visual signals, air waves carry sound signals. The channel is mainly the concern of physicists and engineers and has little to do with meaning, although the physical characteristics of the channel limit the medium and codes that it can carry. Indeed, some codes, such as Morse or semaphore, have been evolved to match the physical characteristics of the channels available. Communication theory is concerned with ways of measuring and maximizing the capacity of a given channel to convey **information**. Care must be taken to distinguish channel from **medium** and **code** which are much more productive concepts for the communication studies student.

JF

See **code, communication theory, medium, signal**

choice ⋆ 'Where there's choice, there's meaning' is a basic precept in communication. ⋆ All **codes** involve **paradigmatic** choices, where the significance of what was chosen can be assessed only by contrasting it with what was not, but could have been. Choice is often paired with *chain* (**syntagm**) to indicate how **language** works.

JF

See **absence, binary opposition, commutation test, difference, language, paradigm**

class/social class ⋆ Social classes are those distinct social formations made up of groups of people who have a similar relationship to the means of **production** in society and, as a result, a common social and cultural position within an unequal system of property ownership, **power** and material rewards. ⋆ As the term refers to the fundamental **determinant** of social **stratification** within modern industrial societies, you should expect to encounter it frequently.

The basic theory of social class, and the one that has shaped all subsequent accounts, was outlined in the work of Karl Marx (1818–83). In the tradition established by Marx, *class relations* provide the key to understanding central aspects of society, culture and history. Within this approach, classes must be understood as fundamental to the social relations associated with particular modes of economic production and organization. For

Marx, the historical development of social and economic relations could be divided into different periods, each of which was characterized by a different mode of production. The production and distribution of material goods is defined as a necessary condition for the existence of any society, and Marx argued that as soon as a society was organized to produce *more* than the bare minimum required for subsistence, it was historically possible for different social classes to emerge. A basic distinction is drawn here between different modes of production and forms of ownership, between societies which are characterized on the one hand by common ownership of the means of producing (forms of communism), and on the other, those in which such ownership is not common, rather it is distributed unequally, and concentrated in the hands of some groups (owners) to the exclusion of others (non-owners).

Societies of this latter type are *class divided*, characterized above all by their relations of exploitation, and hence of domination and subordination. Marx divided them into historical epochs of ancient slaveholding, feudalism and capitalism, though he sub-divided them even further. In the period of ancient civilization the dominant mode of production could be described as slavery, and the means of production were slaves. During feudalism the mode was agricultural and the means land; under capitalism the major mode is industrial, and the means capital, in all its many forms.

In its broadest sense this means that the most significant social division in these societies lies between a majority class that does the productive labour (be they slaves, serfs, or proletariat/working class), and the minority class that privately owns the means of production (landowning citizens, aristocracy, or bourgeois/capitalist class), and because of this is able to expropriate and command the surplus goods and wealth produced by such labour. In other words, the most fundamental conflict of interest is between those who own the means of production and those who do not. In feudal society, the conflict was between those who owned the land and those who did not. In capitalist society it is ultimately between owners and non-owners of capital. The relations between these owning and non-owning classes are therefore defined as primarily exploitative and antagonistic, as their *class interests* inevitably conflict. They pose the basic historical contradiction which can be resolved only by the transformation of the overall mode of production. It is in this sense for Marx that class conflict becomes the 'dynamo' or 'locomotive' of social history and social change. The broad contours of historical development are determined by the struggles between dominant or ruling classes, with their interests in maintaining existing economic and political relations and inequalities, and subordinate classes, with their counter interests in challenging and changing them.

While the principal social division within class societies is between the owning class and the producing class, Marx did recognize that there are other classes (for example, the 'petit-bourgeoisie': shopkeepers and owners of small businesses in capitalism). In addition, it is important to note that neither the owning or dominant class nor the non–owning classes are conceived as unitary. Each class may under certain conditions be divided into different *class fractions* possessing, within limits, different interests. For example, relations between skilled and unskilled labour, or between industrial and finance 'blocs' or representatives of the capital class.

First and foremost then it is useful to think of social classes as socially organized sets of relations within a process of production. Different class positions can be recognized empirically in so far as they confer what Weber called different 'life chances' upon individuals. They govern access to a wide variety of scarce and valued products and services in society. Products such as food and the whole range of consumer commodities, services such as medical care, education, or legal representation. Because of this many attempts to investigate and measure social class have tended to collapse class into its product; and hence pinpoint occupation and wealth as primary indicators of social class position.

It is however important to go beyond this point, and not to restrict class to a convenient way of describing social categories formed by different types of jobs, levels of wealth, property, power and status. What are equally at stake in a full consideration of social class are the ways in which class is recognized, made sense of and responded to within **culture**. Marx suggested that different social classes were characterized by differing **ideologies**,

41

those 'definite forms of social consciousness' (1971, p. 425), which correspond with particular class positions. Furthermore, Marx drew an important distinction between what he called a *class in itself* and a *class for itself*. This distinction hinges on the degree to which people who share a common relationship to the means of production (a class in itself), develop a *class consciousness* and *class identity* which recognizes their commonly exploited situation and interests. This class consciousness, under certain historical conditions, promotes the organized social and political action of a class for itself. In this way class refers not only as is commonly thought to economic or monetary relations, it is central also to the analysis of culture and cultural relations. Culture becomes the terrain in which class relations are made meaningful, and through which dominant and subordinate classes contest **hegemony**. A great deal of the recent work in communication and cultural studies can be seen as sharing a common concern with the interrelationships between classes, culture and communication. Much of this work seeks to analyse how underlying material or economic conflicts and inequalities between and within social classes are expressed and reproduced in cultural relations and representations.

TO

See **base, culture, hegemony, ideology, meaning systems, power**

Further reading Bilton *et al.* (1981); Williams (1976a); Giddens and Held (eds) (1982); Giddens (1982); Turner (1990)

closure ⋆ Often called **ideological** closure, this concept refers to the textual strategies by means of which a viewer or reader is encouraged to make sense of a factual or fictional **narrative** in a particular way, or according to a particular ideological framework. ⋆ Ideological closure is a property of all texts, but the term is most often used in the analysis of newspaper, television or other **representations** whose chief purpose is to relate stories about the public affairs of politics, industry, social and cultural relations, and so on. Closure is a property of **texts** – that is to say, not of the intentions of the producers or the opinions of the viewer/reader – so its mechanisms are ultimately **rhetorical**.

It is a useful concept in media analysis, since it directs our attention to the way that stories are constructed to promote or encourage certain meanings, and how other possible ways of making sense of the event or action have been **absented**, discouraged or closed out.

Closure works at the level of the **sign** as well as at the higher level of the text. In the case of signs, their **multi-accentuality** is 'fixed', as it were, so that when the sign is used (often over and over again) to connote just one of its potential meanings and not others, it seems as though the sign always, necessarily, means this. For instance, the media close the concept of youth: most frequently it connotes not young persons but young male persons, and not just any young male persons but those who are involved in 'antisocial' (*sic*) behaviour. Hence 'youth' is signified by a constellation of **signifiers** which collectively serve to 'close' our very perception of youth: it **means**, naturally, muggers, skinheads, gangs, violence, graffiti, football hooliganism, and so on. If we want to signify 'young persons' other than as social misfits, we cannot easily use the sign 'youth' at all. The media themselves operate a clear distinction between 'youths' and 'kids', 'youngsters', etc.

Closure is also used as a term by **Gestalt** psychologists. Here it refers to the way we **perceive** by filling in gaps within perceived wholes, overlooking any actual interruptions.

JH

See **Gestalt, preferred reading**

code ⋆ A code is a system of **signs** governed by rules agreed (explicitly or implicitly) between the members of the using **culture**. ⋆ This is a definition of a signifying code which is the type that readers of this book are most interested in, but there are also behavioural codes, such as the legal code, or the two codes of rugby football (Union and League). The highway code is both a signifying and a behavioural code. Signifying codes, then, have the following features:

(1) They have a number of units arranged in **paradigms** from which one is chosen.

(2) These chosen units are combined **syntagmatically** into a **message** or **text**.

(3) They convey **meaning** which derives from the agreement among, and shared cultural experience of, their users.

(4) They are transmittable by their appropriate **media** of communication.

(5) They can be a way of classifying, organizing and understanding material, as well as of transmitting or communicating it.

All our social and cultural activities or products are encoded.

The code with the simplest form is the **binary** code, in which the paradigm of units is confined to two – Yes/No, On/Off, $+/-$ or 1/0. This still allows complex syntagms; indeed the most sophisticated computers work through a binary code.

Analogue codes are composed of units which are not distinguishable in themselves, but only in their interpretation (for example, the continuous scale of mouth shape from a slight smile through a grin to a laugh). *Digital* codes have units that are clearly distinguished from each other (for example, verbal language, mathematics or musical notation which has imposed digital differences upon continuous scales of sound). Digital codes are easier to understand and talk about, which is why science uses them, while aesthetic or emotive codes are frequently more analogic.

Logical codes have an agreed and precisely defined paradigm of meanings for their paradigm of units. They work on the first order of **signification** (the denotative) only, and try as far as possible to exclude second order meanings of connotation and myth. The language of mathematics ($5 - 3 = 2$), or of chemical formulae (H_2O), are purely logical codes. Scientific writing and objective reporting aspire to a logical code of language.

Aesthetic codes, on the other hand, work more on the second order of signification (indeed many have no denotative meaning at all); they do not have precisely defined meanings, but tend

44

more to the subjective or **intersubjective**. They rely partly on established **convention**, but also on their ability to embody clues for their own decoding, so that an aesthetic **text** uses codes that are, to a certain extent, unique to it alone, and which can therefore be decoded only by paying close attention to the text itself.

Presentational codes use the body as transmitter, and are tied to the here and now; they tend to be **indexical** in that they indicate aspects of the sender's internal or social state. The main ones are body contact, proximity to another, physical orientation, appearance, head nods, facial expression, gesture, posture, eye movement and contact, and non-verbal aspects of speech (intonation, volume). They are often called the codes of **non-verbal communication** (or NVC). *Representational codes* produce freestanding texts that can be isolated from their sender; they can deal with abstractions, absences and generalizations; and they tend to be **iconic** or **symbolic** (Peirce's terms). They produce books, paintings, films and so on.

There is a range of technical codes in each medium, which are frequently used to convey second order signification, particularly connotation. In photography we can use the codes of focus, lighting, **framing** and camera angle to produce connotative meanings; in film and television the codes of editing, fading and dissolving can perform the same function (or they can signify relationships within the narrative); in music, the Italian directions like *allegro*, *lente* and *staccato* are a technical code signifying the connotations that depend upon how the piece is played.

Also in the second order of signification are the *cultural* codes through which **myths** operate. These are manifest within the texts of a culture, but can also be seen at work in the way that we conceptualize or understand our social world.

JF

See **convention, discourse, elaborated and restricted codes**
Further reading   Fiske (1982); Turner (1990)

cognition/cognitive   ⋆ Cognition refers to the individual's acquisition and application of knowledge; it is the process whereby we assimilate and organize information about events and relationships, so that we may be commonly said to 'know' about the world. ⋆ Within early psychology, the subject area of cognition attracted theorists interested in **perception**, memory, thinking and **language**. The major research technique was introspection, a subjective method which involves looking inwards and studying yourself. This provided some fascinating material as regards observing communication 'within the mind' – for example, James's observations of the 'tip-of-the-tongue' phenomenon where he had partially forgotten a name, and yet knew that he knew it. An adaptation of this phenomenon provides a useful practical exercise in the illustration of memory: collect news and media photographs of moderately famous people and ask a group of colleagues to name them. For each face you will most likely produce a 'tip-of-the-tongue' state for one or two of the group members. The frustration of knowing yet not accurately remembering is heightened if you ask the rest of the group to provide hints – for example, the number of syllables in the surname, or the films and records that the famous people in the pictures produced or recorded. Often this information structures recall, and the person who is in the 'tip-of-the-tongue' state will suddenly and dramatically announce the words that they have been searching for. Such an exercise allows us to observe and discuss strategies for remembering – it virtually puts memory into slow motion because usually cognitive processes occur so quickly that they defy analysis.

With the advent of **behaviourism**, academic interest in introspection and cognition declined because of the desire for scientific **empiricism**. The consequent loss of interest lasted until the 1960s, when the inadequacies of behaviourist approaches to the analysis of complex human behaviour, and the advent of more sophisticated **methodological** techniques, established cognition as an essential research area. As Neisser (1976) states, advances in communications and computer technology encouraged the application of **information processing models** to cognitive activity. Such theorizing went far beyond early introspective attempts, and has contributed much to the understanding of **intrapersonal communication**. Other interests have been directed more towards linguistic development, with Piaget and Vygotsky providing valuable insights into the relationships between thought and language – is one possible without the other?

DS

See **information processing, interpersonal communication, memory, model, perception, schema**
Further reading Miller (1966); Neisser (1976); Phillips (1981); Green and Hicks (1984); Eiser (1986)

cognitive dissonance ⋆ A state of disharmony, inconsistency or conflict between the organized attitudes, beliefs and values within an individual's cognitive system. ⋆ Dissonance theory was developed by Festinger (1957) and suggests that people are **motivated** to restore balance, equilibrium or consonance by reducing such conflict. In a rather static way it proposes that we psychologically strive to maintain an efficient, balanced, and well-organized outlook on the world.

A popular example is the heavy smoker who reads a medical report about the links between smoking and lung cancer. This leads to anxiety because s/he enjoys smoking but does not want to risk such an unpleasant early death. Cognitive dissonance theory predicts that such conflict will force the individual to reduce anxiety produced by contradictory experience. A number of strategies emerge:

(1) The seeking out of information which supports existing **attitudes** (s/he may read other reports that claim no correlation between smoking and cancer).
(2) The outright denial or devaluation of new and contradictory information (bold assertion about the repeated inaccuracies of the medical profession).
(3) Decreasing the importance of the entire dissonant issue by calling into question ultimate beliefs, **values** and prescriptions about the world (for example, stating that all death is unpleasant and inevitable, so what is the problem with cancer?).
(4) Accepting dissonant information and rejecting the

47

existing **cognitive** outlook for that issue – a process that may be central to eventual *attitude change* (for example, stop smoking).

Dissonance theory also suggests that we continually justify and rationalize our actions, even when they appear irrational, inappropriate, or unnecessary. Thus Festinger and Carlsmith (1959) concluded that poorly rather than well-paid subjects found a monotonous laboratory task more interesting. Similarly, Aronson and Mills (1959) claimed that membership of a particular **group** was more highly valued when an embarrassing initiation ceremony had to be completed by each member. Dissonance theory can perhaps be criticized for making the naive assumption that all conflict is aversive; there are obvious occasions when we deliberately seek out risky, uncertain and dissonance-producing situations. There is also a general failure to explain why some people adopt one strategy while others follow another when reducing conflict – this may stem from inattention to social or **cultural** contexts of **interaction**.

DS

See **attitude, persuasion**
Further reading   Festinger (1957); Billig (1982)

collocation ⋆ The tendency of words to co-occur in everyday discourse. ⋆ Thus, *dark* collocates strongly with *night*, in so far as they tend to co-occur. The same could be said of the relationship of *deadly* to *nightshade* or *nuclear* to *weapon*. The study of **meaning**, using this approach, investigates the meaning of a word in terms of its patterns of collocation, on the principle (enunciated by J. R. Firth, a British linguist who first formulated the notion of collocation) that 'you shall know a word by the company it keeps'. (Compare Wittgenstein: 'the meaning of a word is its use in the language'.) Collocation does, however, imply statistical profiles of patterns of co-occurrence. These have proved notoriously difficult to produce until recently when it has become possible to apply sophisticated computational techniques to a very large corpus of data. Recent dictionaries – for instance, the *Collins Cobuild English Language Dictionary* – have been developed using such techniques.

MM

See **semantics**
Further reading Halliday and Hasan (1975)

common sense ⋆ A category of knowledge whose 'truth' is proposed as obvious, natural, inevitable, eternal, unarguable and 'what we always/already know'. Hence, the political philosophy of non-political non-philosophers. ⋆

Historically, the concept of 'common sense' was used in radical polemics against the established official knowledges promoted by church or state. It was held to be a more compelling category of knowledge than traditional dogmas, and was based on the argument that if individual experience and belief contradicted the precepts of the Church, then the dictates of the individual experience should prevail. Hence it was a valuable **rhetorical** device in arguments which Protestants developed against the reactionary medieval Catholic Church, or political radicals used against the established secular state in the nineteenth century. For instance, the unequal distribution of wealth as between the sovereign, aristocracy and middle classes on the one hand, and the labourers and poor on the other, was represented as an offence against common sense in Chartist pamphleteering.

However, this example demonstrates that common sense has no 'contents' – it is a category not a repertoire. For in modern times the mass media in particular have colonized the concept, and use it to 'prove' that the unequal distribution of wealth is, far from being an offence against common sense, actually only explicable *as* common sense – that's the way things are, given other 'common sense' notions like 'human **nature**' (defined as greedy, competitive, untrustworthy, and so on).

Hence common sense is a site of social struggle; contending social groups seek to represent their way of looking at things as being commonsensical. To the extent that one **group** or 'bloc' succeeds in establishing itself as the source and repository of common sense, it is likely to be able to maintain its **hegemony** over other groups whose 'sense' is likely to appear as marginal, alien or even dangerous to those of 'us' who are endowed with the real thing.

JH

See **experience, hegemony, naturalizing**
Further reading   Bennett *et al.* (eds) (1981b); Hartley (1982); Fiske (1989a, 1989b)

communication   ⋆ There are broadly two types of definition of communication. The first sees it as a process by which A sends a message to B upon whom it has an effect. The second sees it as a negotiation and exchange of meaning, in which messages, people–in–cultures and 'reality' interact so as to enable meaning to be produced or understanding to occur. ⋆

The aim of the first is to identify the stages through which communication passes so that each one may be properly studied and its role in and effect upon the whole process clearly identified. Lasswell (1948) does this with his model '*Who* says *what* in *which channel* to *whom* with *what effect*?' Within this approach there are naturally areas of disagreement: one such concerns the importance of the intention to communicate. MacKay (1972) argues that a geologist can extract a lot of information from a rock, but that the rock does not communicate because it has no intention, nor power of choice. Other writers include all the symbolic means by which one person (or other organism) affects another. See Nilson in Sereno and Mortensen (1970) for a good summary of this approach.

The second approach is **structuralist** in that it focuses on the relationship between constituent elements necessary for meaning to occur. These elements fall into three main groups:

(1)   the **text**, its **signs** and **codes**;
(2)   the people who 'read' the text, the cultural and social experience that has formed both them and the signs/codes they use; and
(3)   the awareness of an '*external reality*' to which both text and

people refer. (By 'external reality' we mean that to which a text refers that is other than itself.)

Some authorities such as Saussure emphasize the 'text' group (signs/codes/language), others such as Barthes focus on the text/culture interaction, while those with a more philosophic approach, such as Peirce or Ogden and Richards, pay attention to the 'external reality' which they call **object** or **referent**. The way in which meaning is produced from the interaction between these three groups is the main study of **semiotics**.

JF

communication theory ★ An early attempt to extend the applicability of **information theory** beyond its engineering base into human communication in general. ★ It models communication on a process in which a source **encodes** and then transmits a **message** along a **channel**. This is received and **decoded** at its destination upon which it produces an effect.

Shannon and Weaver (1949) were the first to articulate the theory and produced their basic model:

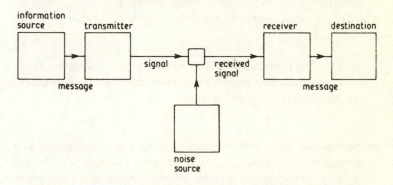

Gerbner (1956) produced an elaborated and more sophisticated version that should be studied after Shannon and Weaver's. The fundamental assumptions of the theory are that the aim of communication is to achieve efficiency, which is reached when the destination decodes the identical message to that encoded at the

51

source. Failure to achieve this is the result of breakdowns or inadequacies at some stage of the process, and setting these right will therefore improve the efficiency.

Communication theory has been subject to considerable criticism since 1949. Its critics accuse it of being interventionist, in that its aims appear to be to increase the ability of the communicator to intervene within, or control, the life of the **receiver**. It also implies that the receiver is passive, and at the mercy of the previous stages in the process, and thus fails to account for other influences upon the effect of the message on the receiver. It emphasizes the skills, techniques and processes of communication, and is therefore favoured by the professionals in the media. It does not address itself to the meaning of the message, nor to the social context or relationship of the people involved. It is a mechanistic, rather than a **semiotic** or social model. However, later workers following this model implicitly or explicitly have compensated for some of these basic deficiencies. Lasswell's (1948) verbal version '*Who* says *what* in *which channel* to *whom* with *what effect*?' has structured most of the sociological and psychological research which has implicitly followed this model. **Content analysis** is also an essentially communication theory view of the message. Much **behaviourist** psychology with its emphasis upon interpersonal skills is another derivation of this model.

JF

See **code, communication, cybernetics, entropy, feedback, information theory, medium, message, redundancy, sender/receiver, signal, symbol, text**

commutation test ⋆ A test used to assess if a particular unit in a **syntagm** carries meaning, and if so, what meaning. ⋆ The test involves changing the unit for another one in the same **paradigm**: this can be done imaginatively or actually. Thus, Fiske (1982) analyses a photograph of blacks confronting police in an inner city street, and by imagination 'commutes' the inner city street to an expensive outer suburb. He concludes that this changes the **meaning** of the syntagm, and that the unit inner-city-street is therefore significant. Commuting the van parked nearby into a car, however, does not change the meaning of the syntagm, and so the van is not seen as a bearer of meaning. By contrasting inner–city–street with expensive–outer–suburb we can begin to assess the meaning of the inner–city–street as a unit of meaning. Commutations in a syntagm can also be made actually and the resulting changes in meaning assessed **empirically** by **audience** study.

JF

See **choice, paradigm, syntagm**

competence ⋆ The word has a specialized sense in linguistics, where it is used to refer to the native speaker's (tacit and intuitive) knowledge of the language. ⋆ Noam Chomsky developed this technical sense of the term as a challenge to what were current trends in American linguistics of the 1950s which declared that **language** could be studied as a purely behavioural phenomenon independently of **meaning** and of underlying mental structure. Chomsky shifted the basic focus of study away from verbal behaviour to our intuitions about language – particularly those that enable any native speaker to distinguish between grammatical and ungrammatical sentences in his or her native language. With these intuitions as its focus, the goal of linguistics became that of describing or **modelling** the rules that go into making up the native speaker's grammar. These rules are descriptive, but ultimately amount to a formal, explicit model of the native speaker's competence. Chomsky was very emphatic that these rules – the grammar – amount to a statement of knowledge and must be clearly distinguished from what actual people do when speaking the language. This he described as **performance** and argued that since speakers of the language slip-up while talking, leaving sentences unfinished, making false-starts and other mistakes, then mere performance could provide no reliable guide to underlying competence. It was thus no use studying what people did if you wanted to find out what they knew. This knowledge, however, was a necessary precondition for performance.

Chomsky's isolation of competence as the descriptive goal of linguistics involved him in some quite deliberate idealizations. Competence was that of 'the ideal speaker hearer in the homogeneous speech community'. It was thus not socio-culturally determined in any way but a basic mental faculty, belonging to all, and part of our genetic inheritance. In this way Chomsky emphasizes the unity of humankind in language – what is for him our common access to the power of speech. But by deliberately overlooking variation in language from situation to situation, he laid himself open to criticism for separating language off from its social context and avoiding issues of institutionalized inequalities in the social valuation of differing fashions of speaking. At the same time, his emphasis on competence also led him to overlook important regularities in the apparent disfluencies of performance which more recent work (see **conversation analysis**) suggests are part of the social purposes of speech.

MM

See **conversation analysis, institutions, langue, parole, performance**

Further Reading   Chomsky (1965); Hymes (1971)

concentration   ⋆ A term referring to the decreasing dispersal of ownership in advanced capitalist economies, where the means of production in market sectors become owned by progressively fewer and larger groups. ⋆   The dynamics and consequences of this process within mass communication industries have formed an important focus for recent research. The highly concentrated structure of these industries is indicated by the *concentration ratio* which expresses the proportion of a market sector owned and controlled by the five leading firms. As Murdock and Golding (1977) have noted: 'By the beginning of the seventies the top five firms in the respective sectors accounted for 71% of daily newspaper circulation, 74% of the homes with commercial television, 78% of the admissions to cinemas, 70% of paperback sales, and 65% of record sales' (p. 25).

Processes involved in this general tendency include integration, diversification and internationalization (Golding 1974), all of which are economic strategies employed by media companies seeking to maintain, if not increase, their control of the market and their profit potential. The large corporate organizations, with interests spread across media and other sectors of the British and international economies, that are the logical result of the process of concentration, are known as *multi media conglomerates*, of which Thorn/EMI and ACC are good examples. The consequences of concentration form the basis for a number of interrelated debates. Central to these debates are the contending perspectives offered by **liberal pluralist** and Marxist theorists. They produce radically different accounts of the dynamics and consequences of ownership and control within media organizations.

In brief, Marxists use such patterns of highly concentrated ownership as evidence for their thesis that the production and distribution of **culture** is determined by the dominant capitalist **class**. Hence they suggest that the output of mass media is ultimately controlled in the interests of that class, serving to legitimate and reproduce their **ideologies**, interests and **power** as opposed to those of subordinate classes. Liberal pluralists reject such a view, arguing that it is too conspiratorial and over unified. From their perspective, the economically concentrated power of media ownership no longer gives total control over output to the proprietorial group, or **elite**. The power of ownership is counterbalanced in their view by the plurality of competing interests represented by diverse **groups** of shareholders and consumers, professional managers and producers, advertisers and trade unions, all of whom are refereed by the state.

TO

See **cultural production, pluralism, power, representation**
Further reading Murdock and Golding (1977); Curran and Seaton (1991); Negrine (1989)

condensation ★ The combination of two or more ideas, desires or memories into a single episode, image, symbol or sign. ★ This blending process implies increased meaning(s) and **motivation for a sign** that is subject to condensation. It is a frequently used concept in **psychoanalytical theory**, where it plays an important **role** in the attempted analysis of dreams and **symbol** formation. Freud suggested that actual remembered events within a dream (the manifest content) may represent a number of underlying varied but repressed wishes and **memories** (the latent content). Condensation thus involves the linking of the **unconscious** with the conscious.

We might, for example, remember dreaming about a door lock. With further thought this might remind us of once, a long time ago, being locked into a room and feeling very frightened. The manifest content of lock (and, by implication, key) may also carry sexual associations. It might further remind us of our recent attempts to unlock the writings of Lacan. All of these latent **meanings** condense upon the one remembered manifest episode.

A further application is an innuendo and pun, where a single word or statement can lead to two interpretations – one open and acceptable, the other secretive and taboo. The unanswered question is why do we find this funny?

DS

See **motivation (of the sign), psychoanalytical theory, ritual condensation**
Further reading Stafford–Clarke (1967)

conformity ⋆ Internalized agreement with rules, norms and conventions which are established by other groups. ⋆ We conform, for example, to the **group**, a **stereotype**, to legal standards, or a religious doctrine. Conformity is to be distinguished from *compliance*. Conformity implies more extreme and 'inner' agreement with **others**, whereas compliance implies a more superficial agreement that may well be based on anticipation of the immediate consequences of disagreement. Compliance is often associated with obedience to authority, as discussed in detail by Milgram (1974), and may form the basis for future conformity as a result of prolonged expedience.

The analysis of conformity has been of particular interest to communication theorists discussing aspects of **persuasion**, **socialization**, **group** dynamics, and intergroup relations. Conformity may be **conscious** or **unconscious**, and the conforming individual may or may not be aware of non–conformist (see **deviance**) **attitudes**. There is the strong possibility that mass media represent the conformist beliefs, opinions and **values** held by an inferred majority of the viewer population, and in so doing reinforce conformity still further. In this respect much recent interest has been expressed in the content and effects of media **stereotyping**.

DS

See **attitude, consensus, deviance, persuasion, stereotype**

Further reading Milgram (1974); Aronson (1980); Rosenbaum (1983); Brown (1986)

consciousness ∗ Awareness of situations, images, sensations or memories at social and psychological levels of analysis. ∗ The term has been extensively used in social science when discussing aspects of social and cultural formations and perceptions of social processes. Thus in Marxist sociology consciousness may refer to awareness of the 'true' state of affairs concerning **power** relations and dominance, or to 'false consciousness', forms of falsification or **myth**, associated with the controlling interests and **ideologies** of dominant classes. One great interest has been in the ways that major social **institutions** relate to everyday '**common sense**' value systems, to the extent that underlying issues concerning social inequality have been misrepresented or else taken for granted: 'that's just the way things are, have always been, and will always be'.

It might be argued that with successful mystification the owners of capital carry on owning whilst the producers of capital carry on producing because of the *un*consciousness. Any change in the status quo will therefore involve contradicting myths, or exposing false premises, in order to raise consciousness.

At the level of individual awareness, the discipline of psychology has been less overtly political in approaching this concept. The crucial feature is that of attending to thoughts, feelings and images, rather than going through the processes of articulation. Within the psychological context there are many types of conscious activity, including daydreaming, remembering night dreams and calculation. Always the individual possesses at least some knowledge, at that point in time, of the respective activity. A useful discussion is offered by the review by Hilgard *et al.* (1979) of the distinction between passive consciousness, where the individual receives information from the environment (as when we sit in the crowd and watch a cricket match), and active consciousness which involves productive mental activity (as when we plan our journey home from the cricket ground). But even this distinction poses problems, especially when asked to consider somebody as totally receptive and unquestioning.

Observation of conscious states often involves the use of **language**, self-report and introspection. This is illustrated by Joyce's (1916) *stream of consciousness* or Freud's technique of *free association*. Psychoanalytically based interest in the latter concerns the clues provided by consciousness about valuable repressed information located within the inferred opposite: an **unconscious**. Indeed, **psychoanalytical theory** can be criticized for an almost exclusive emphasis on unconscious events determining all conscious activity. The reductionist position adopted by many classic psychoanalysts underestimates the power of language and social structure in the shaping, guiding or provision of varying levels of consciousness. It is here that Marxist interpretations of **ideology** resulting from (and in turn regulating) economic inequality become most relevant by way of criticism.

DS

See **archetype, articulation, hegemony, mystification, myth, perception, propaganda, psychoanalytical theory, subconscious, unconscious**.

consciousness/culture industry ⋆ Large-scale social agencies, organizations and practices whose ultimate product is signification; a collective term for the modern communications media. ⋆ The implication of this useful concept is that individual consciousness is not a pre-given or self-evident attribute of persons, at least as far as its 'content', or its characteristic forms and practices, are concerned. Consciousness is a social product generated out of the resources of socially organized sense-making. The 'consciousness of an age', in short, comes from definite institutions and practices. The consciousness industry is usually taken to comprise the **mass communications** media, but might also include institutions like education, religion, and so on. Together these agencies are responsible for reproducing the forms, hierarchies and established senses of consciousness which we as individuals come to 'inhabit' as our identities.

The term was coined by Enzensberger, and is similar to the idea of the *culture industry* (of which the paradigm example is Hollywood in its golden age) proposed by the **Frankfurt school**.

JH

See **class, consciousness, hegemony, ideology, subjectivity**
Further reading Enzensberger (1970)

consensus ⋆ A term used to imply social and cultural unity through shared agreement, particularly those levels of collective agreement, contested, achieved and negotiated between people in social groups and in the wider society as a whole. ⋆ Without some degree of consensus, communication, in all its cultural forms, would be an impossibility, as communication requires at least minimal agreement over **signs** and their **codes** of signification. 'We' communicate, behave and gain identity as members of social groups, cultures and societies, by accepting or modifying within certain limits, their respective consensual frameworks. In this way consensus has been emphasized as a basic source of social unity and social solidarity. Its analysis and explanation represents a sensitive focal point for debate in the study of society, culture and politics.

A traditional divide in this debate lies between two broad positions or **paradigms**, often referred to as 'consensus' and 'conflict' perspectives. The former perspective places emphasis upon a high degree of social consensus, co-operation and stability, as these are assumed to be natural, normal and indeed inevitable conditions for social life. Furthermore, as members of the same society, it is assumed that all people should subscribe to the same culture, share and conform to the same 'central **value** system' or **consensus**. As a result, it is claimed, we all come to share roughly the same interests and have equal stakes in maintaining existing social and political arrangements. In this way the idea of *social* consensus extends into one of *political* consensus, since society becomes represented ideally as a static, harmonious whole, without major and widespread conflicts between different social groups and **classes**, and ideally without **deviance** and opposition. Where disagreements do arise, it is argued that there are adequate, consensually defined, institutional means for both expressing and collectively resolving such 'disensus'. State and political institutions, for example, are defined as central to this process, as they are seen ultimately to operate in the name of consensus, both by guaranteeing equal access and weight for all groups in the collective decision-making procedures of society, and by functioning to regulate and control behaviour which threatens consensual values or goals.

The idea of social and political consensus is not rejected within the opposing conflict perspective, it is however considerably challenged and redefined. In this approach, society is conceived largely in terms of *conflicts* between social groups and classes, whose interests, far from being unified and common, are opposed and incompatible. Some of these groups will be oppressed, subordinate and disadvantaged, whereas others exercise power, and hold positions of material and cultural advantage and privilege. Rather than any *one* overriding social consensus, different groups are formed precisely because of their different, often mutually opposed, experiences, interests, and the very different value systems that these give rise to. Unity and social solidarity are therefore based upon values that are shared and developed within groups with definite interests in common, and must be understood in the context of wider historical conflicts between dominant classes and groups who wish to maintain and reproduce the inequalities of existing social and political relations, and subordinate or oppositional groups who may wish radically to transform them. In this perspective consensus is inextricably linked with the possession of material and cultural power, and the practice of domination – particularly, in so far as this enables and allows dominant groups to define their specific interests and values as those that should be common to all, to represent them as if they have universal 'consensual' authority. In other words, far from being a natural and inevitable source of social agreement, cohesion and stability, consensus is seen as constructed, guided and imposed, a form of 'agreement' which serves to benefit certain dominant groups, at the expense of those occupying subordinate social positions.

In short, there is little consensus about 'consensus', it is a highly contested term and needs to be carefully thought through in the context of the debates it serves to raise.

TO

See **conformity, functionalism, hegemony, ideology, institutions, meaning systems, pluralism, power, rules**
Further reading Cuff and Payne (eds) (1979); Worsley (ed.) (1977); Bilton *et al.* (1981)

conspiracy theory ⋆ A view of the structure and operation of **power** relations, which sees the activities within organizations, **institutions** and the wider society as directly and deliberately controlled by some small, highly co-ordinated, but not necessarily visible, elite. ⋆ The 'hidden' motives of this **elite** usually combine self-interest with the implementation of a variety of social and political conditions that would ensure their dominance. A tendency to emphasize the direct **interpersonal** networks of control and the 'grand strategy' of the 'plot' at the expense of alternative perspectives flaws this approach badly. For example, from this perspective the mass media are conceived as powerful automatic relay mechanisms, directly controlled by certain powerful members of a conspiratorial group, who are able to condition and persuade unsuspecting **audiences** into passive conformity to their schemes. This is a theory with little or no credibility.

TO

See **power**

content analysis ⋆ The analysis of frequencies in manifest content of messages using the identification and counting of key units of content as the basis of its method. ⋆ It stresses the **objectivity** and repeatability of its methods, and uses the **empiricism** of its data to define itself in contrast to more interpretative methods of studying content. It is non–selective, and works on the total **message**, or message system, or upon a statistically constituted sample.

It is a statistical method, and as such is at its best when dealing with large numbers of units, or with a complete message system (for example, television advertisements, the popular press, or political cartoons published in the three weeks before a specific election). It should not be used for analysing a single **text** (see Fiske 1982).

Its results may be expressed as raw figures, but are more frequently and usefully given as percentages. A comparison between sets of figures is usually necessary – the fact that 38 per cent of women in television ads are shown indoors becomes meaningful only when we compare it with the equivalent figure for men – 14 per cent (see table below). Similarly, the proportion of column centimetres devoted by a quality newspaper to, say, politics or entertainment is interesting only when compared to the equivalent figures for a tabloid.

The most problematic part of content analysis is the categorization, that is, how to choose and classify units to be counted. Typical examples are – words; column centimetres; race, class and age of killers and victims in television drama; married and unmarried and engaged males and females in popular fiction; occupations in television drama; and so on. Before any message can be analysed statistically it must be divided into categories of this sort, and it is here that content analysis's claim to objectivity is at its weakest. Texts can be categorized in a potentially infinite number of ways, and the selection of categories deemed to be significant will inevitably involve the sort of value judgements that the method claims to outlaw.

A typical example of the results of a content analysis is:

Settings of male and female characters in television
advertisements

Setting	Males (n = 462)	Females (n = 235)
	%	%
Room of house (other than kitchen)	11	24
Kitchen	3	14
Outdoors	44	19
Business	14	7
Limbo	12	10
School	1	4
(n = total number of units)	Dominick and Rauch (1972)	

context/social context ⋆ A much-used term which is employed
in two major ways: first, it may refer to the immediate and
specific features of a social situation or environment that surround
a particular interaction or communicative interchange; second,
and in a more generally encompassing sense, it may be used to
describe those wider social, political and historical circumstances
and conditions within which certain actions, processes or events
are located and made meaningful. ⋆ In both cases the term
serves to direct attention towards the not necessarily visible, but
none the less **determining** forces which constitute and regulate
social activity.

JF

See **determination**

context of situation ⋆ This term was given special prominence
by the British linguist M. A. K. Halliday to help specify ways
in which language varies according to its situation of use. ⋆
According to Halliday, the selection of linguistic form for an
utterance is partially determined by features of the extra-linguistic
context, or context of situation. Relevant features of context
typically amount to more than the physical environment or

setting of the utterance, but include more especially factors such as the type of social relationship involved, the nature of the medium adopted, the kind of activity in which the utterance is embedded, and the topic being conveyed. As users of the language, then, we are constantly making and recognizing fine adjustments in linguistic selection, depending upon the context of situation. An utterance such as 'I observed the suspect proceeding east along Sauchiehall Street' is unlikely to occur outside court-room testimony; in less formal contexts of situation the same idea is likely to be rendered as 'I saw 'im going towards town'.

Contexts of situation vary from those that are relatively open and negotiable in character (such as family or peer group conver-sation) to those of a more institutionalized and closed nature (such as court room proceedings, media interviews, classroom lessons, and so on). Any society or social formation will feature a number of common, recurring but salient contexts of situation, which Halliday termed *typical* contexts of situation. The totality of these comprise that society's *context of culture*. In this way the term confirms the sociological and anthropological orientation of Halliday's work, with context of situation being a crucial mediating concept between the linguistic order and the social order. Indeed, in developing the concept, Halliday himself acknowledges a debt through the linguist Firth to the anthropologist Malinowski.

As a concept its explanatory power is limited by the difficulties of capturing the dialectical relationship of **language** to situation. On the one hand language is sensitive to its context of situation. On the other hand it is active in defining and constituting that very context of situation. It is difficult to hold both insights simultaneously without some sense of circularity.

MM

See **pragmatics, register, speech event**
Further reading Halliday (1978); Gregory and Carroll (1978); Montgomery (1986)

convention ⋆ A textual or social practice shared by members of a culture or subculture. ⋆ Conventions are frequently, but not necessarily, unstated and taken for granted. They are the ways in which the practices and habituated ways of doing and seeing are spread throughout a **culture**; they derive, therefore, from the shared experience of the members adopting them and they create shared expectations. Conventions work in the same way in both **texts** and social life: a text or piece of behaviour which conforms to convention is easily understood and widely accepted. Conversely, breaking conventions socially or textually produces misunderstandings or resentment or both in others. Ironically it is often through breaking a convention that the convention itself becomes apparent. Conventions are **redundant**, **phatic**, easily decoded and stress **group** or cultural membership.

JF

See **code, norm, realism**

conversation analysis ⋆ The search for patterned regularities in the details of conversational behaviour. ⋆ The approach has its roots in a particular branch of sociology known as ethnomethodology which was basically concerned with identifying the fundamental categories and forms of reasoning used by members of society to make sense of their everyday social world. As such, it was part of a continuing reaction in the human and social sciences against ill-considered and over-optimistic use of quantitive and statistical method.

True to its sociological origins, conversation analysis is interested in verbal interaction primarily as instances of the situated social order. Practitioners of this approach study conversation as a rich source of observable material on how members of society achieve orderliness in their everyday interactions with each other. They view conversations as jointly constructed, practical accomplishments, and seek to display from the close analysis of transcribed talk the methods adopted by participants in achieving this orderliness – the conversational structures to which participants attend and the interpretative work which they undertake. In line with this project, conversation analysis has provided detailed accounts of how the taking of turns is managed in conversation and how turns are linked together in coherent ways. Some types of utterance are predictably related to each other in pairs such as *summons + answer, question + answer* or *greeting + greeting*, and related pairs such as these provide strong linking formats as part of the sequential organisation of talk.

MM

See **discourse interaction/social interaction, pragmatics**
Further reading Atkinson and Heritage (eds) (1984); Levinson (1983)

counterculture ⋆ A collective label, applied to the politicized, largely middle-class, alternative or 'revolutionary' youth sub-cultures of the 1960s and early 1970s. ⋆ The term was adopted in America by theorists such as Marcuse (1972) and Roszak (1971), and served to integrate the **ideologies**, practices and goals of such movements as hippies and student radicals into a broadly unified expression of youthful political protest and resist-ance against the older establishment on both sides of the Atlantic. Unlike the disguised, more fragmentary forms of resistance posed by working-class youth **subcultures**, the countercultural groups, drawing on a middle-class parent **culture**, especially within higher education, articulated a more organized, intellec-tual and political challenge, apparently unified in the face of authority.

In this way the term occupies a significant but unstable position in debates surrounding the importance of different social **class** positions as determinants of the subcultural responses of young people.

TO

See **class, culture, subculture**
Further reading Clarke *et al.* (1976); Brake (1980); Middleton and Muncie (1981); Gordon (1986)

creole ⋆ A creole is a language which develops out of a pidgin language to become the native language of a group. ⋆ For example, the Africans who as slave labour were captured and transported to the 'New World' developed a **pidgin language** in their contacts with white slave traders and plantation owners. It was quite common, however, for them to lack a common language amongst themselves, partly because of the immense linguistic diversity in their West African homelands; and partly because of deliberately repressive policies of segregating individuals from the same language group. While the pidgin language might be adequate for master–slave contact, it was too simple to handle the full range of communicative needs among the Africans themselves. Under such circumstances the simple structures of the pidgin undergo rapid elaboration, especially when it is learnt as a first language by small children. Indeed, its general use in intimate, domestic settings and for sustaining communal life amongst the Africans themselves all contributed to a process of *creolization* whereby a simplified contact language takes on all the complexity of an established language, often in the space of a generation.

The actual process of creolization has escaped close scrutiny, partly because it is more commonly associated with the language of subordinated **groups**. But there is a growing recognition that the process may be an extremely widespread feature of language development and linguistic change. It is not too fanciful to suggest that, since English itself was spawned out of a master–slave relationship between Norman conqueror and Saxon serf, it gained its present hybrid shape (drawing as it does on both Norman French and Anglo-Saxon) through a process of creolization.

MM

See **diachronic, pidgin**,
Further reading Mulhausler (1986); Todd (1984)

cross cultural ⋆ A kind of comparative analysis which prioritizes the relativity of cultural activities. ⋆ Pioneered in social and cultural anthropology, the method is to compare whatever your particular object of study might be with perspectives from other **cultures**. Hence there are cross cultural studies of marriage ceremonies, kinship networks, visual illusions, and so on. A revealing cross cultural comparison is one that shows how apparently 'primitive' cultural forms, such as magic and witchcraft, may in fact be not too dissimilar to so-called 'advanced' forms, such as media representations or scientific **ideologies**.

Cross cultural analysis has proved popular with theorists interested in the relative bases of **norms**, **values**, **rules** and **roles** within societies. With the analysis of **deviance**, for example, it is worth noting that what may be unacceptable to one culture is acceptable to another. However, major difficulties emerge when recognizing that an author's own cultural perspectives may interfere with observation and analysis of a 'foreign' **group**. This is particularly evident when the **languages** of observer and observed differ so markedly.

JH/DS

See **methodology, participant observation**
Further reading   Beattie (1966); Harris (1977); Leach (1982)

culture   ⋆ The social production and reproduction of sense, meaning and consciousness. The sphere of meaning, which unifies the spheres of production (economics) and social relations (politics).
⋆ If you are planning to use the term culture as an analytical concept, or if you encounter its use, it is unlikely that you will ever be able to fix on just one definition that will do for all such occasions.

However, it will often be possible to use or read the word clearly and uncontroversially: Welsh culture, youth culture, a cultured person, Victorian culture, working-class culture, intellectual culture; or even a cultured pearl, bacterial culture, agriculture, cultivation of the soil. The trouble arises when you notice that even in these examples the term culture seems to mean half-a-dozen different things. What on earth do all these things share that can be encompassed by the single term?

The answer, oddly enough, is nothing. The term *culture* is **multi-discursive**; it can be mobilized in a number of different **discourses**. This means you cannot import a fixed definition into any and every context and expect it to make sense. What you have to do is identify the discursive context itself. It may be the discourse of nationalism, fashion, anthropology, literary criticism, viti-culture, Marxism, feminism, **cultural studies**, or even **common sense**. In each case, culture's **meaning** will be determined relationally, or negatively, by its differentiation from others in that discourse, and not positively, by reference to any intrinsic or self-evident properties that are eternally fixed as being quintessentially cultural. Further, the concept of culture cannot be 'verified' by referring its meaning to phenomena or actions or objects out there beyond discourse. What the term refers to (its **referent** as opposed to its **signified**) is determined by the term itself in its discursive context, and not the other way around.

Given this, it will come as no surprise to learn that its established senses and uses result from the history of its usage within various discourses. It stems, originally, from a purely agricultural root; culture as cultivation of the soil, of plants, culture as tillage. By extension, it encompasses the culture of creatures from oysters to bacteria. Cultivation such as this implies not just growth but also deliberate tending of 'natural' stock to transform it into a desired 'cultivar' – a strain with selected, refined or improved characteristics.

Applying all this to people, it is clear that the term offers a fertile metaphor for the cultivation of minds – the deliberate husbandry of 'natural' capacities to produce perfect rulers. It is not without significance that just this usage of the term roughly coincided with the establishment of the first stage of the modern market economy – early agrarian capitalism in the seventeenth and eighteenth centuries. The production of a strain of men who are not 'naturally' (by divine right of succession) fitted to rule but who are nevertheless powerful is made sense of, by those men themselves and for the benefit of others, by the systematic dissemination of the metaphor of culture.

However, the early **hegemony** of the aristocratic landowning capitalists was subjected by the nineteenth century to the altogether more disruptive development of urban, industrial, commercial capital. No sooner was culture established as a term that referred freely to rulers without echoes of rhizomes than economic and political changes began to challenge the naturalized right of the cultured to rule. Entrepreneurial and imperial capitalism appeared to be no respecter of culture. Instead, the term was denounced by Marx (culture which means works of wonder for the rich also means rags and corruption for the poor), and apparently ignored by the capitalist and middle classes alike. It was left to the intelligentsia, especially its liberal–conservative, moralist–humanist literary element, to take up the concept. Here, during the mid-nineteenth century, it began to be honed into quite a precise notion, which is still influential today.

Culture was established, especially by Matthew Arnold and his followers, as the pursuit not of material but of spiritual perfection via the knowledge and practice of 'great' literature, 'fine' art and 'serious' music. Since the goal was perfection not just understanding, and spiritual not material, culture was seen as the training of 'discrimination' and 'appreciation' based on 'responsiveness' to 'the best that has been thought and said in the world'. The cultural critics then strove to prescribe and establish what exactly could be counted as the 'best'. But such critics also tended to see themselves as an embattled community struggling against the encroachments of material civilization and scientific technology to preserve the 'sweetness and light' of culture and disseminate it to the benighted denizens of **mass society**. In such a climate it is not surprising to find that the 'treasures' of culture are assumed to belong to a pre-industrial past and a non-industrial **consciousness**. Modern proponents of this concept of culture-as-embattled-perfection have been influential in offering an ideology to highly placed **elites** in government, administrative, intellectual and even **broadcasting** circles within which their *sectional* interests can be represented as *general* interests.

Culture has not yet recovered from this history. The concept itself has undergone a period of decolonization. It is argued by those who object to the elitist notion of culture that it dispossesses most people, leaving a 'cultured' few and an 'uncultured' majority. Further, there seems to be an uncanny degree of fit between this division of culture and other social divisions – for instance those of **class**, **gender** and **race**. It seems that the cultural critics' discourse of 'excellence' works not so much to preserve timeless and universal treasures but, much more immediately though less obviously, to translate class and other kinds of social primacy into **cultural capital**. The struggle to dismantle the supremacy of elite, high English culture was championed first by Hoggart (1957) and Williams (1958). Their initiative has been taken up in the form of **cultural studies**, in which the concept of culture has undergone a radical transformation, moving towards the formulation offered at the heading of this entry. Since the late 1960s the notion of culture has been reworked largely in terms of Marxist, feminist and multi-culturalist approaches. Although the issues are by no means clarified, let alone resolved, they can be stated. Culture is now seen as a determining and not just a determined part of social activity, and therefore culture is a significant sphere for the reproduction of social power inequalities.

JH

See **class, difference, discourse, hegemony, ideology, language, nature, popular, reality, signification, structuralism, subjectivity**

Further reading Williams (1981); Turner (1990)

cultural studies ⋆ Cultural studies has focused on the relations between social relations and meanings – or more exactly on the way social divisions are made meaningful. ⋆ In general terms, culture is seen as the sphere in which **class**, **gender**, **race** and other inequalities are **naturalized** and **represented** in forms which sever (as far as possible) the connection between these and economic and political inequalities. Conversely, culture is also the means by and through which various subordinate groups live and resist their subordination. Culture is, then, the terrain on which **hegemony** is struggled for and established, and hence it is the site of 'cultural struggles'.

Clearly this approach to culture differs markedly from that of the 'cultural critics' for whom culture is the sphere of art, **aesthetics** and moral/creative values. Most importantly, cultural studies seeks to account for cultural differences and practices not by reference to intrinsic or eternal values (how good?), but by reference to the overall map of social relations (in whose interests?). Thus any distinction between 'cultured' and 'uncultured' people or practices that has been inherited from the **elite** tradition of cultural criticism is now seen in **class** terms. The distinctions themselves and the evaluations and 'discriminations' associated with them are analysed (not assumed): they are ideological representations.

The shape of cultural studies has been directly influenced by this struggle to decolonize the inherited concept, and to criticize its tendency to supress its own role in reproducing class and other inequalities. Thus, cultural studies has developed a body of work which attempts to recover and place the cultures of hitherto neglected groups. Initially this entailed attention to the historical development and forms of working-class culture, and analysis of contemporary forms of **popular culture** and media.

Unlike traditional academic disciplines, cultural studies did not have (or seek) a well-defined intellectual or disciplinary domain. It flourished at the margins of and by successive encounters with different institutionalized **discourses**, especially those of literary studies, sociology and history; and to a lesser extent of linguistics, **semiotics**, anthropology and **psychoanalysis**. Partly as a result, and partly in response to the intellectual and political upheavals of the 1960s (which saw rapid developments internationally in **structuralism**, **semiotics**, Marxism, feminism) cultural studies entered a period of intensive theoretical work. The aim was to understand how culture (the social production of sense and consciousness) should be specified in itself and in relation to economics (production) and politics (social relations).

This required the elaboration of explicit and historically grounded theoretical **models**, and the reworking of certain central organizing concepts (for example, **class**, **ideology**, **hegemony**, **language**, **subjectivity**). Meanwhile, attention at the empirical level was focused on ethnographic and textual studies of those cultural practices and forms that seemed to show how people exploit the available cultural discourses to resist the authority of dominant ideology. In particular, spectacular youth **subcultures** (teds, mods, bike-boys, hippies, skinheads, punks) were studied as instances of 'resistance through **rituals**'.

Subsequently, advances in feminist theory and politics challenged the monopoly of attention given to male subcultural activities. Cultural studies is currently at the stage of coming to terms with both feminism and **multi-culturalism**. The outcome of these encounters is not as yet fully worked through.

Throughout its short history, cultural studies has been characterized by attention to the politics of both methods of study and academic disciplines. There has been a continuing criticism of the **ideologies** of **objectivity** and **empiricism**, and cultural studies makes explicit what other academic disciplines often leave implicit – that the production of knowledge is always done either in the interests of those who hold **power** or of those who contest that hold.

JH

Further reading Hall *et al.* (eds) (1980); Turner (1990); Carey (1989); Grossberg *et al.* (eds) (1992)

cultural capital ∗ Originating specifically in the work of Pierre Bourdieu, this term describes the unequal distribution of cultural practices, values and competences characteristic of capitalist societies. ∗ Just as different social **classes** and **groups** are defined in terms of their differences in their access to economic capital, and hence material **power**, so Bourdieu argues they must be seen to possess correspondingly unequal cultural capital and symbolic power. Bourdieu's prime focus has been the educational system, which he suggests operates as a 'market place' for the distribution, exchange and grading of diverse cultural capital, hence reproducing underlying class relations. The term provides a useful shorthand for these complex issues; it can and should be extended to discussions of **gender**, **race** and other social divisions.

TO

See **class, culture, cultural reproduction, discourse, hegemony, lifestyle**

Further reading Bourdieu (1984); Garnham and Williams (1980); Featherstone (1987); Robbins (1991); Murdock (1989)

cultural imperialism ∗ Both an integral part and product of a more general process of imperialism, whereby certain economically dominant nations systematically develop and extend their economic, political and cultural control over other countries.

★ In a direct sense this gives rise to global relations of dominance, subordination and dependency between the wealth and power of advanced capitalist **nations** (especially the USA and western Europe), and the relatively powerless underdeveloped countries (notably Third World countries and nation states in South America, Asia and Africa). Cultural imperialism refers to important aspects of this process, namely the ways in which the transmission of certain products, fashions and styles *from* the dominant nations *to* the dependent markets leads to the creation of particular patterns of demand and consumption which are underpinned by and endorse the cultural **values**, ideals and practices of their dominant origin. In this manner the local **cultures** of developing nations become dominated and in varying degrees invaded, displaced and challenged by foreign, often western, cultures. Multi-national corporations play an important **role** in this process, as their aim is to facilitate the spread of their output throughout the global economy; ultimately this involves the international dissemination of **ideologies** consonant with the capitalist system.

The mass media are one of the most influential institutionalized means whereby this general process is organized and achieved, and the term *media imperialism* is often used to highlight their specific role. Analysis of world-wide media relations reveals what Boyd-Barrett (1977) has termed 'the uni-directional nature of international media flow'. This entails the one-way export of media products such as films, television programmes, records, news and advertisements, *from* a highly restricted number of internationally dominant sources of media production (notably the USA) *to* media systems in developing national and cultural **contexts**.

TO

See **globalization**
Further reading Boyd-Barrett (1977); Tunstall (1977); Smith (1980); Tomlinson (1991)

cultural production ★ The social production of sense, **meaning** or **consciousness**. The industrial production of cultural commodities. ⋆ Cultural production is a term gaining currency to emphasize the **institutionalized** and social character of **culture**, as opposed to the widely held belief that culture is the result of **individual** inspirations and imagination (see Wolff 1981).

For a specific application of the term to an analysis of broadcast television and cinema, see Ellis (1982).

JM

cultural reproduction ⋆ The overall process by which a social formation attempts to maintain and perpetuate the structures, forms and established corpus of sense-making: the effort to capture and fix the future representations and discourses of a society so as to reproduce its existing power relations. ⋆ This term is most commonly used in **cultural studies** to denote the way the cultural sphere acts as an arena for contending social interests to engage in a continuing stuggle over **signification**. The outcome is, at any one time, a greater or lesser degree of obviousness for the definitions and signifying practices of the dominant interests. Cultural reproduction, then, is the process of attempting to **naturalize** and legitimate the social authority of dominant interests (usually understood in **class/race/gender** terms). However, cultural reproduction also includes responses and resistances to, and departures from, the legitimated forms and practices of sense making. Thus reproduction in this context is a relational term, implying not a predetermined or uncontradictory linear transmission of the present into the future, but a complex network of personal and institutional relations with conflicting as well as congruent purposes. *What* is reproduced, then, is not a foregone conclusion, but results from the relative strength and weakness of the cultural forces that are in play in a given place and time.

JH

See **socialization**

cybernetics ⋆ The study of self-regulating systems, in which the effect of an action is fed back to its source in order that the originator may make any necessary adjustments to its subsequent actions. ⋆ Thus a thermostat feeds back information to a central heating boiler which then adjusts its output according to the room temperature, or a sensor in a robot's arm feeds back information to the control system. The feedback of the **receiver**'s reaction to the **sender** is the cybernetic concept of most relevance to the study of communication.

JF

See **feedback**

deep structure ⋆ A way of representing the structure of a sentence in as abstract a form as possible. ⋆ For any **language** the structure of sentences may be represented at two levels – at the level of the surface structure and at the level of the deep structure. The representation of the surface structure is closer to the shape of the sentence as it is used. Representation of the deep structure is more abstract and attempts to capture more basic and general features of its organization. The distinction derives from the work of the American linguist Noam Chomsky who justified it by arguing that deep structural representations were necessary to account for contrasting surface phenomena such as ambiguity on the one hand, and structurally dissimilar sentences which mean the same thing on the other hand.

In the case of ambiguity, the surface structure of a sentence such as 'the shooting of the hunters was terrible' may be made sense of in at least two ways – either 'the hunters shot badly' or 'it was bad that the hunters were shot'. These two ways of making sense of the sentence correspond to two alternative deep structures that may underlie the surface. In one deep structure the hunters are the subject of the action of shooting; in the other deep structure the hunters are the object of the action of shooting. This sentence, therefore, has at least two possible deep structures.

In the case of sentences which seem dissimilar in their structure, a common pattern may none the less underlie them. For example, 'the government banned the programme' is *on the surface* dissimilar from the sentence 'the programme was banned by the government'. But while the order of elements is very different in the two sentences the basic meaning is the same. Here it is because the two differing surface structures share an identical, underlying deep structure.

In Chomsky's work he then proposed a set of special rules which relate the two levels of representation to each other. Deep structures are **transformed** into surface structures by the operation of **transformational rules** which change the deep structure by re-ordering elements and inserting or deleting them. The notion, however, need not be restricted to the sentences of a language. It can also be applied to a range of **cultural** objects such as dreams, **myths** and stories. Superficially dissimilar myths may be related through a common deep structure. Or a story may be retold from a differing point of view so that the two versions are related to each through sharing a common deep structure.

MM

See **syntax, transformation**
Further reading Chomsky (1965, 1968)

defence mechanism ⋆ A process or technique by which the individual attempts to protect his or her self from pending danger and hence maintains some sense of security. ⋆ A concept used extensively in **psychoanalytical theory**, defence can be accomplished in a number of ways. Always the purpose is to reduce anxiety, avoid pain, or dismiss self-criticism. The major techniques for defence include (i) **identification**, where the **individual** adopts the goals and values of others, and in this sense attains defence because of **group** support; (ii) rationalization, where criticized behaviour is justified by plausible explanation that may not always be completely relevant; (iii) regression, where there is a reversion to earlier psychological states (for example, childhood) that are characterized by impulsivity and less complexity; and (iv) **projection**, where unacceptable characteristics of the self are attributed, perhaps falsely, to other people.

A more experimental analysis has been offered by **cognitive** psychologists interested in **perception**. Some evidence suggests that people block, or more slowly recognize, threatening or unpleasant **stimuli** that are shown for brief periods of time: a phenomenon relevant to the discussion of **censorship** and repression. However, as Dixon (1971) suggests, the situation is far from clear when so many perceptual defence **experiments** require subjects to report or recognize socially unacceptable information. Any delay can be attributed to hesitation or embarrassment rather than genuine censorship or misperception.

DS

See **projection, psychoanalytical theory**
Further reading Stafford-Clarke (1967); Dixon (1971)

deixis ⋆ Words or expressions whose precise meaning always depends upon their particular **context of situation** ⋆ *Deictic* items in effect point outwards (*deixis* is derived ultimately from the Greek word 'to show') from the text to the extra-linguistic context. They include words such as *this, that, here, there, us, you,* etc. Deictic items may be seen as falling into three major categories: *person deixis* such as *I, you, he/she/it, we, they, me,* mine, us, ours, them, theirs; temporal diexis such as *now, then, yesterday, today, tomorrow;* and *place deixis* such as *here, there, away, this, that.*

Part of the interest of such apparently commonplace items is the way in which they shift their meaning from context to context by referring to different entities: thus '*I*' refers to whoever is speaking at the moment of utterance. This can pose problems during early language development. Precisely because the referent is always shifting, children take time to identify the meaning of deictic terms and can mistakenly reverse their application, saying – for example – 'pick you up, Daddy' instead of 'pick me up, Daddy'.

Deixis is also interesting for the way in which it raises crucially important issues about **language** and **meaning**. Consideration of deictic terms helps to show how the meaning of many utterances does not reside purely in the words themselves, but depends also upon the **context** in which the words were uttered. For it is only by reference to context that we can recover the particular meaning of particular deictic expressions.

MM

See **context of situation, pragmatics, reference**
Further reading Levinson (1983); Lyons (1977)

dependency theory ⋆ A theory that postulates that the mass media are so crucial to our society that we are dependent upon them for certain social functions. ⋆ It derives from a **functionalist** view of society and proposes that we depend on the media for information about our environment, for the transmission of cultural **values**, for entertainment, and for the identification and interpretation of key social issues. Without the media to perform these necessary functions we, as individuals, would enter a state of **anomie** or social alienation, and society as we know it today would collapse. The theory is now outdated and discredited because it overprioritizes the media and ignores the role of other social **institutions** such as the family, education, religion, politics, and so on.

TO

See **functionalism**
Further reading DeFleur and Ball–Rokeach (1975); McQuail and Windahl (1981)

deregulation ⋆ A 1980s term originating from the USA, which refers to the systematic restructuring of forms of public provision and control and their replacement with those derived more directly from commercial, market operations. ⋆ In UK and other national contexts, deregulation has been part of the influential rhetoric which has been used both to describe and to effect the privatization of major public sector industries. Previously organized as state funded and controlled agencies, public monopolies, providing and guaranteeing public services, sectors such as health, telecommunications, gas, electricity and other services have been reorganized to compete more directly according to market forces of profitability, investment and consumer demand. The *de* in deregulation therefore implies the positive removal or 'rolling back' of the power of the state and public authority as sectors are 'opened up' to commercial competition.

Advocates of deregulation generally suggest that the most effective and efficient forms of provision and service are those provided on the commercial market. Against this, critics have argued that 'de'regulation is in effect 're'regulation, the transfer of assets and control from public to private hands, with the consequent loss of democratic accountability and social responsibility. In this way arguments about deregulation often present strongly contrasting visions of future consumers and **consumption**. For those on the political right, deregulation is the key to expanded choice and quality of services. For those on the left, deregulation leads to the stark reinstatement of the divide between those consumers who can and those who cannot afford to participate, own or control.

At a less general level than broad debates about the politics and cultural impact of deregulation is a series of issues concerning the mass media, notably developments in the organization and provision of broadcasting services. In the UK context, for example, considerable argument has been sparked by the Conservative government's policies for deregulating television and radio services. This has also encompassed the expansion of satellite and other new media and information technologies.

TO

See **public service broadcasting**
Further reading   McQuail and Siune (eds) (1986); Negrine (1989); Scannell (1989, 1990)

determination   ∗ The process by which social and historical conditions establish the limits within which cultural products and social activity can be formed, and which enable them to take their specific form. ∗   In social theory, phenomena that present themselves for direct observation (**empirical** facts) are rarely taken at face value, since empirical facts never *simply* present themselves for direct observation. Any act or object exists within a structure of relationships with others in its system, and with other systems. At the same time it exists with antecedent preconditions. The relationships and preconditions that make possible the definite (empirical) form and substance of an object or act are said to *determine* it.

There may be said to be *levels* of determination within a social system and historical epoch: so, for example, the actual programmes broadcast by a given television **channel** will be determined by that channel's financial resources, policies, personnel, and so on, and by its relations with other channels and other social agencies (for example, the law, the government).

However, the channel itself and its relationships with other agencies will themselves be determined at a 'higher' level by, for instance, the prevailing ideological and economic structure of the society in which the channel operates. Since what we are describing is the relation between social acts and agencies, and not a linear process of cause and effect, there is no *ultimate determinant*.

Furthermore, determination is not to be equated with causes since a governing antecedent or structurally organized system produces no necessary or inevitable outcome, but rather a limited (and hence in principle a predictable) choice of possible outcomes. Determination then isn't the same as **determinism**.

The concept of determination is important in the study of **culture** and **communication**, since it comes into play when we seek to account for the actual forms and practices of cultural production in a given time and place. The question is whether these forms and practices determine the social and political relations that characterize the society, or whether social, political and economic relations determine the forms of culture and communication. Perhaps an even more interesting question is the extent to which, and the precise way in which, each determines the other.

JH

See **articulation, base**

determinism ⋆ The assertion that all or at least a wide range of social and cultural phenomena directly derive their form, structure and direction from other underlying or fundamental forces. ⋆ The concept forms a couplet with the issues and problems associated with **autonomy**, and is the subject of contest on similar levels. At the general or structural level of analysis it appears in a variety of particular forms, which would include:

Economic determinism, where all social and cultural processes are held to be directly reducible to underlying economic and material relations.

Technological determinism, where social change is seen as a direct result of fundamental technological development and innovation (see Williams 1974).

Biological determinism, where specified biological instinctive or natural drives and needs become over-emphasized as determinants of social and communicative interaction and wider social process. This is often opposed to social or cultural determinism, forming the basis for what has become known as the '**nature**-nurture' debate.

The issues at stake here, in these and other examples, are largely concerned with degrees of weighting – all social and cultural theories face problems of reconciling ideas of **determination** and structure with notions of **autonomy** and action. Determinism is the tendency to ignore or suppress the latter, often as a result of over-estimation of the power of the former. Other examples of the general label being specifically mobilized would include *linguistic determinism*, *psychological determinism* and *cultural determinism*. In all of these cases, as in the examples cited above, the term tends to carry a *negative* connotation.

TO

See **autonomy, determination**
Further reading Worsley (ed.) (1977); Williams (1974)

deviance ⋆ A term used to refer to behaviour which infringes social rules, or disrupts the expectations of others, and as a result often attracts social penalty or punishment. ⋆ The occurrence of deviance is generally accepted to be an inevitable and even integral part of all societies: 'what is normal, simply, is the existence of criminality' (Durkheim 1950, p. 65). The nature of deviance however, as many social anthropologists have suggested, differs markedly between both social **contexts** and historical periods. Deviance is therefore best viewed as a social construct, and the ways in which different societies and social situations are characterized by different **rules**, and hence by wide varieties of activities defined as deviant, have been a prominent focus for research and enquiry. While all people break and contravene rules at some time, not all people are subsequently regarded or labelled as deviants. Deviant labels, or **roles**, such as 'robber', 'murderer', 'scrounger', 'drug addict', and so on, operate as Rock (1973) has suggested, 'to locate such deviants in social networks which are structurally removed from us. Furthermore most of us have no wish to reduce this distance' (p. 29).

Our knowledge of such roles and activities, and the **meanings** and **values** assigned to them, are central components of the way the society and **groups** we belong to organize and control our beliefs and understandings about the social world. Popular, often **common sense** explanations, have tended to see deviance as the result of physical or psychological inadequacy or 'defect' on the part of the deviant individual. Contemporary approaches reject this emphasis, and instead widen the focus of enquiry to examine the **interactions** and **power** relations between what Box (1971) has called 'rule breakers', 'rule markers' and 'rule enforcers'. Cohen (1971), for example, has urged that 'the concept of crime is meaningful only in terms of certain acts being prohibited by the state, and a problem can only be a problem to somebody. So whenever we see terms such as deviance and social problem, we must ask: "Says Who?" ' (p. 17).

A great deal of mass media output informs us about varieties and forms of deviance. In so doing the media serve as important reference points for our definitions of the 'good', the 'bad' and the 'ugly'; the normal and abnormal; the legitimate and non-legitimate, and so on. Not surprisingly the media coverage and presentation of deviance and social problems have constituted an important focus for much recent research.

TO

See **amplification, consensus, labelling, moral panic, norms, rules**

Further reading Rock (1973); Box (1971); Cohen and Young (eds) (1981); Cohen (1980); Hartley (1982); Bilton *et al.* (1981); Downes and Rock (1982)

diachronic ⋆ To study something diachronically is to study it as a system changing over time. ⋆ The term *diachronic* is particularly associated with the work of the Swiss linguist Ferdinand de Saussure who set up a distinction in linguistic study between studying **language** as a system of **meanings** at one moment in time (*synchronic linguistics*) and studying changes in the system of meanings from one temporal point to another (*diachronic linguistics*). When he formulated this distinction (first made public in his 1911 lectures) the linguistics of his day was still primarily concerned with historical analysis. It was thus concerned with the origins of language and families of languages; with changes in pronunciation from one period to another; and with tracing changes in the meaning of individual words from their origin in a source language. Saussure regarded these endeavours as fundamentally flawed, because they were atomistic and neglected the interrelated components of the system by focusing on isolated elements. The proper historical study of language depended, for Saussure, on initially describing the overall shape of the language, synchronically, before proceeding to the description of its change over time. Synchronic study thus became, in Saussure's view, logically prior to diachronic study; and the latter became – in effect – the comparison of temporally discrete synchronic states.

In this sense, Saussure was not, as has sometimes been claimed, against the historical study of language. On the contrary, he was concerned to establish the historical study of language (*diachrony*) on a sounder footing. However, one effect of his *Course in General Linguistics* was to re-orientate the whole direction of linguistic research away from the study of historical change and on to the current state of the language, so that historical linguistics has, until recently, suffered a long period of neglect.

MM

See **synchronic**
Further reading Culler (1976); Saussure (1974)

dialect ⋆ A dialect is a socially or regionally marked version of a language made up of distinctive patterns of sentence construction, vocabulary and pronunciation. The use of one dialect rather than another depends basically upon the social class and regional origins of the speaker. ⋆ Examples of dialect differences in English cover a wide range of phenomena and include matters such as: the use of multiple negation ('I hadn't got nothing to fall back on') which is common in some dialects of English but not in others; variation in vocabulary (the same object – a sports shoe, for instance – may be differently designated in different dialects, as *plimsoll, dap, sandy pump,* etc. in different parts of the UK); and distinctive patterns of pronunciation (such as using a glottal stop instead of /t/ in words such as *bitter, Luton, letter, bottle, butter,* which is common in parts of London).

The latter kind of variation, purely in terms of sound, is also known as **accent**; accent, however, refers *only* to pronunciation, and is thus not as inclusive a term as dialect which embraces a wider range of linguistic variation. Indeed in the UK it is possible to find the standard dialect being spoken in a range of regional accents.

Everyone speaks a dialect, whether it be a non-standard regional dialect or the standard dialect. The standard UK dialect itself evolved out of a particular regional dialect of the south-east English Midlands and gained pre-eminence not because of any intrinsic linguistic superiority, but simply because it was the dialect spoken in that part of the country that was particularly influential in the emergence of the modern UK **nation** state. It was the dialect spoken at the universities of Oxford and Cambridge, and by important sections of the mercantile class. Thus, its growing adoption from the fifteenth century onwards as the preferred dialect in education, in certain key professions such as the law, and indeed for written communication in general, is more a question of historical contingency than any special linguistic qualities.

Its adoption as a standard dialect, particularly for written communication, leads to normative pressure on other less socially prestigious dialects. This in turn gives rise to the mistaken view that the norms of the standard are inherently more correct than those of other dialects – a judgement which is unconsciously based on social factors rather than a linguistic consideration. From a linguistic viewpoint all dialects are equal in their ability to communicate the intentions of their users, even though a particular dialect can become identified with a particular communicative role.

MM

See **accent, code, diglossia, standard language, variety**
Further reading   Hughes and Trudgill (1979); Montgomery (1986)

dialogic ⋆ A property of all signification, that of being structured as dialogue. ⋆ The term was coined by Volosinov (1973) in order to stress the continuous, interactive, generative process of **language**, as opposed to the Saussurian emphasis on its abstract, structural **form**. Volosinov insists that all language is expressive of social relations, and hence that every individual utterance is structured as dialogue. That is, the way an utterance is organized by a speaker/writer is **oriented** towards an anticipated response in the hearer/reader.

Furthermore, once the utterance is received by its addressee, it results in meaning and understanding only through a dialogic interaction with what Volosinov calls 'inner speech' – a kind of internal dialogue that not only renders **signs** into sense, but simultaneously takes the process further by generating a response that is capable of being uttered as the next 'moment' of the dialogue.

Volosinov insists that this feature of **signification** is not tied to speech alone, but characterizes all utterances. Even monologues or soliloquies (speech without an addressee) are internally structured as dialogue. The same goes for utterances whose addressees are neither present nor known to the addresser – for example, books and media output. This book is dialogic in that each word, sentence, entry, and the book as a whole, is oriented towards a supposed addressee, and thus takes account of anticipated responses in the way it is selected, organized and sequenced.

JH

See **author/ship, multi–accentuality, orientation**

diegesis ⋆ From the Greek for *narration*, the word has been taken up in textual criticism (often as the adjective – *diegetic*) to identify whatever is described or imagined as the content of a narrative, as opposed to its **rhetorical** or **formal** features; the world 'inside' the tale, not the mode of its telling. The term is frequently found in cinema studies to distinguish the fictional world portrayed on screen from any artistic or technical features. ⋆

As with so many concepts, this one is most interesting if you consider it 'negatively' – the contrast between diegetic and non-diegetic aspects of any narrative, whether factual (e.g., news, documentary) or fictional, in the print or screen media. Characters, action and dialogue are usually diegetic, while music, voice-over, captions, inter-titles or **authorial** interventions are usually non-diegetic – they don't arise from the fictional world itself.

Having said this, it is only fair to add that nothing is *essentially* diegetic or non-diegetic. Music is diegetic if played by a character, but not if played by an off-screen orchestra with no part in the plot. This contrast is joked with in *Blazing Saddles* where the apparently non-diegetic music is suddenly revealed to be its opposite – the entire Count Basie Orchestra appears in the 'Western' setting, and the Count himself waves to one of the lead characters. Music can be both diegetic and non-diegetic simultaneously – a character singing (in the rain) to the accompaniment of unseen strings, for instance.

Even such diegetic fundamentals as character can be shifted between diegetic and non-diegetic roles. The film-maker Jean-Luc Godard plays with the contrast by having a fictional couple halt in mid-dialogue to step out of character and introduce themselves directly to the viewer. Alfred Hitchcock, in a comparable joke, always appears discreetly in his films as a walk-on, forcing clued-up spectators to attend to both diegetic and non-diegetic aspects at once.

In news, verisimilitude is created by mixing (diegetic) **actuality** and ambient sound with (non-diegetic) voice-over commentary. Often it is very hard to distinguish diegetic from non-diegetic textual features in a story. The non-diegetic voice-over commentary of documentary can in turn be re-fictionalized, notably in American gangster films and shows (*The Untouchables* on television or Roger Corman's *The St Valentine's Day Massacre* in cinema), and then this re-fictionalization becomes so imperative that it has only to be quoted to render a version of the genre 'true' (Cissy Spacek's voice-over in *Badlands*). Such mutual impregnations of reality and representation, actuality and fiction, fertilize our diegetic age.

JH

difference ⋆ A concept from linguistic philosophy, specifically the writings of the Swiss Ferdinand de Saussure and the Algerian–French Jacques Derrida, which has become a focus for attempts to understand the fundamental capacity of language and writing to mean. ⋆

For Saussure, difference is that attribute of the **language**-system (**langue**) which allows its elements to be distinguished from one another and so to **signify**. At its simplest, the system of differences operates at the **phonemic** level, allowing a very restricted number of differentiated sounds (forty-four in English) in various combinations to signify a potentially infinite range of meanings. Working to this exemplary model it is possible to claim that difference is the foundation of **meaning**.

For Derrida, however, this is only the start of the problem, a start signalled by spelling difference 'incorrectly' – '*différance*'. Derrida criticizes what he calls the *metaphysics of presence* as a recurring theme throughout western philosophy. This is the ideal (metaphysical) situation in which speech (but not writing) is supposed to yield up to the speaker a pure, transparent correspondence between *sound* and *sense*; i.e. between language and **consciousness**. In short, meaning (thought) is *self-present* in speaking (language).

Derrida disagrees. For him, the traditional distinction between speech and writing, privileging speech as somehow original or pure, cannot be sustained. Writing, because of its distance (in space and time) from its source, and because of its capacity for dissimulation, is a traditional problem for western philosophy –

an impediment to the desire or craving for language to act as the obedient vehicle for thought. For Derrida, writing is not an impure '*supplement*' to speech, but is its *precondition*; the very characteristics of writing that led Saussure (and the phenomenologist Edmund Husserl) to set it apart from speech are those that Derrida finds it impossible to leave out of account. However, it is not his project to replace speech as the model of sense-making with writing; his quarry is the *opposition* speech/writing in linguistic philosophy, and the 'metaphysical' tradition which seeks to arbitrate between the two terms in that opposition.

The notion of *différance* is one that Derrida would certainly refuse to call a concept, key or otherwise – his project is not to settle or to define meanings but to *unsettle* them. It encompasses the post-Saussurian idea of differing, adds to it the Derridean idea of deferring (postponement of what could be present to another time – an 'absent presence' of meaning), and represents these paradoxical ideas (differing suggests non-identity; deferring suggests sameness albeit postponed, perhaps endlessly) in a word whose startling 'misspelling' can be discerned only through writing (since *différance* is pronounced orally the *same* way as the word from which it differs, *différence*).

Derrida's work was especially influential in the 1970s and early 1980s when the Saussurian terminology of signification was becoming well known. After Derrida, it wasn't possible to claim that **signifiers** referred to **signifieds** (an absent presence); on the contrary, signifiers refer only to themselves, and meaning is generated by a differential play of signifiers in an endless, self-referential chain, beyond which it is not possible to go for verification. That is to say, there is no '**experience**' or '**reality**' beyond signification which can act as a test or warrant of its veracity, for all experience and reality is already a **representation** in **signification**. Representation, far from being a duplicitous, textual, tainted 'expression' of otherwise pure thought, is all we've got – **perception** itself is already a representation, and pure consciousness cannot be 'expressed' since it is the differentiating activity of signification that constitutes consciousness. Finally, it isn't possible any more to claim with confidence that individual **subjects** 'have' an identity (self-presence, self-knowledge), since identity is a product of difference – of the endless play of signifiers in the (absent) system of language.

Derrida co-wrote the script for **postmodernism** (subtitled 'the textualist's revenge') by positing the world as a text. His philosophy of doubt and radical scepticism led to the 'deconstructionist' movement, especially influential in America (see **structuralism**).

Interestingly, there's a 'politics of signification' attached to the very notion of difference. Some would argue that Derridean post-structuralism ends up in an idealist, solipsistic, anti-materialist cul-de-sac, where the materialist contention that social existence determines consciousness is short-circuited, giving a new lease of life to an Alice in Wonderland version of critical practice which allows the world to mean whatever the critic decides (this is a particularly apt criticism of some examples of deconstruction). On the other hand, some have argued that Derridean doubt, scepticism and self-reflexivity are not radical philosophical positions at all, because these qualities have been central planks of western philosophy since Aristotle and Plato. If so, this makes Derridean practice paradoxically a conservative force in intellectual culture, despite its unsettling implications.

JH

See **authorship, binary opposition, culture, discourse, individualism, postmodernism, subjectivity**
Further reading   Norris (1982); Lawson (1985)

diglossia   ⋆ The presence within a speech community of two related, but contrasting, linguistic varieties – one of which is high status, the other low status – which are used in complementary contexts. ⋆   Thus the high variety will most likely be used for news **broadcasts**, religious services, newspaper editorials and traditional poetry, whereas the low variety will be used for everyday conversation, sports commentary, soap opera and other informal contexts. Clear examples of diglossia are to be found in the Arabic-speaking world. In most, if not all, Arab countries two varieties of Arabic exist side by side – Colloquial Arabic learnt informally at home as the first language, and Classical Arabic acquired by explicit instruction at school. The grammar, pronunciation, and some of the vocabulary of the two forms of Arabic are different. The language of the Qur'an – the sacred text of Islam – is in Classical Arabic; and partly for this reason the high variety – Classical Arabic – is fairly uniform right through the Arabic-speaking world, despite strong regional variations in the local variety of Colloquial Arabic. Indeed, the availability throughout the Arab world of Classical Arabic helps to guarantee a degree of mutual intelligibility when speakers of quite divergent forms of Colloquial Arabic meet. Other diglossic situations may be found in Greece (between Classical Greek and Demotic Greek) and in Switzerland (between High German and Swiss German). While English-speaking communities do not seem to display such strong internal division into two contrasting varieties, it is still possible to recognize a cline or scale of competing varieties which are accorded differing degrees of prestige.

MM

See **accent, anti-language, code, creole, dialect, pidgin, standard language**
Further reading　Ferguson (1972)

discourse (adjective = discursive)　★ A term now quite widely used in a number of different disciplines and schools of thought, often with different purposes. Most uncontroversially, it is used in linguistics to refer to verbal utterances of greater magnitude than the sentence. ★ *Discourse analysis* is concerned not only with complex utterances by one speaker, but more frequently with the turn-taking interaction between two or more, and with the linguistic rules and conventions that are taken to be in play and governing such discourses in their given context.

However, the concept of discourse has also developed, separately, out of post-**structuralism** and **semiotics**. Here it really represents an attempt to fix, within one term, some of the theoretical ground gained in the early days of the structuralist enterprise. To grasp its significance you have to remember that in this early period structuralism/semiotics was above all an oppositional intellectual force, whose proponents were attempting to criticize and transform the inherited habits of thought and analysis about the question of where meaning comes from. Traditionally, and even now most 'obviously', meaning was ascribed to objects 'out there' in the world, and to the inner essences and feelings of individuals. Structuralism took issue with these ideas, insisting that **meaning** is an effect of **signification**, and that signification is a property not of the world out there nor of individual people, but of **language**. It follows that both the world out there and individual consciousness are themselves comprehensible only as *products*, not *sources*, of language/signification. We are what we say, and the world is what we say it is. But the problem with this conclusion is that it is too free-floating and abstract; it gives the impression that – not only in principle but also in practice – the world and the word can mean whatever we like.

Life isn't so simple. The abstract concept of 'language' proved inadequate to account for the historical, political and cultural 'fixing' of certain meanings, and their constant reproduction and circulation via established kinds of speech, forms of representation, and in particular institutional settings. This is the point at which the concept of discourse began to supplant the now flabby and imprecise notion of 'language'. Unlike 'language', the term *discourse* itself is both a noun and a verb. So it is easier to retain the sense of discourse as an *act*, where the noun 'language' often seems to refer to a *thing*. In its established usages, discourse referred both to the interactive process and the end result of thought and communication. Discourse is the social process of making and reproducing sense(s).

Once taken up by structuralism, largely through the writings of Michel Foucault, the concept of discourse proved useful to represent both a very general theoretical notion and numbers of specific discourses.

The general theoretical notion is that while meaning can be generated only from the **langue** or abstract system of language, and while we can apprehend the world only through language systems, the fact remains that the resources of language-in-general are and always have been subjected to the historical developments and conflicts of social relations in general. In short, although **langue** may be abstract, meaning never is. Discourses are the product of social, historical and institutional formations, and meanings are produced by these institutionalized discourses. It follows that the potentially infinite senses any language system is capable of producing are always limited and fixed by the structure of social relations which prevails in a given time and place, and which is itself represented through various discourses.

Thus individuals don't simply learn languages as abstract skills. On the contrary, everyone is predated by established discourses in which various **subjectivities** are **represented** already – for instance, those of **class**, **gender**, nation, ethnicity, age, family and individuality. We establish and **experience** our own individuality by 'inhabiting' numbers of such discursive **subjectivities** (some of which confirm each other; others however coexist far from peacefully). The theory of discourse proposes that individuality itself is the site, as it were, on which socially produced and historically established discourses are reproduced and regulated.

Once the general theoretical notion of discourse has been achieved, attention turns to *specific discourses* in which socially established sense is encountered and contested. These range from **media** discourses like television and news, to **institutionalized** discourses like medicine, literature and science. Discourses are structured and interrelated; some are more prestigious, legitimated and hence 'more obvious' than others, while there are discourses that have an uphill struggle to win any recognition at all. Thus discourses are **power** relations. It follows that much of the social sense-making we're subjected to – in the media, at school, in conversation – is the working through of **ideological** struggle between discourses: a good contemporary example is that between the discourses of (legitimated, naturalized) patriarchy and (emergent, marginalized) feminism. Textual analysis can be employed to follow the moves in this struggle, by showing how particular texts take up elements of different discourses and **articulate** them (that is, 'knit them together').

However, though discourses may be traced in **texts**, and though texts may be the means by which discursive knowledges are circulated, established or suppressed, discourses are not themselves textual.

JH

Further reading   For discourse analysis in linguistics see Coulthard and Montgomery (eds) (1981); for the concept of discourse in post-structuralism see Sturrock (ed.) (1979), introduction and chapter on Michel Foucault

displacement ⋆ The process by which the importance or significance of something is transferred (displaced) on to something else by a process similar to metaphoric transposition. ⋆

For Marx, displacement was part of the way **ideology** works to misrepresent reality. For instance, Dorfman and Mattelart (1975) show that there are no (or very few) working-class characters in the typical Donald Duck comic: but that criminals are all given working-**class** characteristics. These characteristics, they suggest, are displaced on to the criminals, thus justifying at the **subconscious** level (on which ideology works) the absence of the working class from the middle-class capitalist world of Ducksville, presenting them as 'really' socially deviant.

For psychologists, the major focus of interest has been in the redirecting and rechannelling of energy away from a **frustrating** goal and towards a more vulnerable target. Displacement becomes an important consideration whenever we refer to symbolism because it refers to a querying of surface meaning. There are three common applications:

(1) In the analysis of intra- and inter-**group** relations, studies of frustration and aggression have concentrated on instances where frustrating obstacles are too powerful to remove or avoid. This then leads to the displacement of aggression towards a more vulnerable target that is less likely to retaliate. One example might include the victimization of relatively powerless 'ethnic minorities' by more powerful **others** who are nevertheless frustrated by still more powerful **authorities**. Hence explanations of **prejudice**, discrimination and scapegoating emerge.

(2) In the investigation of short-term **memory**, items can be displaced by more recently processed information and may therefore be forgotten and more difficult to retrieve. For example, we may forget the beginning of an

argument if overwhelmed by subsequent information. The term 'displacement' is preferred to 'lost' because with appropriate reminder cues previously forgotten information can be remembered.

(3) In **psychoanalytical theory** the emphasis is placed upon mental imagery and the transference of psychic energy from one **symbol** to another. For example, **images** remembered from dreams may symbolize more essential but less socially acceptable aspects of sexual behaviour. Displacement leads to the process of *sublimation*, the replacement of objects that have primary significance with more removed symbols. In so doing there is a decrease in involvement and emotional significance through the distancing of symbolizing objects from their more meaningful representations. The basic assumption here is that we find it difficult to confront basic and hedonistic desires that are punished and repressed at an early stage within **socialization**.

DS

See **identification, projection, voyeur**
Further reading Dorfman and Mattelart (1975); Hilgard *et al.* (1979)

distinctive feature(s) ⋆ A term from structural linguistics that describes those features of a **sign** which distinguish it from others in the same **paradigm**. ⋆ This is an important concept for those theorists who believe that the meaning of a sign is determined largely by its relationship with other signs. Distinctive features are found in both the **signifier** and the **signified**.

Distinctive features of the **signifier**: The *a* in *last* can be pronounced in a number of ways depending on the national or regional accent of the speaker. What matters is that it is perceptively different from the vowel sounds in *lest*, *list*, *lost* or *lust*. As long as the sounds *lest*, *list*, *lost* and *lust* have features that are distinctive from *all* the ways of pronouncing *last*, all five words will have distinctive '**meanings**'. Similarly, the significance of, for example, pinstriped trousers resides in the features that distinguish them from grey flannel trousers or from blue and white striped chef's trousers. In these examples the distinctive features belong to the units in the **sign** system (that is, the signifiers).

Distinctive features of the **signified**: We can understand the meaning of the term 'youth', for example, only when we identify those features that distinguish it from 'adult' and 'child'. The word 'cow' will mean to a city dweller 'a farm animal distinguished from a horse or pig', but to a farmer it will be distinguished significantly from a heifer, a calf, a bull, and so on. In these examples the distinctive features belong to the concepts by which we order, categorize and understand our social experience (that is, the signifieds).

The importance of distinctive features gives rise to the dictum that 'We can only know what a sign means by looking at what it does *not*'.

JF

See **choice, paradigm, sign, signifier/signified, value**

---

dramaturgy ⋆ The study of everyday life by way of analogy with theatre. ⋆ As Harré (1979) reminds us, the dramaturgical framework is one of the oldest **models** referred to by observers and analysts of social action. Notions of performance, scene setting and **role** play become central to interpretations of actors on a stage of life who are following through scripts which have been constructed by prior performances and performers. Much interest was shown in the theatrical **analogy** by **symbolic interactionists** associated with the Chicago school of sociology (Mead 1934). Goffman's (1971) interpretations of impression management, public behaviour and interaction **rituals** further strengthened applications of such a model: especially when ethnographers were seeking an understanding of various communities which appeared to be rehearsing routines and acts in a variety of contexts. One example includes Scott's (1968) observations of people at racetracks, where a virtual cast of characters – with one or two gambling stars – are seen to follow through various scenes as they back various runners and see them win or lose. But for all of the appeal in applying such a simplistic framework to everyday action, the reader should remain critical of its validity on all occasions. One particular problem concerns its descriptive power but explanatory weakness: very rarely do dramaturgists ask why do people play these parts, and where do they originate from? Furthermore, the analogy with theatre has only partially been applied: for example, can we so confidently assume directors, audiences, stage-hands and critics within the same contexts as players, who act out some invisible script? Dramaturgy also neglects the importance and frequency of spontaneous action which either improvises, ad libs or even rejects some form of scripted action. Despite these criticisms, the model retains a prominent position in the analysis of groups who are observed within 'the field' – especially as this constitutes an alternative to the experimental study of social interaction associated with the social psychology laboratory.

DS

See **encounter, ethnography, facework, non-verbal communication, ritual, role, symbolic interactionism**
Further reading   Hare (1985); Goffman (1971)

dyad   ⋆ Two people engaged in face-to-face interaction. ⋆   As the smallest group the dyad is characterized by the degree of reciprocity and communication between the two members. A **group** of eight members cannot be viewed as four dyads on any one occasion; communication process and networks differ radically with such an increase in group size.

Dyads might include married couples, solicitor and client, or teacher and student, while dyadic communication is characterized by a virtual relaying of information between the two individuals. Speech will obviously be used in many cases but other *non-verbal* cues may complement or even replace spoken **language** completely, as in the case of **interaction** between parent and newborn child. It is this dyad, and later the **primary group**, that allows for the development of *interpersonal* behaviour and acquisition of **meaning**(s) from the **signs**, cues and words given by the other member. As Laing (1969) emphasizes, our interpretation of the **other**'s actions in turn affects that other's future actions because of his or her **perception** of our interpretation. Thus a **transactional** basis for dyadic communication is recognized. Let us return to the example of mother–child dyad. The mother certainly socializes the child in a number of ways, but we can also argue that the child socializes the mother, as when the mother departs from conventional (verbal and non-verbal) codes in order to secure more effective understandings for both interactants. It becomes more appropriate to include participants within the transactional process rather than **sender** and **receiver** as suggested by a more linear, **hypodermic needle model** of communication.

DS

See **encounter, facework, group, interpersonal communication, non-verbal communication, other, primary group**
Further reading Tajfel and Fraser (1978); Aronson (ed.) (1988); Burton and Dimbleby (1988)

E

effects/effects tradition ★ A heavily loaded term, traditionally and still commonly used to refer to the supposed direct consequences and impact of media messages on individuals. The term now also serves to describe a particular tradition of media study.

★ Historically the **media** have been accused of encouraging people into a broad succession of activities and behaviours that they would otherwise not consider, and into accepting beliefs, **values** and ideas that they would otherwise not entertain. Notably the dominant preoccupations informing such claims, and the vast amount of research that they have generated, have been with *negative* effects, the media *causing* those social and psychological activities defined and classified as 'problems' or threats of an 'anti-social', 'harmful' or 'dangerous' nature. Thus a succession of **moral panics**, often orchestrated by the media themselves, have amplified public concern about the effects of the media, in terms of their causing violence, juvenile delinquency, permissiveness and other social problems. Certain **groups** and sections of the population have been consistently identified as especially vulnerable to such direct effects: for example, children, young people and the 'uneducated'.

There can be little doubt that the introduction, development and presence of the various mass media have had some kinds of 'effects' and 'influences' on society as a whole: for example, in the spheres of education and politics, and in consequence upon social groups and individuals. However, the very complexities of these issues and relationships have tended to be minimized and masked in the face of the assumption that the all-powerful media can and do *cause* direct effects on individuals. The interweaving of academic research with the contours of public and political opinion, the interests of media industries and organizations, around this narrow question of effects has dominated and served to define a considerable amount of debate and research (see, for example, the debate surrounding so-called 'copycat riots' in UK cities in the summer of 1981: Tumber 1982; Herridge 1983).

As McQuail (1977) and others have suggested, this 'effects' focus and tradition moved from the unquestioned assumption of media power and direct influence, crystallized in the **hypodermic needle model** of media effects, to a preoccupation with the **empirical** measurement and demonstration of the processes involved in the communication of effects. Paradoxically, it was this application of methods of empirical investigation that produced a reversal and rethinking of earlier assumptions. By the late 1960s the lack of convincing evidence to prove direct unmediated effects forced a reconsideration of the problems and processes involved. Whereas effects research had a marked tendency to treat **audience** members as isolated individuals, cut off from everything but the media, subsequent work has concentrated on restoring the **individual** to a **context** of social and discursive relations, on the assumption that this situation shapes the individual's **decoding** and responses to media messages. This move requires a general widening of perspective, to the point where questions of particular short-term effect must be located within a more general consideration and analysis of the media's role in longer-term processes of social and **cultural reproduction**, and the **determination** and construction of **meanings**. Hall (1977) has called this 'media effectivity'.

Claims that the media produce or cause effect X or Y must be treated with circumspection; their 'obviousness' and apparently factual nature should be countered by rigorous and critical examination of the assumptions underlying them.

TO

See **audience, campaign, discourse, hypodermic needle model, uses and gratifications**
Further reading McQuail (1977); Morley (1980); Halloran (1977); Murdock and McCron (1979); Noble (1975); McQuail and Windahl (1981); McLeod *et al.* (1991)

elaborated and restricted codes ★ Bernstein's (1971) famous categorization of the different types of language used in different social situations. ★

The *elaborated code* is used in social relations where there is an expectation of **individual** differences, and which therefore encourage the expression of **meanings** that are discrete to the speaker. Meanings of this sort have to be verbalized precisely and accurately in order to make them available to the listener, and so the elaborated code requires a large vocabulary and a complex syntax. It is thus relatively unpredictable, or of low **redundancy**.

The *restricted code*, on the other hand, encourages the expression of **group** membership rather than of individual differences, and depends upon a context of shared assumptions, common social experience and shared expectations. It therefore needs a smaller vocabulary, and a simpler syntax: it is a highly redundant code. The codes of **non-verbal communication** (NVC) play a vital role alongside the restricted code; indeed, Bernstein suggests that new information or individual difference is expressed solely through the codes of NVC: with the elaborated code they are unimportant, if not actually unnecessary.

The elaborated code is more independent of its immediate context, it deals effectively with abstractions, absences and generalizations; the restricted code is better suited to the here and now and to the concrete. The elaborated code is the **discourse** of formal training or education; the restricted needs common social experience or background. Hence the elaborated code is generally accorded higher status in our society, suits the characteristic social relations of the higher status groups, and is propagated and rewarded by our education system. The restricted code is given correspondingly lower status, suits the typical social relations of the lower status groups, and is discouraged in most schools.

It is unfortunate that the distinction between the two codes fits our **class** differences so neatly, because it tempts us to look for the causes of this distinction in factors like class, education and intelligence. Bernstein is at pains to stress that this is not so – the difference is generated by the different types of social relations, not directly by the class, education or in any way by the intelligence of the speaker. He shows how tightly knit middle–class groups such as the officers' mess, public schools or legal and religious societies use restricted codes. But he does admit that the educated middle class has access to both restricted and elaborated codes, whereas the less well educated working class is confined to the restricted.

It is interesting to extend this concept beyond verbal language into art and other cultural forms. High culture works of art tend to use elaborated codes, whether they be works of literature, drama, music, dance, painting or sculpture. Works in mass or folk culture, however, tend to use restricted codes, because they operate through shared tastes and common social bonds and do not express, as do the high culture works, the individual uniqueness and originality of the artist.

JF

See **broadcasting, class, code, culture, narrowcasting**
Further reading Atkinson (1985)

elite ⋆ A fragment of the dominant section of a social formation that exercises or claims social and cultural leadership by virtue of some assumed qualities of excellence which are held to belong exclusively to that fragment. ⋆ The excellence usually claimed by elites in the cultural sphere is of an intellectual, creative or artistic nature; often presented as the ability to discriminate or judge better than others. The term thus implies a relation – usually between an elite and the *mass* (over whom the elite claims leadership). Both *mass* and *elite* are misleading terms, owing more to political debate than to analytical rigour. However, both have been influential in studies of the media, where the concept of an elite has been used both to describe the media professionals who produce mass communication, and, paradoxically, to separate the mass media from an 'elite' **culture** which is itself used as a yardstick to judge (usually with contempt) media products. You should not use the term as a neutral discriptive category, then, because it tends to reproduce the very kinds of **ideological** assumptions that analysis should expose, not replicate.

JH

See **mass society theory**

empiricism ⋆ An approach emphasizing the importance of observable, measurable and quantifiable evidence. ⋆ Three basic assumptions are evident: (i) empiricism assumes a universal, **objective** reality available for study; (ii) it assumes that we are able to devise methods of studying this reality objectively; (iii) it assumes that hypotheses explaining this reality are therefore capable of proof or disproof. As Fiske (1982) suggests, the empirical method 'fits neatly with the commonsense, science-based picture of the world' (p. 119).

The empirical method thus seeks verification through controlled, repeatable but public discussion. The presumable aim of the empiricist is that of receiving unanimous scientific support because nobody has disproved his/her argument. In other words, all of the evidence is in total agreement.

The major problem is that these assumptions are rarely, if ever, possible. Admittedly, repeated observation is possible within **experimental** conditions, where a number of variables are systematically manipulated within a highly controlled environment. It is not however feasible to explain or describe complex real life situations by way of experimental **analogies** – especially when the experimenters themselves may differ so markedly in their theoretical **orientations**, **methodologies**, **ideology** and **languages**.

DS

See **behaviourism, methodology, objectivity, positivism**
Further reading Fiske (1982)

encounter ⋆ A meeting between two or more people who engage in interaction. ⋆ The term has been especially favoured for its noun (as opposed to verb) status: for example, 'an encounter' (as opposed to 'an interaction'). Encounters may be characterized by various **rituals** and routines which are well rehearsed and relatively meaningless (A: 'Hi, how are you?', B: 'Fine, see you'; A: 'See you'). They are more often associated with meetings which may be unexpected, intimate or even hostile. Theorists from a variety of schools have attempted to identify the basic components of interaction associated with social encounters – to such an extent that pages of analysis can follow on from the briefest of meetings, especially when verbal content is linked with body language.

Closely linked to the concept of encounter is encounter **group**, which encourages open criticism in a frank and direct way of delegated group members – although this is supposed to be therapeutic, it is an experience that can also be destructive for people who are not prepared for such an ordeal!

DS

See **dramaturgy, facework, interpersonal communication, non-verbal communication, ritual**
Further reading Argyle (1987, 1988)

entailment ∗ A technical term from **semantics** used to designate a sentence that may be inferred from another sentence as its necessary logical consequence. ∗ Thus, the sentence 'John is a bachelor' entails the sentence 'John is unmarried'.

MM

See **implicature, semantics**

entertainment ∗ An **ideological** concept, ranking as one of the more successful **rhetorical** ploys of the twentieth century. It seems to refer effortlessly to a regime of universally intelligible mainstream output from the print, live and electronic media, encompassing audio–visual, narrative and performative genres. It is, however, a complex condensation of individual gratifications, textual forms and industrial organization. ∗

Entertainment as a concept is ideological because it is used to justify **discursive** practices which, while aimed at audience maximization and the reduction of unit costs, are represented as neutral or apolitical, plausible (or legible) not by reference to the commercial imperatives of the entertainment industry but by reference to the assumed demands of a fictionalized **audience** or public. The idea of entertainment is trotted out to justify representations that can on other grounds be citicized for **racism**, sexism, metropolitanism and the rest. In short, don't be beguiled by claims that something offensive is 'only entertainment'.

JH

entropy ⋆ Unpredictability in the content or form of a message: a term from communication theory. ⋆ Entropy in the **content** is the equivalent of high information, and frequently requires **redundancy** to be introduced into the form for effective, easy **communication**. Entropy in the **form** is usually the result of breaking existing **conventions**, usually for aesthetic or imaginative reasons. Entropy correlates with **information** on the level of content, and is opposed to redundancy on both levels.

JF

See **information theory, redundancy**

escapism ⋆ A process which has been defined in largely psychological terms and which enables the individual to withdraw from unpleasant or threatening situations by recourse to preferred symbolic or imaginative states. ⋆ Getting away from a particular context is not always possible. Just as there is a process of leaving, there is also an association with entering a different frame of reference, and one that offers some form of comfort. In **psychoanalytical theory** such escape follows on from confrontation with insurmountable, **frustrating** objects or events. The person may therefore withdraw from that situation and fantasize through imagination and the sophisticated use of imagery.

Escapism can be viewed as a **defence mechanism**, and may frequently involve **identification** with **others**, sometimes referred to as *heroes/heroines*, who are perceived as being more powerful and successful in overcoming frustrating obstacles. An ideal self-image can even replace others as the adulated person in *fantasy*. Escape can further be aided by external cues as with organized activity (for example, games) or **media texts** that guide imagination and imagery while also allowing for individual creativity.

A general concern with escapism has been prominently evidenced in the study of both media **audiences** and media **content**. The popularity of certain media, notably cinema, has been explained in terms of the audience's need to escape from a variety of pressures and constraints associated with everyday life. **Uses and gratifications** theorists, for example, commonly substitute the term *diversion* for escapism, to imply that audiences use media to escape from the mundane routines, problems and frustrations of the real world – and thereby achieve emotional release. In this sense the media **text** is seen as offering, in varying degrees, forms of **symbolic** escape. Studies such as these are often challenged because they rarely question *what* the audience is escaping *into*. The text is assumed to be unproblematic, and escapism is seen as being a function of the audience, not of the text.

DS

See **catharsis, defence mechanism, identification, uses and gratifications, voyeur**

ethnic ⋆ A descriptive label for a group, implicitly defined in terms of racial or national characteristics, where the main emphasis falls on cultural practices and beliefs. ⋆ The concept can be usefully applied to **minorities** which either have been set apart or have desired separation according to distinct cultural attitudes and traditions. On the other hand, we do not usually refer to 'ethnic majorities' associated with national groupings and identities – is it possible, for example, to argue for an 'ethnic quality' to the English in England? It would seem that such a quaint label can only be attached to **nation**-groups when located abroad, and furthermore when those **groups** do not constitute part of a ruling

107

elite. For example, there may be an 'ethnic' description of Hispanics in New York – but not of the English in India.

The popularity of the term belies its vagueness – note how many overlaps can be counted between an ethnic grouping and religion, colour (but not **gender**), or nationality. In some ways it has found favour with politicians and academics who search for more delicate ways of describing groups who differ from the nation state and who have some shared identity (either secured for themselves, or with such cultural values placed upon them): it may be more convenient (if mystifying), for example, to say 'London's ethnic groups' than 'Pakistani, Indians, West Indian and Chinese living in London'.

A closely related concept is *ethnocentricism*, as discussed by Allport (1980). This refers more to the process of looking inwards to the **values**, beliefs and histories of one's own group, and which may be seen as a form of insularity by outsiders. Ethnocentric tendencies have often been linked with persecution, and especially **racism** at levels of both oppressor and victim. For the persecutor, ethnocentrism leads to the valuing of national identity and to the seeing of different cultures or communities located within that nation as inferior, a threat, or a weakness. The targets of what Adorno *et al*. (1950) call such authoritarian personalities may also be characterized by ethnocentrism, but with a preservation of culture which outsiders view as foreign. In essence, the bigot views insularity as a snub, whilst forgetting that his or her own discrimination and insularity fosters alienation and distrust – or simply a lack of opportunity to communicate.

The development of ethnic values can therefore be seen either as a form of self-protection, or as a positive move for the acceptance of people within society. The importance of historical process cannot be underplayed here – what may be an ethnic group for today was an 'immigrant problem' of yesterday. Indeed, it might even be argued that the search for 'authentic' ethnic identity and experience lies at the heart of some forms of modern tourism.

DS

See **culture, minority, prejudice, race**
Further reading Montgomery (1986)

ethnography ⋆ A method of fieldwork research, largely derived from anthropology, where the researcher attempts to enter into the culture of a particular group and provide an account of meanings and activities 'from the inside'. ⋆ The method emphasizes the cultural distance that the researchers have to bridge if they are to make intelligible the community or **group** under study. The ethnographer draws on a wide range of sources to paint a picture of a social group, and participates 'in people's daily lives for an extended period of time, watching what happens, listening to what is said, asking questions' (Hammersley and Atkinson 1983). In so doing, ethnography especially values the **language** community – so much so that this method is also linked with **conversational analysis**. Whilst ethnography is usually linked with sub-branches of anthropology or sociology, especially for instance the Chicago school of **symbolic interactionism**, we should note overlaps with aspects of **participant observation** in psychology.

The skilled ethnographer aims to understand **cultural values** within collectives and communities that are essentially meaningful to those people so involved. A further level of communication is then achieved through the writing-up of such observations, in that ethnographic literature will typically provide verbatim quotes, life histories and **case studies**: these publications are often accessible to a wide range of readers because of the researcher's respect for a faithful and detailed recounting of events that actually happened.

Examples of ethnographic study include Beynon's (1985) study of secondary school classes in South Wales, or Barbera-Stein's (1979) study of day-care centres for pre-school children, or Saunders and Turner's (1987) observations of betting offices. Whatever the purpose of investigation, the onus is on going into the field and achieving qualitative analysis of **groups** that are defined as sharing particular cultural values. While this has achieved much support as an alternative to the sterile laboratory study or superficial, quantitative **questionnaire** survey, we should be careful about the underlying implications about a 'real world out there' being distinct from the social researcher's academic framework. Indeed, ethnographic literature sometimes reflects a researcher's search for **ethnic** identity, rather than an interpretation of ethnic values.

Whilst this method has many advantages in both illustrating theory and involving practical research work, certain criticisms should also be noted. Observations can be overt or covert – the latter implying a degree of infiltration by the researcher, and the possibility of disclosing information that would misrepresent or damage group members in some way. This ethical query is accompanied by the possibility of researchers 'raiding' cultures for evidence which supports pre–existing hypotheses or theories – qualitative material can so easily be manipulated and selectively edited. But assuming the integrity of the researcher, there is also the very real possibility of ethnographers providing a functional account of how groups operate and perceive their worlds, without including more structural perspectives on that group's economic and power relations within a social order. In essence, there may be an abundance of description but a scarcity of explanation or theory-building.

Another concern addresses the difficulty of researchers actually reaching an understanding of another group's perceptions and/or **languages** – especially when barriers such as social **class** exist (note how few middle–class groups are subjected to ethnographic scrutiny). Finally, if integration between researcher and group is achieved, we should ask what happens to those people left behind when that researcher finishes the project and moves on to something new.

DS

See **methodology, parole, participant observation**
Further reading Hammersley and Atkinson (1983); Turner (1990); Atkinson (1990)

ex-nomination   ⋆ A term coined by Barthes (1973) to show how the economic determinants of a society are absent from representations of that society – they are literally un-named.   ⋆   Barthes's own example of ex-nomination is *capitalism*. This is named quite easily in the *economic* **discourses** of western societies – it is uncontroversial to say that we live within a capitalist economy. However, Barthes points out, the situation is not so simple in *political* discourses. There are no capitalist parties as such, even though certain political and governmental parties may see themselves as 'supporters' of capitalist 'enterprise'. When we move on to the **ideological** discourses of **representations**, capitalism is completely ex-nominated – the connection between familiar **myths**, **meanings** and forms of representation on the one hand and capitalism on the other hand is erased. These forms are **naturalized** into **common sense**, so that eventually it seems odd to suggest that **realism**, for instance, should be understood as 'bourgeois' realism, or that the obvious, self-evident properties of 'reality' are actually products of an established way of looking at it, and not properties of the natural world itself.

The concept of ex-nomination can be extended to encompass other aspects of modern **cultures**, and in so doing its further implications can be worked out. Just as capitalism is ex-nominated in the movement from economics through politics to ideology, so we find that there are ex-nominating processes involved in representations of **gender**, **race** and nation. Whereas it is frequently the case that women are represented first as women, and then in other terms, for men this is not so. They are represented in terms of their job, action, character or whatever – their gender is 'beyond **discourse**', as it were: it does not need to be named. So we find newspaper headlines that tell of 'Senator and Girl in Crash', or 'Beauty of the Siege – Cheery Heroine was a Lifesaver', or 'Sexy Anna Tops Poll'. In each case the woman is defined by her looks, body or procreative ability, whereas men are very rarely 'nominated' in this way.

Similarly, the ex-nominating process can be observed in representations of race and nation. That is, black people and non-English nationals (including the other UK nations of Wales, Scotland and Northern Ireland) are **signified** as 'belonging' to their respective race or nation, whereas for English whites there is no need to name these attributes.

It can be argued then that wherever a qualifying adjective seems redundant we are in the presence of ex-nomination – where we can speak of people without specifying their age, **class**, region, **gender, race** or **nation**.

JH

See **ideology, naturalizing**

111

experience ⋆ A term much used in **common sense** conceptualizations of what it is that determines knowledge, forms of expression or culture. ⋆ Usually imputed to the **individual** person (and then, perhaps, aggregated up to larger **groups** like the neighbourhood, community or nation), experience is taken to be a prime *source* of **meaning**.

It is widely argued, then, that we must pay due deference to experience, whether our own or that of groups we wish to study and understand. And many arguments about the 'true significance' or 'quality' of a given **text** (factual or fictional, analytic or 'creative') are centred on whether or not it is 'faithful' to 'authentic' experience.

The term has become controversial within **cultural studies**, because it has been used – especially by historians of the working class or of ordinary life – as the justification for particular interpretations of a group or period; and thence it has been used to underpin various **ideological** positions which seek to promote the interests of such groups. Thus, 'we must base our politics on the experience of the people we represent'. The trouble with this position is that the 'experience' of powerless groups includes negative as well as positive elements, including, above all, deep-rooted sexism and **racism**. So 'experience' turns out to be a two-edged weapon.

This is partly because of a serious theoretical error in the way the term has hitherto been used. It is taken to be the *source* of meaning – out of the experiences of people and groups are built their **culture**, forms of expression, ideologies, and so on. That is impossible, since without cultural and **signifying** or **discursive** systems which predate the individual, and which form the resources out of which an individuality can be constructed for/by each person, there wouldn't be anything to experience *with*. In short, experience is not the precondition for meaning, but vice versa. As a result of this conclusion, increasing attention has been focused on experience as an object of study in itself rather than as an explanatory term. Such analysis includes attention to the use of the term as a taken-for-granted (untheorized) concept in academic **discourses** (like psychology) as well as in media, literary and similar contexts.

JH

See **culture, discourse, individual/ism, subjectivity**
Further reading   Donald (1982)

experiment ⋆ A scientifically controlled situation or process where selected variables are isolated and investigated empirically in order to test a hypothesis. ⋆ For example, an experimental programme designed to test for the effectiveness of an advertisement might have as the *dependent variable* the **audience's** choice of the advertised product. This could be affected by such *independent variables* as colour and quality of product packaging, male or female presenters within the advertisement, and so on. A series of experiments that manipulates each independent variable (or combination of variables) to the exclusion of others (and other combinations) is carefully designed to identify just which components of the advertisement is/are most effective in **persuading** the buyer.

Biases in the design and execution of experiments, and the subsequent interpretation of experimental data, have been frequently noted (see, for example, Jung 1971). Often, though not always, laboratories are artificial set-ups used for experimentation. This is because variables cannot always be manipulated naturally, and neither can the effects of such manipulation be observed within the real 'outside' world. The problem with this is that the experimenter designs a highly artificial situation which stands in the way of confident extrapolation to non-laboratory encounters. Experiments therefore face two major considerations. First, the degree to which laboratory tests may represent 'real life' settings. Second, the degree to which the experimental sample represents a total population. Both points raise a general problem concerning the validity and generalizability of laboratory-based and experimentally produced data.

The experimental method has proved to be popular in the **effects tradition** and with investigation of the **hypodermic needle model** of communication. A typical set-up would involve a control as well as an experimental condition. Just as the experimental group encounters 'abnormal' conditions the control group offers some parallel with the 'normal' state of affairs. Any differences in observed behaviour patterns are supposedly attributable to experimental manipulations. For example, we might be interested in the effects of television **violence** on children. Our investigation will have to try to separate out the different effects of watching non-violent television from watching violent programmes and from not watching any television at all. Three **groups** of people would be investigated:

Group A: views a violent programme
Group B: views a non-violent programme
Group C: does not watch television at all

Group C constitutes a control group because it acts as a base against which we can measure the effects of television exposure, regardless of content. All children within these groups would be tested in some way – both before and after viewing (groups A and B) or some other activity (group C). Their respective performances would then be compared.

It is, however, difficult to control for all interfering variables that may be at play when investigating such communication. For example, simply being in a laboratory and a victim of some contrived situation may easily influence the behaviours of control subjects. It is important to remain critical of claims concerning **empiricism** and **objectivity** as regards the inclusion of control groups within experimental design.

DS

See **empiricism, methodology, objectivity, positivism**
Further reading Miller (1984); Harris (1986); Aronson (ed.) (1988)

F

facework ⋆ A term referring to aspects of public performances by actors that are identified within social settings. ⋆ At first glance the obvious association is with eye contact and facial expression, but facework should also be linked with more general aspects of body **language** and even **conversation**. In this sense 'face' means the line of contact between actors who are located within what Goffman (1971) calls a 'front' region of performance. For example, facework for a restaurant waitress involves the wearing of uniform, the asking of certain questions but not others, the taking of orders, and obedience to certain other codes of conduct when in the presence of customers (or proprieters). But when out of their company (what Goffman calls back-stage) the rules for interaction quickly change – in the kitchen they may say rude things, smoke a cigarette, joke around and even have a meal.

A useful topic involves the analysis of facework for a social group of your choosing. Facework can be interpreted according to various themes – such as costume, posture and catch-phrases. Much facework relies on support from others who are in the same 'team' and who can help out if things do not go according to plan (or who can improvise when performances get boring). Even more interesting is the identification of 'props' used by participant actors to complement facework and *impression management* – these can range from the use of physical objects (for example, dinner plates) to more permanent aids that cannot be quickly adopted or dropped (for example, make-up).

Despite the practical appeal of the facework concept, it should be noted that there are problems with a front-stage/back-stage divide. If we assume that facework is linked with public perform-ance, then when back-stage we are still engaged in acting – but this time with a different group of people or **audience** and with different roles and rules. Consequently, you may question whether we completely drop this dramatic mask of communi-cation. Furthermore, many **symbolic interactionists** who pur-sue this theme of **dramaturgy** give the impression that facework is the key dimension in analysing **encounters**: after all, what is there behind the public self, and are we always conscious of our performance? Mead's (1934) distinction between the 'I' and the 'me' seems to have led to a preoccupation with the latter concept amongst theorists interested in theatres as the metaphor for every-day life.

DS

See **dramaturgy, encounter, non-verbal communica-tion**

Further reading Goffman (1971); Burns (1992)

feedback ⋆ A term from **cybernetics**, though now closely associ-ated with communication **models** and **communication theory**. It is taken to be the process by which the decoder's reaction to the message is transmitted back to the encoder. ⋆ It then becomes the **encoder's** means of knowing how the **mess-age** has been received. Thus it allows for changes in transmission, encoding or **medium** to achieve the encoder's desired reaction.

The process models of communication frequently categorize the media according to their opportunities for feedback, and generally relate feedback to efficiency. Thus the mass media, noticeboards or a tannoy system which allow for limited or delayed feedback are seen as less efficient means of passing infor-mation than face-to-face communication, or the telephone. Similarly, some claim that the lecture is less effective than the seminar.

We should note that adding a feedback loop to a linear process model does not make that model circular or dynamic – it is there to increase the effectiveness of the linear process.

JF

See **cybernetics**

Fordism/post-Fordism ★ Distinctive stages in the historical organization of production in twentieth-century industrial societies. ★ The terms are also commonly used as shorthand for broader changes in **cultural** and political relations and processes, which gives them a wider remit than solely describing modes of industrial **production**. The concepts, however, draw on the reputation of Henry Ford, historically credited as the first industrialist to *mass produce* a *standardized product* at a price which was affordable and made possible *mass consumption*. This system, *Fordism*, was characterized by large-scale industrial plant and investment; an inflexible, mechanized production line; and rigid and repetitive routines of labour process and 'scientific management'. The logic of this type of organization, as Ford noted, was that customers could have an automobile in any colour they desired – as long as it was black; and this is a useful metaphor for the relations between producers and consumers embodied in the early form, operating to rigid, standardized rules of production, which restricted the development of differentiated 'consumer culture'. Whilst the Fordist phase is held to be characteristic of advanced western economies, especially in the postwar period, some of its key tenets – standardization and centralization for instance – were also associated with developments in Soviet and other worldwide industrial cultures.

Post-Fordism implies a distinctive historical shift, whereby new economic markets and cultures have been opened principally by means of new computer-based information technologies. In contrast to Fordism, the post-Fordist age is usually associated with smaller, more flexible units of production, able to cater responsively for much greater ranges or types of segmented and specialized consumer demands. Post-Fordism is associated with changes in the politics and economics of major western states from the 1980s onwards. Central processes identified by the

117

concept include: the decline of old 'mass' or 'heavy' industries and the appearance of new, 'sunrise', micro–chip sectors, more flexibility in decentralized networks of labour and work organization, together with tendencies towards global relations of production and **consumption**. Finally, it is suggested that a key feature is the development of multiplicities of **lifestyles** and different consumer practices.

Debate continues about the utility and precise implications of the two concepts and the kinds of transition implicit in their application. Undoubtedly these debates have considerable relevance in the analysis and understanding of *contemporary* culture and communication and those aspects which might legitimately be regarded as historically distinctive and significant.

TO

See   **globalization, lifestyle, mass society, postmodernism**
Further reading   Harvey (1989)

foregrounding   ⋆ A communicative element may be said to be foregrounded when it is made the focus of attention for its own sake. ⋆   The term derives from the work of the Russian and Czech Formalists during the 1920s who developed the concept as part of a theory which argued that literature was a specialized and distinctive mode of communication. Literature (and poetry in particular) was different from everyday communication because of the systematic foregrounding of selected linguistic components. These stood out against the background of everyday communicative norms in one of two ways – either by rule-breaking or by rule-making. Thus, one kind of foregrounding consists of manipulating the normal rules of linguistic communication by bending or breaking them, as in the following poem by e.e. cummings:

Me up at does

out of the floor
quietly Stare

a poisoned mouse

still who alive

is asking What
have i done that

You wouldn't have

Amongst other things, the first four lines scramble the more usual
ordering of elements in an English clause, which in normal prose
writing would be likely to read 'a poisoned mouse does quietly
stare up at me out of the floor'. This is one of several ways
(including, for example, the adoption of unusual patterns of
punctuation) in which the poem breaks the normal rules of
English.

Another kind of foregrounding involves the superimposition
of extra rules or patterns beyond those required to ensure intelligibility. The use of rhyme, alliteration and metrical rhythm
amount to just such patternings at the level of sound in poetry.

Foregrounding may also be achieved through additional syntactic patterning as in the following short poem by Shelley:

> One word is too often profaned
>   For me to profane it;
> One feeling too falsely disdained
>   For thee to disdain it;
> One hope is too like despair
>   For prudence to smother;
> And pity from thee more dear
>   Than that from another.

The first four lines of the poem are built up from a simple
syntactic pattern of the following type:

    One -X- (is) too -Y- -Z-ed
        For -M- to -Z- it;

where X = noun; Y = adverb; Z = verb stem; and M =
pronoun. The pattern is so strong at the beginning of the poem
that the second pair of lines exactly parallels the syntax of the first
pair. The rhetorical force of the last two lines, however, derives –
in part at least – from the way in which it breaks from the pattern

119

established so strongly at beginning. In both these ways, therefore, by rule-making and rule-breaking are elements of the language foregrounded.

According to the Formalists this foregrounding was more than **language** calling attention to itself. 'Making strange' the language in this way was in fact part of making everyday experiences unfamiliar. By manipulating the rules of the language, literature extends its communicative possibilities, frees itself from its automatic ways of rendering the world, and achieves special **rhetorical** effects.

However, a crucial shortcoming of the Formalist account is the way in which it neglected to notice some of the identical processes at work in non-literary texts. Parallel structures of syntax, for instance, may be found quite commonly in political speeches, advertising and other kinds of persuasive discourse. Thus, when Neil Kinnock (a UK Labour politician) produces the following sentences in the course of a speech, he is adopting precisely the kind of repetitive syntactic patterning identified by the Formalists as peculiar to poetry:

> We are ruled by a Government
> whose rhetoric is resolution but whose reality is industrial
> ruin,
> whose rhetoric is efficiency but whose reality is
> collapse.
> Their rhetoric is morality,
> their reality is unemployment, which splits or scatters
> families.

And similar kinds of syntactic patterning may also be found in advertising:

> *PERFUMERY*
> THE PERFUME YOU WEAR SAYS A LOT ABOUT YOU
> The range we have says something about us.
> Nothing triggers memories as strongly as scent.
> Just a hint of a familiar fragrance brings back that Time.
> That Place.
> That Person.

Names are forgettable
Even photos fade,
But perfume lingers.

Here again, as with the poem and the speech, we can find in the first two lines of the advert a parallel syntactic structure:

The -X- -Y- -Z- says -N- about -Y-

where X = noun; Y = pronoun; Z = verb; and N = quantifying expression. We also have quite marked sound patterning with an identical initial sound used in the words 'familiar', 'fragrance', 'forgettable', 'photos', 'fade', and 'place', 'person', 'perfume'. In the light of evidence such as this, it would seem that the attempt of the Formalists to identify poetry (or even 'literariness') with foregrounded features of language is impossible to sustain. Instead, what counts as poetry seems to be as much a matter of social judgements as textual properties. However, this does not mean that the notion of foregrounding is thereby only of historical interest. It is noticeable, for instance, that the kind of extract singled out above from a political speech is precisely that part of the speech most likely to elicit applause in the context of its initial delivery, and the part most likely to be excerpted for subsequent news broadcasts. Foregrounded uses of language, therefore, seem to be strongly associated outside literature with **rhetoric** – with acts of verbal **persuasion** – and the notion of foregrounding retains its interest as part of this broader study.

MM

See **code, metaphor, rules, text**
Further reading   Atkinson (1984); Bennett (1979); Leech (1966)

form and content   ⋆ A deceptively simple pair of words that refer to the fact that all signs have a physical existence (that is, form), and refer to something other than themselves (that is, content). ⋆ The simplicity is deceptive because it can, and often does, lead to the misconception that the content is pre-existent, waiting to be given an appropriate form – what has been called the 'vulgar packaging' **model** of communication. In this the **message** (or content) is **encoded** into **signs** (form), transmitted and then **decoded**, that is, the form is peeled off to reveal the content rather like taking the paper off a parcel. Incidentally one of the weaknesses of **content analysis** is that it takes no account of the form that each unit of content takes.

In fact neither the form nor content can exist without the other, and each is affected by the other to the extent that the separation between the two is a (dubious) analytical exercise only, and cannot exist in reality. These terms can therefore be related to **signifier** and **signified** – which are equally interdependent, and which exist for analytical convenience only, but which have more rigorous definitions and are part of a more precisely articulated model of **signification**.

Literary criticism is particularly prone to talk about 'form', indeed one dominant school of criticism of a generation ago was 'Formalism'. The word 'form' has been used so widely and loosely that it is due for a rest, and students should be chary of using it; likewise 'content'.

JF

See **content analysis, sign, signifier/signified**

frame ★ A concept referring to the organization of social knowledge and experience. ★ Goffman (1974) has demonstrated how we frame reality in everyday life in order to comprehend and respond to social situations. The frame **analogy** has proved extremely useful when analysing social **interaction**, because it marks out an **encounter** or episode as separate from other encounters or episodes. In the same way a frame around a painting marks out a clear boundary between wall and picture.

The term has also been employed in the study of the mass media. Media frames are principles of selection – **codes** of emphasis, interpretation and presentation. Media producers routinely use them to organize media output and **discourses**, whether verbal or visual. In this context media frames enable news journalists, for example, to process and 'package' large amounts of diverse and often contradictory information, quickly and routinely. These frames are therefore an important **institutionalized** part of the **encoding** of mass media **texts**, and may play a key role in structuring **audience** decodings.

DS

See **codes, news values, preferred reading**
Further reading Goffman (1974); Tuchman (1978); Gitlin (1980); Hall *et al*. (eds) (1980)

Frankfurt school ∗ A group of German intellectuals, loosely united in their efforts to develop a revolutionary philosophical variant of western Marxism, known as 'critical theory'. ∗ Taking its collective name from the Institute of Social Research founded in Frankfurt in 1923, the school was forced to leave Germany and emigrated to the USA during the 1930s, although it was later formally re-established in Frankfurt in 1953. Principal figures of the school are Max Horkheimer (with interests in philosophy, sociology and social psychology), Theodor Adorno (sociology, philosophy and the critical study of music), Herbert Marcuse (philosophy and politics), Erich Fromm (psychoanalyst, social psychologist) and Walter Benjamin (sociology of literature, art, and photography). The work of Jürgen Habermas (philosopher and sociologist) provides the most recent attempt to continue and develop the school's traditions. In general these theorists share and are united by a concern to analyse the nature and consequences of a variety of economic, political and cultural changes, that they define as fundamental to capitalist societies of their time. Their overriding aim is to generate progressive and positive social development through their work by exposing the underlying contradictions of **class** societies.

Their **context** and **experiences** are strongly evidenced in the major themes and questions they choose to confront. These include explanations of the rise of Fascism, and the decline of revolutionary movements, and a focal concern for what they identify as the increasingly authoritarian and bureaucratic tendencies of modern western societies. During their period in the USA, these themes were developed in their analysis of the mass media, which they called the *culture industry*. They argued that the culture industry had logically emerged to perform a highly manipulative role in advanced capitalist societies, serving to contain and subvert forms of oppositional or critical **consciousness** on behalf of the dominant capitalist class. While there are differing interpretations of this and other strands of their work, most commentators have emphasized the pessimism that permeates their analysis, and the potentially contradictory marriage of 'mass' and 'class' perspectives that such work represents.

TO

See **class, consciousness industry, mass society**
Further reading Held (1980); Bennett (1977); Morley (1980); Adorno (1991)

functionalism/structural functionalism ⋆ A theoretical perspective that views societies as integrated, harmonious, cohesive 'wholes' or 'social systems', where all parts ideally function to maintain equilibrium, consensus and social order. ⋆ Rather like an organism, or body, societies are analysed in terms of their constituent parts, or 'sub-systems', all of which have to function efficiently if the overall 'health' and well-being of the organism or society are to be maintained. Thus the functionalist perspective on any feature of a society or **group** would question what function that feature performs for the social 'whole'. For example, what are the functions of **language**, of mass media systems and so on, how do they serve to maintain equilibrium and **consensus**, and how are they functionally interrelated to other social systems?

Associated particularly with the sociology of Emile Durkheim (1858–1917) and Talcott Parsons (1902–79), structural functionalism became the dominant form of social theory in America during the 1940s and 1950s, underpinning much work on communication and mass communication. Merton (1957) refined this form of analysis in a number of ways, particularly by suggesting that consequences which are favourable or 'functional' for one **institution** or group in society, may be what he called 'dysfunctional' for others. He also distinguished between manifest (socially intended) functions, and latent (unintended) functions, of particular actions and processes. Lasswell (1948) and Lazarsfeld and Merton (1948) provide interesting examples of functionalist approaches to communication and mass communication. A more recent functionalist perspective on the mass media is provided by Wright (1975), who proposed the following inventory of questions:

	(1)	manifest	(3)	functions	
What are the		and		and	of mass communicated
	(2)	latent	(4)	dysfunctions	

(5)	surveillance (news)	for the	(9)	society
(6)	correlation (selection)		(10)	individual
(7)	cultural transmission		(11)	subgroups
(8)	entertainment		(12)	cultural systems?

Functionalism has been subject to criticism on many levels, and no longer retains its previous dominant position. Of particular importance here are suggestions that as a perspective it overemphasizes consensus between groups in society, thus absenting conflict from social relations. It also fails to provide an adequate account of social change and transformation.

TO

See **consensus, uses and gratifications**
Further reading Cuff and Payne (eds) (1979); Bilton *et al*. (1981); Cohen (1968); Wright (1975); Schramm and Roberts (eds) (1971)

gatekeeper ⋆ A term originating in American social psychological and sociological traditions, used to describe those personnel, such as editors, who occupy strategic decision-making positions within news media organizations. ⋆ It is part of an essentially mechanistic **model**, which sees news as the outcome of a 'flow' or **channel** of raw information that has passed the selective filters or 'gates' of a news bureaucracy. Professional communicators are divided in this model into either 'news gatherers' or 'news processors', according to their stage of involvement in the production process. In the first stage reporters and journalists collect 'raw' news, in the second this material is selected and abbreviated by gatekeepers who, through their selective control, literally make the news. In other words they 'open the gate' for some bits of information, which they deem newsworthy, and 'close the gate' upon others.

Their prime professional function is to make **objective**, **impartial** decisions vital to the final news product, and most gatekeeper studies attempt to gauge those pressures that influence or prejudice such decisions. These pressures are usually seen to stem from (i) the gatekeepers' **subjective value** system, likes and dislikes; (ii) their immediate work situation; and (iii) those identifiable legal, bureaucratic and commercial controls that constrain gatekeepers' decisions.

The gatekeeper concept is now generally regarded as over-simplified and of little utility. Historically it does mark an important stage in the analysis of mass media communicators. The most often cited example is White (1950).

TO

Further reading Chibnall (1977); Tunstall (1970); Hall *et al.* (1978); McQuail and Windahl (1981); Schudson (1991)

gender ⋆ The cultural differentiation of male from female. ⋆ Gender is all **culture** and no nature: the only natural aspect of gender is *sexual* differentiation – a bio/physiological difference upon which is balanced a rickety but enormously elaborate cultural structure of differences which are used to classify and make meaningful the social relations of the human species. Whenever sexual differences are taken as *meaningful*, we are in the presence not of sex but of gender. The point of insisting on this distinction between sex and gender is that nothing very much can be done about human physiology in the short run, but culture can be transformed. So arguments about what is 'essentially' male or female, or 'masculine' or 'feminine', often justify gender differences as being 'only natural', but this justification is 'only **ideological**'. Gender is a human and a **signifying** division; its 'source' in nature is neither here nor there.

JH

See **binary opposition, patriarchy, power**

genre ⋆ The recognized paradigmatic sets into which the total output of a given medium (film, television, writing) is classified. ⋆ Typically, individual movies, programmes or books are recognized as 'belonging' to a particular genre – say the Western, horror or musical in cinema; or the police series, sitcom or soap opera in television. The upshot of this recognition is that the viewer/reader/critic will orient his or her reactions to what's there according to the expectations generated by recognizing the genre in the first place. You don't judge a Western for not being musical enough, and you don't judge a musical for not being horrific enough. If you laugh at a police series, or thrill to a car chase in a sitcom, then either the programme is deliberately playing with genre expectations, or you are **aberrantly decoding** it.

It is hard to isolate the precise characteristics of a given genre, and to arrive at a finite list of all the different genres (whether of one particular **medium** or across them all). Further, you can't isolate what kind of characteristics indicate distinctions between genres – it's not just subject matter, nor just **style**, nor is it simply the establishment of distinct **conventions** appropriate to each genre. It is all of these, but because **paradigms** don't behave like shopping lists you can find occasions when the addition of just one film to the Western genre, for instance, changes that genre as a whole – even though the Western in question may display few of the recognized conventions, styles or subject matters traditionally associated with its genre. *Butch Cassidy and the Sundance Kid*, *The Wild Bunch* and *Badlands* have all been credited with this effect on the Western genre. Genres, then, are dynamic paradigms, not formulaic lists, and you cannot describe them by their intrinsic properties. Even so, they do have a material effect on the organization of both our responses to a film, and the way the industry itself **institutionalizes** its output – there were whole studios which concentrated on particular genres (MGM on musicals and Warners on gangsters, for example), and individual actors, directors and writers will often be identified wholly with just one genre – Hitchcock, Huston, Berkeley, and so on.

In effect, then, genres are agents of ideological **closure** – they limit the **meaning**-potential of a given **text**, and they limit the commercial risk of the producer corporations. But they are constantly transformed by the addition of new examples, so that in the end you have to conclude that there's no such thing as a 'typical' Western, even though you can recognize one when you see it. To account for this we need to understand genre as a property of the relations between texts, and hence of **signification**. This means that genres can be defined only negatively, or relationally, by the difference that is perceived between the work in question and those that (i) belong to different genres, and (ii) other instances from the same genre-paradigm. It follows that there is no intrinsic set of properties which defines one or all genres in any one or all media for all time. The set of genres in play at a particular historical moment will determine how each one is understood, and how each individual text will fit the available categories. So much so, in fact, that one and the same text can belong to different genres in different countries or times. An example of this might be the film *Double Indemnity* which started out as a thriller, but is now often revived as an instance of *film noir*.

JH

See **closure, paradigm**
Further reading Corner (1991), Berger (1992)

Gestalt ⋆ The recognition of wholeness and overall form rather than of individual component elements. ⋆ The Gestalt movement of the early and mid-twentieth century emphasized that the whole is different from the sum of the parts. The major theorists (Wertheimer, Kohler, Koffka and Lewin) realized that an understanding of all of the parts within any given structure will not provide a complete understanding of the total structure. Instead, **meaning** derives from the interrelationships of those parts, and of each part of the whole. For example, we tend to see a series of interrupted squares rather than eighteen straight lines:

Similarly, we tend to hear speech rather than isolated utterances when listening to conversation.

Gestalt theory is of particular relevance to the study of **groups**. Our knowledge of a number of **individual** students cannot predict how that group will behave once the individual members get together for a seminar. Gestalt perspectives may also be useful when interpreting an **audience's** reactions to media **texts**. Although individual scenes may be identified within a half-hour drama the global and overall impression of the programme will depend on the interrelationships of actors and actresses within a total **narrative** sequence of settings and character relations. A further consideration is that of the **cultural** and contextual Gestalt of each individual viewer.

DS

See **closure**
Further reading Schellenberg (1978)

globalization ∗ The growth and acceleration of economic and cultural networks which operate on a worldwide scale and basis. ∗ Globalization is strongly linked with debates about 'world **culture**', and emerged as a critical concept in the late 1980s. The term refers to that whole complex of flows and processes which have increasingly transcended national boundaries in the last twenty years. The growth of 'global culture' has resulted from major shifts and developments in multinational markets and corporations, communication and media technologies and their world systems of **production** and **consumption**. The process is distinguished from **cultural imperialism** in that it is conceived as more complex and total, and less organized or predictable in its outcomes.

For some recent writers, the cultural experience of globalization and the mishmash of world cultures which result can be seen as a telling aspect of the **postmodern** condition. From this point of view, the late twentieth century has seen decisive changes in the influence of national cultural and economic structures and their historical boundaries and 'securities' have increasingly had to confront the realities of international and global integration. The results of these processes have been termed a new and distinctive cultural *space* – the global – which both erodes and destabilizes older established forms of the national culture and identity. These are replaced, it is suggested, by a global–local dimension, and everyday, situated cultures are now routinely saturated with references to the global. Central to this process has been the emergence of communication technologies and media networks which allow for faster, more extensive, interdependent forms of worldwide exchange, travel and interaction. The rapid developments and contradictions in these and other processes and their impact on diverse forms of cultural and social life provide a continuing and urgent site for debate and research. It is important that cultural and communication studies should recognize and respond to these global transformations.

TO

See **cultural imperialism, Fordism/post-Fordism, post-modernism**

Further reading Tomlinson (1991); Featherstone (ed.) (1990); Sreberny-Mohammadi (1991)

group ⋆ A collection of people who have some shared interest or goal. ⋆ Social psychologists and sociologists have recognized many types of group. A small group is characterized by sustained **interaction** between members via **role** playing, goal setting and the development of affective relations. Examples include the family, a friendship circle and a work group. For larger groups the loss of one member does not usually have serious implications for that group's structure and functioning. Examples might include a television **audience** or a lecture theatre full of students.

Groups can be formal or informal in terms of intimacy and role playing between members, and they can be relatively structured in recognizing leaders and deputies or unstructured in not having such a rigid pattern for relationships. Other commonly used dichotomies include **primary**–secondary, temporary–permanent, and **autonomous**–dependent. An alternative and usually more specific classification procedure involves the recognition of different types of group goals or **contexts** associated with all of each group's members. Descriptions include peer and reference groups, committees, panels, juries, therapy groups and school classes. The host of categories that emerge suggests that only rarely does the **individual** belong to one group at any point in time. Instead, a variety of groups, sometimes experienced simultaneously, are considered essential for **socialization**.

The emergence of group identity and manifesto as recognized by both members and members of other groups has attracted much discussion of intergroup relations, group dynamics and communication, and conflict. Billig (1982) concentrates on the bases of **ideology** in this respect, and emphasizes that any

131

discussion of groups must include sociological, historical and economic factors as well as social psychological ones. As such the group transcends any one single analysis based on the individual's **perception** of that group. In so doing a more electric understanding may be reached concerning the discussion of, for example, patriotism, nationalism and **class** consciousness.

DS

See **audience, dyad, primary group**
Further reading Tajfel and Fraser (eds) (1978); Billig (1982); Robinson (1984); Burton and Dimbleby (1988)

H

hegemony ★ A concept developed by Gramsci in the 1930s and taken up in cultural studies, where it refers principally to the ability in certain historical periods of the dominant classes to exercise social and cultural leadership, and by these means – rather than by direct coercion of subordinate classes – to maintain their power over the economic, political and cultural direction of the nation. ★ The crucial aspect of the notion of hegemony is not that it operates by forcing people against their conscious will or better judgement to concede power to the already-powerful, but that it describes a situation whereby our consent is actively sought for those ways of making sense of the world which 'happen' to fit in with the interests of the hegemonic alliance of **classes**, or *power bloc*. Hence our active participation in understanding ourselves, our social relations and the world at large results in our complicity in our own subordination.

Once you've grasped that hegemony describes the winning of consent to unequal class relations, you will need to take the concept further; to understand that it is being used in **cultural** analysis. This may include attention to those cultural forms, like propaganda or advertising for instance, whose avowed intention is to promote a certain party or product. But such deliberate manipulations of **images** and **meanings** might in fact be taken as evidence that successful hegemony has *not* been achieved, since there is clearly some felt need to explain the doings of the

133

powerful in terms not readily available to the people at whom the propaganda is aimed. In **cultural studies**, therefore, the concept of hegemony is more often to be found in those studies which seek to show how everyday meanings, representations and activities are organized and made sense of in such a way as to render the class interests of the dominant 'bloc' into an apparently natural, inevitable, eternal and hence unarguable general interest, with a claim on everybody.

Thus studies which concentrate on the hegemonic aspect of culture will focus on those forms and **institutions** which are usually taken to be **impartial** or neutral; representative of everybody without apparent reference to class, **race** or **gender**. Such institutions are the state, the law, the educational system, the media and the family. These institutions are prolific producers of sense, knowledges and meanings – they are cultural agencies whose importance lies just as much in their role as organizers and producers of individual and social consciousness as in their more obvious 'stated' functions. Although they are **relatively autonomous** from one another, peopled by different personnel with different professional skills and ideologies, nevertheless these cultural agencies collectively form the site on which hegemony can be established and exercised. They can, in short, be 'captured' or 'colonized' by a power bloc which consists of not only the dominant economic class but also its 'allies' and *subaltern classes*, from professionals and managers to intellectuals of various kinds and subordinate class *fractions* who perceive their interests as congruent to or identical with those of the dominant group itself.

It follows that hegemony operates in the realm of **consciousness** and **representations**; its success is most likely when the totality of social, cultural and individual **experience** is capable of being made sense of in terms that are defined, established and put into circulation by the power bloc. In short, hegemony **naturalizes** what is historically a class **ideology**, and renders it into the form of **common sense**. The upshot is that **power** can be exercised not as force but as 'authority'; and 'cultural' aspects of life are de-politicized. Those strategies for making sense of one's self and the world that are most easily available and officially encouraged appear not as strategies but as natural (unarguable) properties of 'human nature'. Alternative strategies – based on oppositional politics or counter-hegemonic consciousness – not only appear as 'unofficial' in this context, but also are likely to be represented as literally non-sense; impossible to imagine, incapable of being represented.

However, the continuing conflicts of interest between classes, which forms of ownership and the industrial organization of production cannot help but continuously reproduce, ensure that hegemony can never be total. There are always emergent forms of consciousness and representation which may be mobilized in opposition to the hegemonic order. This means that a lot of work, called *ideological labour*, goes into the struggle between hegemonic and counter-hegemonic forms. And what's at stake in the long term in this struggle can be political and economic power itself.

JH

See **bardic function, class, culture, ideology, power, socialization**
Further reading   Turner (1990); Hardt (1992)

hero/heroine   * An individual who is worshipped and idolized because of his or her morality, excellence and bravery. Heroes/ heroines may be actual people, and may be culturally reproduced in textual forms.   *   Accordingly, heroic names can range from Pelé to Mandela, Mother Teresa to Greta Garbo, Hercules to Superwoman, or Admiral Nelson to Bertrand Russell. Whether real or imagined, such **images** appear in the face of adversity and with what is taken to be an essential *goodness* to reveal our own shortcomings. More often than not heroes/heroines are ideal types that have at least in part been exaggerated by media representations (in which case they are closely related to **star** images), but which always go beyond **individual** identity through epitomizing a body of **cultural values** and moral beliefs. In so doing, heroes/heroines are integral to socialization and forms of identification. In addition to the concept of idol we should also emphasize martyrdom, which refers to the cruel and unjust death of a hero/heroine – Steve Biko is but one example.

135

Heroic figures are often identified through **binary opposi-tions**, wherein they stand in contrast to morally corrupt villains. Indeed we can ask whether one always depends on the other for their continued existence, and whether so much narrative depends on this opposition – for instance, Sherlock Holmes versus the evil Moriarty. Going beyond fiction we have fact, and the construction of hero/villain **stereotypes** in real life: Kennedy versus Khrushchev in the Cold War, Scargill versus McGregor in the British coal strike of more recent times. Much depends, of course, on which side you are on. The essential **subjectivity** of such images can be further applied to **gender** differences: compare, for example, the female 'dumb blonde' heroine with the male strong-silent type of hero.

A final point concerns the emergence of *anti-heroes/heroines*. Strictly speaking these should be villainous characters because of their weakness, corruption or even cruelty. Yet there now seems to be an in-between category which combines heroic/villainous elements together. You may want to debate the reasons for such an emergence – one explanation might be based on a saturated market for heroic images, wherein images of morality and excel-lence have become abundant, clichéd and even boring.

DS

See **archetype, identification, image, projection, star, stereotype**
Further reading Dyer (1979a, 1987)

homeostasis ⋆ The maintenance of equilibrium; a state or process that maintains balance at some optimal level. ⋆ A popular ana-logy is that of the thermostat, which is turned on when one temperature **threshold** is crossed, and is switched off once another higher temperature threshold is crossed. Homeostasis has proved to be a valuable concept in the analysis of, for example, **motivation**, **non-verbal communication**, and even the organization of **attitudes** within **cognitive** belief systems.

DS

See **threshold**

homology ★ A reproduction or repetition of a structure. ★ The diagrammatic map of London's Underground is a homology of the real thing – the stations and lines bear the same structural relationship to each other – but it is not an **iconic** map. A **model** of the communication process is a homology in that it represents the relationship of the elements involved. The term *homology* is often opposed to analogy or **analogue** which is a reproduction of the **form** rather than the structure. Each episode of a formulaic television series, for example, *Minder* or *Baywatch*, is a homologue of the others in that series. That is, whatever the story, the structure is the same.

JF

hypodermic needle model ★ A mechanistic and unsophisticated model of the media–audience relationship, which sees the media as 'injecting' values, ideas and information directly into each individual in a passive and atomized audience, thereby producing a direct and unmediated effect. ★ Growing out of concern and pessimism surrounding the rapid expansion of electronic media, particularly in the USA in the 1930s and 1940s, this **model** is a popular extension of the stimulus–response framework that underpinned much early writing on **audiences** and media **effects**. Its reduction of the mass communication process to a syringe-like operation, whereby media messages ('plug-in drugs') are fed directly into the **individual** minds of a mass audience, has been consistently challenged and rejected by more recent re-search. It bears the hallmarks of fears surrounding the negative effects of media **power** or omnipotence, and is still encountered in debates such as that concerning the mass media and **violence** in society. It has close links with other **metaphors** drawn between media **messages** and 'diseases' or 'infections', contagiously transmitted, causing impaired 'health' of the individual viewers or listeners.

TO

See **audience, effects, narcotization**
Further reading Halloran (1977); McQuail and Windahl (1981)

icon/iconic * Type of **sign** in which there is a marked physical or perceptual resemblance between the **signifier** and that for which it stands * Thus the black pictorial element of some road signs – depicting rocks falling, deer, or a man with a shovel – may be said to be **iconic**. But the use of a red border or a blue background on road signs is not iconic because there is no necessary relation between the blue or the red and what the colours signify. In the latter case the relationship is purely arbitrary and **conventional**; in the former case it is **motivated**. Representational painting – traditional portrait painting, for example – may be considered iconic, as are most forms of photographic reproduction. Cinema and television, in particular, rely in their visual dimension principally upon iconic modes of signification. This ensures a more easy intelligibility than written prose (where the mode of signification is purely arbitrary); but conventions do none the less play their part even in these most natural-looking of media. One has only to consider how **styles** or **genres** of television and cinema have shifted so much over time for this to be evident. The term is particularly useful in **communication studies** precisely as a way of distinguishing between the types of signification predominant in the differing media.

Religious icons – images of Christ, for example, or of one of the saints – provide an interesting special case of the iconic: to some believers, they have the spiritual power of the person depicted, who is thus 'present' by virtue of the depiction in a particularly compelling fashion.

MM

See **convention, genre, index, motivation, object, sign, symbol**
Further reading   Peirce (1931–58); Saussure (1974); Wollen (1972)

identification   ⋆ The process by which the individual merges at least some of another's identity with his or her own. ⋆   As Rycroft (1968) states, identification can involve (i) the extension of identity *into* someone else; (ii) the borrowing of identity *from* someone else; or (iii) the confusion of identity *with* someone else.

Identification can be viewed as a **defence mechanism** whereby self-criticism leads to adoption of another's identity, where that other appears capable of coping with such a threat. Sometimes we may emulate, or even create, a type of **hero/heroine** that succeeds in overcoming the major frustrations encountered within everyday life. Such identification may be with some **mythical** entity constructed through fantasy, with media **images**, or with first-hand experience of **others** within **groups** (see Rank 1924, for a more detailed **psychoanalytical** account).

Identification has also been extensively discussed when referring to primary and secondary identification within **socialization**: in the former there is little differentiation between the self and external **objects** whereas in the latter the person **perceives** him or herself as separated from other objects – yet identifies with at least some of them.

DS

See **defence mechanism, escapism, interpellation, socialization, voyeur**
Further reading   Rank (1924); Mortensen (ed.) (1979); Nash (1985); Leiss *et al.* (1986)

ideology   ⋆ The social relations of signification (knowledge and **consciousness**) in class societies. ⋆   Often condensed to refer to the products of those relations; knowledges and **representations** characteristic of or in the interests of a **class**. By extension, it refs to the same products, but these may be seen as characteristic of **groups** other than classes – ranging from **gender** (male ideology) to jobs (**occupational ideology**). Ideology is seen as any knowledge that is posed as natural or generally applicable, particularly when its social origins are suppressed, **ex-nominated** or deemed irrelevant. Hence, and especially in more recent **cultural/communication studies**, ideology is seen as the practice of reproducing social relations of inequality within the sphere of **signification** and **discourse**.

Ideology as a theoretical concept comes from Marxism. In classic Marxism, the **forms**, **contents** and purposes of knowledges, representations and **consciousness** are not understood as abstracted from the material and social activities of production and class antagonism. On the contrary, the activity of production gives rise directly to knowledge of nature, and this knowledge of nature is directed towards further and increasing production by bringing all its myriad aspects as closely into line with general natural 'laws' as possible.

It is Marx's contention that knowledge of society springs in the same way, directly from class antagonism. But whereas knowledge of nature may be (at least in principle) of benefit to all classes, knowledge of society is produced and reproduced in the interests of those who are for the time being in a position of social supremacy (the ruling class). Thus, for Marx, knowledge of society differs from knowledge of nature by representing *as* natural those social arrangements that are in fact historically contingent. This is the starting point for a theory of ideology. The fundamental premises on which the Marxist concept of ideology is based are expressed in two of Marx's most celebrated contentions:

The mode of production of material life conditions the social, political and intellectual life process in general. It is not the consciousness of men that determines their being, but, on the contrary, their social being that determines their consciousness.

The individuals composing the ruling class possess among other things consciousness, and therefore think. In so far,

140

therefore, as they rule as a class and determine the extent and compass of an epoch, it is self-evident that they do this in its whole range, hence among other things rule also as thinkers, as producers of ideas, and regulate the production and distribution of the ideas of their age: thus their ideas are the ruling ideas of the epoch.

(Marx 1977, pp. 176, 389)

If the ideas of the ruling class are the ruling ideas of an epoch, then 'bourgeois ideology', for instance, should not be understood simply as what individual members of the bourgeois class think, but as the prevailing ways of making sense that are established throughout bourgeois society. These ways of making sense may be produced and distributed not by the ruling class directly, but by relatively **autonomous** and apparently fragmented groups, ranging from intellectuals and teachers to media professionals and hairdressers.

The contention that social being determines consciousness gives rise to the Marxist notion of *false consciousness*. In case of the ruling class itself, false consciousness occurs when that class imagines that its position in society is determined by the laws of God or nature – as in the doctrine of the divine right of kings for feudal monarchs, or the doctrine of **individualism** and the conception of society as a social contract in bourgeois philosophy. False consciousness for subordinate classes occurs when they make sense of their social and individual circumstances in terms supplied by the prevailing ideology, rather than in terms of their own class interests in opposition to the dominant classes. In this context, ideology is seen as the production and distribution of ideas in the interests of the ruling classes.

Thus ideology is the means by which ruling economic classes generalize and extend their supremacy across the whole range of social activity, and **naturalize** it in the process, so that their rule is accepted as natural and inevitable; and therefore legitimate and binding.

For Marx, not all knowledge of society is necessarily ideological. In particular, the science of historical materialism (Marxism) itself could not be seen as an ideology, given the notion of ideology as an illusory knowledge. The understanding gained in the struggle to change both society and nature is partial and limited and can be mistaken but, for Marxists, the **objective** existence of natural and historical laws is not open to question, nor is the belief that materialist science provides the means to bring those laws into knowledge.

The concept of ideology has proved very influential in the study of communication and culture. So much so, in fact, that it has become somewhat over-extended in use. In particular, ideology has been reduced to a mere **reflection** of the economic **base** in some popularized versions of Marxism. As a result, ideology is often confined to the **superstructure**, where it is defined in terms of 'bodies' of thought, beliefs, ideas, and so on which reduces it from a conceptualization of social relations and practices to a set of **empirical** things.

Just as language is hard to analyse if you look at words rather than the laws which produce words, so the reduction of ideology to ideas does not explain their production or forms. Thus the concept needed to be re-theorized, and this led to the notion of *ideology in general*. This notion is associated especially with Althusser (1971), for whom ideology is the mechanism which turns individuals into **subjects**, but is also implicit in Volosinov (1973). It implies that all knowledge, whether scientific or otherwise, is produced within **language**, and that language is never a transparent medium through which truth can be observed. Hence all language is seen as ideological, and truth as a product not a motivator of language. It follows from this that no specific discourse (including Marxism itself) is exempt from ideology. Instead, there are at any one time numbers of contending ideological discourses in play within an overall social formation, and that what is at stake in the way they are produced, deployed, regulated, institutionalized and resisted is not only knowledge but also power.

However, at the level of specific ideologies, it is clear that ideology isn't a unitary medium that we inhabit like fishes in the medium of the sea. Even within what is often called *dominant ideology* there are contending and conflicting positions – as between, say, different educational philosophies and policies. And ideology is always encountered in **institutional** forms and local circumstances which ensure that there is never a complete fit between dominant class interests and dominant ideology. Further, however naturalized and successful dominant ideologies might seem, they are always in contention with resistances to them from 'below', either in the form of coherent alternatives (feminism, Marxism) or as practical accommodations/rejections (see **subcultures**).

The concept of ideology has become central in the study of the media in particular and communication in general. It is useful in insisting that not only is there no 'natural' meaning inherent in an event or object, but also the meanings into which events and objects are constructed are always socially oriented – aligned with class, gender, race or other interests. Further, ideology is not a set of things but an active practice, either working on the changing circumstances of social activity to reproduce familiar and regulated senses, or struggling to resist established and naturalized sense thus to transform the means of sense-making into new, alternative or oppositional forms, which will generate meanings aligned to different social interests.

JH

Further reading   Cormack (1992); Hall (1982); Larrain (1979); Turner (1990)

ideological state apparatuses   ⋆ The material or institutional form taken by ideology in specified historical circumstances in class societies.   ⋆   Known in the trade as ISAs, and distinguished from RSAs or *repressive state apparatuses*, the two terms were coined by the French Marxist philosopher Louis Althusser (1971).

RSAs are the complex of coercive or regulatory forces available to and directly under the control of the state. They include the penal system, the police, the army, the legislature and government administration. These are distinguished by their legitimated authority to command (whether we like it or not).

ISAs, on the other hand, are various **social institutions** that arise within civil society (the sphere of the private, as opposed to the state). They too perform regulatory functions, and reproduce ideology 'on behalf of' the state. They include education, the family, religion, the legal system, the party-political system, **culture** and communication. They are characterized by consent rather than coercion, and by their **relative autonomy** from the dominant economic class or its representatives in the state.

The function of ISAs is to reproduce our submission to the relations of **production** – to discipline us into the kind of **subjectivity** most conducive to the maintenance and continuity of the existing relations of production. They do it by representing **class** interests as both natural and neutral. They translate class into other terms. For instance, education is neutral because all are equal in front of the examination. But only certain ideologies pass exams. The legal system is neutral because all are equal in front of the law. But only certain acts are criminalized, and only certain ideological subjects are convicted. The media are neutral because their **representations** of the social world are **impartial**. But only certain ideologies are represented as worthy of impartial treatment, others are not. The party-political *system* is neutral, because within it all positions and opinions can be voiced: except for non-party, extra-parliamentary political voices.

JH

Further reading   Althusser (1971)

image   ⋆ Originally meant a visual **representation** of reality – either physically (as in a picture or photograph) or in the imagination (as in literature or in music). Now it commonly means a fabrication or public impression created to appeal to the audience rather than to reproduce reality: it implies a degree of falseness in so far as the reality rarely matches up to the image. ⋆   In this sense we talk about the image of a consumer product or of a politician.

JF

See   **icon, symbol**

impartiality   ⋆ The doctrine of not taking sides in the reporting of public affairs in the broadcast (but not newspaper) media. ⋆

144

Impartiality is the practical and pragmatic exercise of an accommodation between **broadcasters** and parliamentary political parties (especially the two governmental parties). It is a strategy whereby reporters are supposed to take account of (i) a full *range* of views and opinions; (ii) the relative *weight* of opinion (this means that established or orthodox views get priority over challenges to them); and (iii) *changes* that occur in the range and weight of opinion over time.

Traditionally, impartiality had to be exercised *within* programmes. That is, if you quote a Tory view you must quote a Labour view in the same programme. Increasingly, however, the notion of impartiality *between* programmes is gaining acceptance. Here the idea is that if the subject demands it you can give just one position in a single programme, knowing that others will give the opposing view at another time. This development results largely from pressure from broadcasters themselves, some of whom wish to establish 'positioned journalism' that doesn't pretend not to have its own point of view, while others simply object to having to stop a good story in its tracks while 'the two sides' slug it out.

Impartiality is often distinguished from two other concepts, namely *balance* and *neutrality*. It is supposed to overcome their shortcomings. Balance is the allocation of equal time to opposing viewpoints, where what is said is less important than the time it is said in. Neutrality is the indiscriminate **accessing** of any and every viewpoint without any principle of selection. This is deemed unsatisfactory because parliamentary politicians don't take kindly to air-time being given to **groups** or parties dedicated to the overthrow of parliamentary politics. Thus communist, nationalist and socialist parties operating outside the parliamentary framework are denied access without broadcasters having to admit that they're failing to be impartial – they're just not neutral. As a result, the doctrine of impartiality can be seen as a major prop to the parliamentary (two–party) *system*. It is, of course, a statutory requirement laid on broadcasters by Parliament.

JH

See **accessing**

implicature (conversational)   ⋆ A conversational implicature is the kind of meaning conveyed implicitly rather than explicitly by an utterance.   ⋆   The term is important in **pragmatics** and derives from the work of the philosopher H. P. Grice (1975) who in a quite radical way contrasted the logic of philosophy with that of everyday conversation. In particular, he pointed out how utterances in everyday conversation often mean much more than they actually say. In order to explain how this can be so, he proposed that conversation proceeds on the basis of a fundamental principle – the *co-operative principle*. This can be summed up under four basic maxims, or ground-rules, which conversationalists tacitly follow:

(1) the *maxim of quality* states that speakers should be truthful and should not say things which they believe to be false or for which they lack sufficient evidence;

(2) the *maxim of quantity* requires that speakers should be as informative as is required by the purposes of the conversation and should say neither too little nor too much:

(3) the *maxim of relevance* states that what speakers say should fit in with and relate to the purposes of the conversation at that point;

(4) the *maxim of manner* requires that speakers should avoid obscurity, prolixity and ambiguity.

It is on the assumption that these maxims still hold in some way, even when they appear to have been 'flouted', that we make sense of conversation. What happens briefly is this: when a maxim has apparently been flouted by an utterance we try and derive some meaning from it that will leave the maxim and the co-operative principle in place. This inferred, non-manifest meaning is the implicature. Thus, B's reply in the following exchange does not seem literally to meet the terms of A's question:

A: Where's Bill?
B: There's a yellow VW outside Sue's house.

In this sense it apparently flouts at least the maxims of quantity and relevance and thereby fails to conform to the co-operative principle. In practice, however, we assume B to be co-operative at some deeper level and look for some proposition that would link B's actual reply with some manifestly relevant and co-operative reply to the question. In this case B effectively conveys that 'if Bill has a yellow VW, then he may be in Sue's house'.

The notion of conversational implicature provides an important way of going beyond highly literal and strictly logical approaches to meaning: it is a way of emphasizing how the meaning of an utterance lies not just in the words we use but in the deductions and inferences that may be made on the basis of them. But the idea is not without its difficulties. There is considerable debate about exactly how many maxims you need to define adequately the co-operative principle. Some commentators have proposed as many as eight or more. Others have suggested that they can all be reduced to the one maxim, 'be relevant'. Nor is it certain how strong is the co-operative principle itself. Some speech **genres** – such as adversarial cross-examination in the court room, the combative political interview on television, or the full-blown marital quarrel – would seem to exhibit serious, systematic, and fundamental departures from the co-operative principle. And yet, for the theory of implicature to work, it is not a principle that can be variably applied.

MM

See **pragmatics, semantics**
Further reading Levinson (1983); Leech (1983); Grice (1975)

independence ⋆ A concept of scale and opposition, with no intrinsic features. ⋆ Independent film and video production, for instance, includes an incommensurable array of different personnel and practices, each defined contingently as independent against a specific mainstream. Thus: Hollywood directors working outside the major studios are independent – e.g., Stanley Kubrick. Countries outside the major film production centres (Los Angeles and Bombay) compete in the international film market as independents – so the multi-million-dollar-grossing Australian film *Crocodile Dundee*, second only to *Top Gun* in its release year (1986) in both American and world markets, is an independent film.

Types of independence differ. They are organized around different mobilizing **discourses**: community, avant garde, agit-prop (i.e. *agitation and propaganda*), art, connoisseurship, free enterprise, etc. In each case the mobilizing discourse produces specific sets of practices. In one country's overall **cultural production**, independence often signals a production or practice that works more or less self-consciously against the grain of mainstream **entertainment**. Such independence may imply:

(1) different, alternative or oppositional processes of **production** (for instance, working against traditional divisions and hierarchies of labour);

(2) different **aesthetics** (**experimentation** at the level of **image**, narration and structure, promoting attention to meaning-construction, rather than to 'show-and-tell' plots with 'tennis-match dialogue');

(3) a self-reflexive concern with the practitioner's role as well as with subject matter or financial returns;

(4) different relations with **audiences** (getting away from 'bums on seats' towards active engagement with audiences as spectators or as participants);

(5) serving a defined audience 'constituency' rather than the 'mass' (e.g., women, workers, a region or community, people involved in political, social or environmental action).

In addition *independent* has been made to describe funding-sources; the term is a euphemism for 'capitalist' or 'commercial' in the British broadcasting scene, where the main commercial channels in both television and radio (ITV and ILR) and their regulatory bodies (the ITC and Radio Authority) are dubbed independent – presumably of state ownership. At the same time the 'independent film sector' uses the term to help secure public funds from bodies like the Arts Council, British Film Institute and local councils for low-budget non-commercial production. Hence the same term has been found useful at the opposite extremes of the film world.

JH

index ⋆ One of Peirce's three categories of **sign**. An index is a sign that is connected to its **object**, either casually or existentially – it appears to be a part of that to which it refers. ⋆ Thus smoke is an index of fire, spots an index of measles, or a snarl that of anger. Monaco (1977) suggests that indexes (or indices – both forms of the plural are found) are used in film **metonymically**; he gives the example of a roll of banknotes left on a sleeping woman's pillow as an index of prostitution. Cartoonists typically use metonymical indexes – Churchill's cigar, Ted Heath's nose and teeth, Hitler's moustache. There is also a more symbolic form of index, as in a cartoon of a fat employer berating his thin employees – the fat belly is an index of his prosperity and, by extension, of the fat profits squeezed out of the indexically thin employees.

JF

See **icon, metonymy, symbol**

individual ⋆ A synonym for *person*, derived from a medieval conceptualization of the nature of God – three persons but indivisible. ⋆ By extension an adjective for that which cannot be divided further – an oppositional term to collectivities or generalities of various kinds. When the term is used without any notion of contrast to a **group** and is applied to people, it is being used in a way that the *OED* dismisses as 'now chiefly as a colloquial vulgarism, or as a term of disparagement'. But, of course, it is in just this sense that the term *individual* is most familiar nowadays.

JH

individualism ⋆ The mainspring of bourgeois/capitalist philosophy; the doctrine that individuals are the starting-point and source of human action. ⋆ That is, each person 'owns' his or her capacities (especially their capacity to labour) and is not in debt to society (or to, for instance, a feudal overlord) for these capacities. Hence individuals are free to sell their labour power for whatever can be had for it, and are not obliged to consider anyone else in the process. This 'freedom' of the individual, then, is what underlies the operation of the 'free' market economy. The only inhibitors of individual freedom in this model are *competition* (where what can be had for labour power is limited by the value it can command in a competitive market) and *contract* (where each individual's social relations take the form of *commodity exchanges*: for example, labour for wages with mutually binding conditions).

Individualism is rarely discussed in studies of communication, but its assumptions are implicit in a great variety of theorizing on the subject. The most common occurrence is for the notion of the free individual, who is essentially complete and taken to be the source of action and meaning, to form the 'unit' of study. So, according to this notion, communication takes place when individuals *exchange* messages (the contract model); or audiences are made up of aggregates of individuals (abstracted from discursive, economic and political relations except in so far as these can be rendered as variables *within* an individual); or social forces are understood as *deriving from* individual actions.

The alternative perspective to individualism certainly doesn't deny the existence or action of individual people. However, it does maintain that their existence and action is the *product* and not the *source* of social relations and signifying systems. As a result, the term *individual* has been displaced in, for instance, **structuralist**, **semiotic**, Marxist and feminist writings by the concept of **subjectivity**.

JH

See **subjectivity**
Further reading   Macpherson (1962); Thomson (1977)

information processing   ∗ An approach usually associated with computer **analogies** that identify a flow of information within a system.   ∗   Often the identifiable stages include the scanning and selection of a **stimulus** array, the interpretation of such information, storage structures, storage processes, mechanisms of retrieval from storage, and presentation of retrieved or processed information. With the **cognitive** bases of communication, such a framework has often been associated with the processing of information through the substages of **sensation**, **perception**, **memory**, **thinking**, and **language** within an information-processing **model**. When reading this **text**, for example, the sensation stage might involve the 'seeing' of many letters. We then perceive words and sentences. This can be accomplished only through past experience that allows for recognition through memory. However, the more meaningful underlying themes appear with our reflections and thoughts about recognized statements. Thinking itself is assumed to have complex relations with language. All of which determines subsequent perception: you may decide to re-read the page.

Descriptions and explanations of communication that rely on information processing frequently incorporate box-type diagrams that refer to information flow, **feedback** loops, **gatekeepers**, storage space and decision points. Indeed this might be a major disadvantage because important aspects of communication may be overlooked should such a model be taken too literally. For example, it becomes difficult to distinguish consistently between **thinking** and **language**, despite the fact that boundaries are suggested by many theorists. Can you think without language?

DS

See **cognition, communication theory, information theory, language, memory, model, perception, thinking**
Further reading Lindsay and Norman (1977); McCroskey and Wheeless (1976)

information theory ⋆ A mathematical theory designed to measure the amount of information that can be transmitted along a defined **channel** and to identify ways of maximizing the efficiency of this process. ⋆ The term *information* is used in a specialist sense to refer to the predictability of the **signal**, that is, its physical **form**, not its **meaning**. Broadly, the theory states that the less predictable a signal is, the greater the information it conveys. A signal high in information is said to be **entropic**, one with low information is **redundant**. Information is frequently measured in *bits* (an abbreviation for 'binary digits'). A bit is the basic **binary opposition** which is expressible as 0:1. If we take a dictionary of 250,000 words, we can say that each word contains

151

eighteen 'bits' of information (information, remember, refers to the predictability of the word itself, not to its meaning). This is because we need to make choices between 'Is it in the first half?' (0), and 'Is it in the second half?' (1). Answering this eighteen times will identify any word in the dictionary. This word may then be expressed binarily – for example, '0110100 . . . etc.' Information theory is now confined largely to computer-based information-processing systems, though some psychologists use it as a model for human **cognition**.

JF

See **communication theory, cybernetics, entropy, redundancy**
Further reading Shannon and Weaver (1949); Cherry (1957)

institutions/social institutions ⋆ Those enduring regulatory and organizing structures of any society, which constrain and control individuals and individuality. ⋆ We tend to think of institutions, in an everyday sense, as buildings, often places to be avoided, such as prisons, courts, factories, schools or hospitals. While they are embodied in this bricks-and-mortar sense, the term more precisely refers to the underlying principles and **values** according to which *many* social and cultural practices are organized and co-ordinated. Accordingly, while we may enter into and leave institutions, as we employ the term in everyday discourse, in fact they more or less permanently both surround and enter into us, as a (or *the*) condition of our social existence. What we refer to as 'our home', for example, is an institution in itself. It represents the meeting-point for other institutions of privacy, property, wealth, knowledge, kinship and gender relations, and so on, all of which give rise to the **rules**, **codes** and relations of 'our' domestic lives.

Even for this to be written and read, we have to draw on what Berger and Berger (1976) have called 'the social institution above all others' – **language**. This is because language is the fundamental means by which the flux of **experience** and **sensation** is translated into a social reality, classified, ordered, given or denied meaning and significance. The ability to use language, and other means of communication, is so central precisely because it makes possible the organization and mobilization of experience. The social and material environment is organized into nameable 'things', imbued with meanings. Language serves as the basis for social relations, the institution whereby social reality is constantly and collectively (re)negotiated, (re)produced and challenged. It is however important to recognize the essential interconnectedness and fusion of institutions. No one institution ever operates in isolation from others, as if in a vacuum. It may be useful to think of *all* social institutions in terms of the varying degrees to which they represent historical and continuing social responses to conflicts at the levels of:

(1) *Economy*, concerned with the production and distribution of material goods and wealth.
(2) *Politics*, concerned with the exercise of **power** and processes of social regulation.
(3) *Culture*, concerned with the production, exchange and reproduction of meanings.

Seeing institutions in this way involves recognizing that they combine certain important identifying features, which generally appear to be external to the **individual**. The 'language' and the 'law', for example, both seem to exist 'outside' of the actions and demands of individuals (see, for example, **langue** and **parole**). Second, this 'outsideness' is partly defined by its constraining or coercive power and authority over individuals. In Goffman's (1968) terms, 'every institution has encompassing tendencies'. Some, such as prisons and mental hospitals, as he suggests, can be regarded as *total institutions* in terms of the high degree of power and direct regulation they exert over their 'inmates'. For others, their apparent externality and control is guaranteed by their apparent timelessness; by the fact that often, like the buildings, they were there before us, and may survive us as apparently 'natural', 'normal' even 'unchanging' features of social life.

Given their social and cultural centrality, it is not surprising that the study of institutions has served as a broad focus for theoretical and **empirical** problems and debate. Their characteristics and functions are defined differently by contesting theoretical perspectives. A triangle of recurrent problems has fuelled this contest.

First, the problem of **determination**: to what extent and by what means do institutions control, constitute and hence determine *all* individual action and communication – are we all, always, institutional 'agents' or 'inmates'?

Second, the central issue of *whose control?*: to what extent do institutions represent the particular values, interests and legitimized power of dominant groups or classes in society, as opposed to reflecting an overall social **consensus**?

Third, the wider historical issue of the **role** of institutions in social and cultural change, especially the potential tensions and contradictions between their reproductive (conservative) tendencies and their transformative (innovative) capacities.

In short, social institutions, in both their material and discursive forms should perhaps form *the* prime focus for the study of culture and communication. They are the major social sources of **codes**, **rules**, and relations.

TO

See **discourse, language, power, role, rules**
Further reading Berger and Berger (1976); Goffman (1968); Douglas (1987)

interaction/social interaction ⋆ The exchange and negotiation of meaning between two or more participants located within social contexts. ⋆ With social interaction the major focus is on communication and reciprocation between **code** and **rule**-givers, users and constructors. When we are being interviewed we are locked into a social **context** for interaction because somebody else is there and interested in what we have to say. Similarly when catching a bus we are engaging in the exchange of information with the driver and with the other passengers. Frequently, a number of codes will be involved at both the verbal and non-verbal levels. The analysis of social interaction should therefore consider not only the present social context but also all of those things that we bring to the situation. Hence such issues as **role**, **rule**, **power**, **socialization**, **group** membership, **conformity**, **motivation**, **prejudice** and **perception** become as relevant as **non-verbal communication**, **language** and **code**.

The phrase 'social interaction' has perhaps been used too frequently within communication studies – to the point of obscuring any one agreed interpretation. It would be inappropriate, for example, to describe an **audience** as 'socially interacting' when reading a book, or witnessing the death of Hamlet within a hushed and darkened theatre. There may well be **symbolic interaction**, but because of the lack of observable reciprocation from others the social criteria are not satisfied. The argument is complex, especially when we recognize the **cultural** contexts associated with the exchange and negotiation of **meaning**.

TO

See **dyad, encounter, facework, group, interpersonal communication, non-verbal communication**
Further reading Burton and Dimbleby (1988); Forgas (1985); Beechey and Donald (1985); Eiser (1986)

interpellation ⋆ A term from the writings of the French Marxist political philosopher Louis Althusser, referring to what he takes to be the process by which ideology 'hails' individuals as its subject. Sometimes translated as 'appelation'. ⋆ Individuals are said to be interpellated by the **discursive**, linguistic, symbolic order outside of which it is impossible to live. Thus, for Althusserians, **ideology** is general and inescapable, as well as being a material product of ideological state apparatuses. Interpellation is the very mechanism by which people are subjected to ideology, and it is usually understood as a textual operation of **'audience** positioning'. Both the notion of interpellation and that of 'ideology in general' have been criticized since the early 1970s, when they were most influential, as being too essentialist and abstract. If interpellation is understood as 'hailing' (as in 'Oi! You!'), the question of what or who is calling must sooner or later arise. If the answer is 'ideology in general' we certainly avoid **conspiracy theory**, but this doesn't take us very far in understanding specific ideological operations.

However, interpellation can be useful as a concept when applied to specific **discourses**, rather than to the operation of transhistorical general forces on abstract **subjects**. For example, Laclau

(1977) writes of a struggle between discourses in prewar Germany, where the discourse of 'old Prussianism' interpellated a 'nationalist and authoritarian' subject, while 'in Nazi discourse . . . the interpellated subject was a racial one' (pp. 116–42). In this kind of usage, interpellation has something in common with the concepts of **mode of address**, **orientation** and **preferred reading**, with the added conceptual advantage that it presumes the politics of discourse.

JH

interpersonal communication ∗ Communication between people that is unmediated by media technology, such as television, print, radio or film. ∗ It is a concept frequently referred to by social psychologists interested in communication between and within **groups**. Theories of interpersonal communication range from an evolutionary angle that suggests a genetic basis for gregariousness and communication between members of a species (for example, Lorenz 1966; Morris 1977) through to a **behaviourist** approach that posits an increase in the frequency of interpersonal **responses** resulting from selective reinforcement (for example, Skinner 1953). As with many **nature**–nurture arguments it is unwise to fall into an either–or trap, especially when there is little conclusive evidence either way.

Another popular dichotomy is between highly structured communication and more creative or spontaneous conversation. The former refers to a host of **rules**, **rituals**, and **codes** which are developed through **experience** and rehearsal (Goffman 1967). The latter refers to adventure and ad-libbing, which essentially recognizes a helical basis (Dance 1967) where the end point of an encounter is unknown to most or all participants. Interpersonal communication is often contrasted with intrapersonal forms, that is, when communication takes place within the individual.

DS

See **dramaturgy, dyad, facework, group, interaction, language, non-verbal communication, norm, role, rules, socialization**

156

Further reading   Roloff and Miller (1987); Duck (1986); Argyle (1987); Burton and Dimbleby (1988)

interpretant   ⋆ For Peirce, the effect of the sign in the mind of the user, which he calls 'the proper significate effect'. It is not a person, but a mental effect deriving from the user's previous experience of the **sign** and of its **object**. ⋆ It corresponds to Ogden and Richards's (1949) term **reference**. Peirce's theory of how signs mean can be modelled thus:

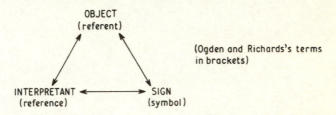

This model demonstrates how closely Peirce's and Ogden and Richards's terms correspond. (See **reference** for Ogden and Richards's model.)

JF

See   **object, reference, referent, sign, symbol**
Further reading   Fiske (1982)

intersubjectivity   ⋆ Those responses to communication that occur in the individual, but which are not, paradoxically, individual in nature. They are shared, to a degree, by all members of a culture or subculture. ⋆   Thus a photograph taken in soft focus with a warm pinkish lighting may evoke **subjective** responses of sentimentality: but it does this through shared **conventions** operating on the second order of **signification** (in this case, **connotation**). My subjective experience of sentimentality may be unique to me, but the connotation of the photograph will be shared by other members of my **culture**. This area of shared subjective responses is intersubjectivity and it is one of the most important means by which a culture affects its members and through which cultural identity is affirmed. It is crucial to an understanding of

157

connotation and **myth**, for second order meanings operate within the area of intersubjectivity. It therefore becomes the site for the work of **ideology**.

JF

See   **ideology, signification, subject**

K

kinesics ⋆ The study of movement and gesture. ⋆ Kinesthetic sense is essential for posture, equilibrium, and general movement or change of position. Kinetics refers to the science of motion that is affected by force, while kinetic art refers to the inclusion of motion between some or all parts of painting and sculpture. *Autokinesis* involves the attribution of change to objects that are in fact static within the environment. The autokinetic effect, for example, involves **perceived** movement of a stationary point of light in a darkened room. Finally, kinesics is associated with the study of the visual mode that is especially involved with body motion and **non-verbal communication**.

DS

See **interpersonal communication, non-verbal communication**

Further reading Birdwhistle (1970); McCroskey and Wheeless (1976)

L

labelling theory ⋆ A perspective which considers that **deviance** is not an intrinsic quality of specific social acts, but rather the consequence of social definition, whereby deviant 'labels' are applied to those activities. ⋆ The approach is especially associated with the work of Becker (1963) who suggests that societies and social **groups** 'create deviance by making those rules whose infraction constitutes deviance, and by applying them to particular people, and labelling them as outsiders' (p. 9). In this sense therefore, behaviour considered as deviant is 'wrong' because it is defined as such by other people, particularly those groups in society who have the power to ensure that their definitions, or 'labels', carry most weight and legitimacy. All actions may be labelled as **deviant** in one **social context** or situation, but not in another, when committed by one person or group, and not by others. Deviant labels are therefore applied to certain forms of behaviour within specific social contexts and historical conditions.

Language is perhaps the fundamental reservoir and medium for any labelling process, serving to organize and represent the moral and social contours and relations of different groups in society. Terms such as delinquent, convict, shoplifter, coward, and so on, do not simply operate neutrally to signify the breaking of certain **rules**. They also confirm a dominant or **consensual** orientation *against* such activities.

The mass media are a major **institutional** source for the

transmission and legitimation of such labels, especially in their often **stereotypical** coverage of groups whose behaviour does not conform to dominant social **norms** and **values**. RIOTERS!, MUGGERS!, EXTREMISTS!, HOOLIGANS!, JUNKIES!, and many other such labels, are part of the often dramatic social construction of what Cohen (1972), has called society's 'folk devils'. The importance of these mass mediated labels lies in the ways in which they are engaged with or decoded by their differing **audiences**. First, in a direct sense they propose 'the nature of "consensus" by pointing to concrete examples of what it is *not*' (Murdock 1981, p. 207). Second, and as a result of their *encoding* and **orientation**, their degrees of credibility are highly related to the acceptance of a basic, often unstated, set of consensual or dominant assumptions and values concerning *how* society should be organized and controlled.

Processes and acts of labelling and counter-labelling are in play as a central component of everyday **social interaction**. They and their institutional forms, realized in (among others) interaction with mass media **texts**, are vital in creating, sustaining and controlling our notions, values and modes of social control.

TO

See **consensus, deviance, institutions, moral panic, stereotype**
Further reading Bilton *et al.* (1981); Downes and Rock (1982); Cohen and Young (eds) (1981)

language ⋆ Usually taken to refer to the whole body of words (vocabulary) and ways of combining them (grammar) that is used by a **nation**, people or **race**. But the term has become associated with various specialized usages and problems in the study of communication. ⋆ The ordinary usage of the term tends to assume that language is (i) a specific language, like Welsh or English; (ii) a nomenclature – an instrument for naming objects that exist out there in the world; and (iii) an instrument for expressing thoughts that exist inside the head.

None of these usages has survived intact in the study of

communication. First, language is studied as a *general capacity*, not as an aggregate of individual languages. Second, the relations between thoughts, words and external objects have been the focus of much theorizing, the result of which is, at the very least, to put in question any idea that words simply name objects or express thoughts. Both these ideas assume language to be a mere reflection of something else that is (it follows) not language – in this case thoughts and objects. The objection to such an assumption is that it denies any active force to language, reducing it to a mere instrument, and that it fails to take into account the extent to which both thoughts and objects can be known only through their representation in some form of language.

Just as atomic physics started by isolating individual atoms but ended up by identifying much smaller particles and forces, so linguistics has identified language as comprising structures and rules operating between elements within words. The most basic is the **phoneme**, or unit of recognizably distinct sound that figures in a particular language. Different languages have different phonemes (there's no /j/ in Welsh, and no /ll/, /ch/, /rh/ in English). But all languages operate with a finite number of phonemes which can then be combined to form words. So language is no longer seen as a 'body of words', but rather as a generative structure or **langue** which is capable of producing **signs**. Beyond phonemic analysis, linguistics has developed around the study of **semantics** and syntax (rules of combination).

Linguistics has traditionally centred on speech. **Semiotics**, on the other hand, has taken over the Saussurian model of language and used it to analyse all kinds of **signification** other than speech – writing, architecture, television, cinema, food, fashion and furniture, for instance. There is no doubt that such sign systems do signify (that is, the way their elements can be selected and combined does serve to communicate meanings), but whether they do it *as* languages or *like* language remains a matter for debate.

Within communication and cultural studies there is widespread agreement that whether they are studied as languages or as language-like, signifying systems of all kinds share certain characteristics. These are: (i) **meaning** is not a result of the intrinsic properties of individual signs or words, but of the systematic relations between the different elements; (ii) language is not an **empirical** thing but a social capacity; (iii) **individuals** are not the source of language but its product – language thinks itself out, as it were, in individuals. Language always escapes the individual and even the social will. Some of the more important concepts and terms associated with the study of language are included under separate entries.

JH

See **code, discourse, langue/parole, non-verbal communication, paradigm/syntagm, phonemic/phonetic, semiotics, sign, signification, signifier/signified, structuralism, synchronic/diachronic**

Further reading Culler (1976); Halliday (1978); Montgomery (1986)

language, functions of ∗ The purposes which language can be made to serve in different situations. ∗ Although we may regard language primarily as a means of making statements which are true or false (the *referential function*), or as an instrument for the communication of ideas (the *ideational function*), this is only part of the total picture. Thus, while the referential or ideational function may be seen as prominent in news reporting, science writing, court room testimony, and so on, several other functions have come to be identified as important in everyday language use. One well-known account of language function is supplied by Jakobson (1960), who identified the *phatic*, the *regulatory* (or 'conative', as he called it), the *emotive*, the *aesthetic* (or 'poetic' as he called it), and the *metalinguistic* functions as equally deserving of attention.

Many situations, for instance, involve a use of language where issues of truth value are not at stake. Consider, for instance, situations such as telephoning a friend. If you ask 'How's things?' or 'How are you?', you are quite likely to be answered: 'Fine.' Subsequent conversation, of course, may well reveal that your interlocutor has one leg in plaster and can walk only with crutches. And yet you would not thereby consider the initial response – 'Fine' – to be untruthful. This is because we commonly use language not just for articulating ideas but for making and sustaining contact, often using quite ritualized formulae which are almost devoid of content. This use is known as the **phatic** *function* of language. Conversations about the weather between relative strangers at UK bus stops are elaborate exercises in the phatic function.

Language is also used to affect the actions and dispositions of others by commands, requests, instructions, and other more subtle acts of verbal persuasion. The language of air-traffic control, of advertising and of political campaigns relies heavily on this function, which is known as the *regulatory* or *conative function*.

In the case of the regulatory function the focus of the language is on the actions and dispositions of the addressee. In contrast to this, language may be used to express the feelings and dispositions of the speaker irrespective of whether an audience is present at all. This is known as the *emotive function* – language used (sometimes involuntarily) for the expression of feelings. Scratching the long-cherished LP record is likely to lead to an outburst of the emotive function.

Language may also be used as a source of intrinsic pleasure. Young children learning their first language may derive great pleasure from playing with the sound properties of language – repeating and modulating sound sequences, sometimes without regard for their communicative potential, as in the following sequence between twins aged thirty-three months:

A: zacky sue
B: (*laughing*) zacky sue zacky sue (*both laugh*) ah
A: appy
B: olp olt olt
A: oppy oppy
B: appy appy (*laughing*).

(after Keenan 1974, p. 171)

This kind of spontaneous linguistic play occurs amongst children whether on their own or in company right through the period of language development. Not only does it seem integral to the process of learning the first language: it seems not too fanciful to suggest that such activity may form the basis for later poetic uses of language. The general name for this kind of activity is the *aesthetic function*. More or less self-conscious playing with language operates in differing linguistic domains, involving not only sound-play as in rhyme and alliteration but also punning, ambiguity, grammatical rule-breaking and so on. Nor is it restricted to poetry proper. Advertising, for example, employs language as much in its aesthetic function as in its conative.

Another important, if sometimes overlooked, function is the use of language to explore and reflect upon itself, known as the *metalinguistic function*. A surprising amount of everyday discourse turns out to be *metalinguistic* – from the television interviewer's 'Is what you're saying then Prime Minister . . .?' to someone in an argument complaining 'That doesn't make sense'. Grammar books and dictionaries, of course, rely heavily on the *metalinguistic function*, as does a book like this especially at moments when it supplies definitions of terms.

The notion of function is important in the study of language principally because it helps to emphasize the way in which language is much more than a tool for thinking with or a vehicle for conveying information. In this way, functional perspectives tend to stress a range of other pressures upon language, and other possibilities for its use, than the need to express some kind of 'propositional content' in a strict logical form which may be measured for its truth value. Thus, it is claimed from a functional perspective that language does a great deal more than defining and expressing concepts. Indeed the linguist Halliday has argued that when children are learning their first language they use it in the first instance much more to affect and interact with their social environment than to convey information. Halliday's account of language is generally functionalist in character, being predicated on the claim that many aspects of its organization are ultimately derived from the functions or purposes that it serves.

The main drawback with the functional perspective is the difficulty of reaching rigorous definitions of the main language functions. Some accounts suggest three; others suggest as many as seven. A more recent approach known as **speech act theory** focuses more specifically on stipulating in detail a precise range of actions which discrete utterances are capable of performing.

MM

See **speech act**
Further reading   Halliday (1973); Jakobson (1960)

langue   ∗ In Saussurian linguistics, the abstract system of signs and conventions underlying individual acts of speaking. ∗   The role of langue, therefore, may be seen as analogous to that of the musical score that underlies individual performances of a symphony or the rules of chess that make possible an unlimited variety of actual games. The symphony, for instance, exists independently of its individual performances – in which false notes may occur, distinctive choices of tempo may be adopted, and so on. Likewise, chess may be played with many different sequences of moves, on many sizes of board, with different kinds of piece, and yet remain chess as long as the basic rules of the game are observed. In the same way, for English or Swahili or Gujarati, there is a common storehouse of basic, necessary conventions or rules which speakers of that language follow when framing their utterances. It is these conventions that constitute the langue for that language; and it is by following such shared conventions that intelligibility is guaranteed between speakers of that language. In this sense, langue is very much a social product shared between members of a social body as a whole and out of the control of any one individual.

As with so many important terms in modern linguistics, the notion of langue was developed initially in the work of the Swiss linguist Ferdinand de Saussure. For him, contrasting langue with **parole** was an important methodological step in isolating the object of linguistic enquiry by focusing on the **institution** (langue) rather than the event (parole). The distinction is similarly formulated in much modern linguistics, whether as **competence** versus **performance** in the work of Chomsky – or potential linguistic behaviour versus actual linguistic behaviour in the work of Halliday. In **structuralism** and in **semiotics** the notion of langue was extended to embrace other kinds of the sign than the purely linguistic one. Thus, patterns of kinship, the social organization of furniture, food, and fashion have all been considered as examples of underlying systems.

MM

See **code, competence, parole, syntagm**
Further reading Saussure (1974); Culler (1976)

lifestyle ★ Distinctive configurations of cultural identity and practice which are associated particularly with modern conditions and forms of cultural consumption. ★ The term is used in a number of often contradictory ways, although it provides an important focus for attention in studies of **culture** and communication in the 1990s.

The idea of lifestyle may be used to describe the particular patterns and distinctive features constituting any **group's** or **individual's** 'style of life'. In this sense the term has been used in a rather anthropological fashion, implying that our 'individuality' and identity are framed within wider collective structures and '**choices**'. Lifestyles are conceived as 'fragments' of any modern social formation, indexing the degrees of '**choice**', '**difference**' and creative or resistant cultural possibilities contained within it. The emphasis tends therefore to be on lifestyles as particular forms of **symbolic** expression of certain lived material and social circumstances.

In contrast to this, the term is also used to refer to significant **rhetorics** and **discourses** in play in the production or regulation of modern cultural life. From this perspective lifestyles are understood essentially as manufactured, especially by modern advertising and marketing agencies and their practices. Appeals to particular kinds of 'lifestyle' have become increasingly central in advertising and the rise of consumer culture in the post-1950. Some critics of this have seen 'lifestyles' as modern euphemisms for social **class** and have restated the contradictions between material and symbolic relations in modern economies. For other writers, however, the concept has a more useful analytical value in its ability to pinpoint key features of life in the advanced or **postmodern** state.

In summary, the term is best approached as a focus for several important issues confronting the study of contemporary cultural life. Key debates concern the degree to which lifestyles are conceived as primarily symbolic codes and practices and understood as relatively autonomous. Second, the extent to which the culture of lifestyles allows for genuine pluralities of expression, including resistance, as opposed to 'disguised' forms of uniformity and 'choice'. In turn, these issues invoke fundamental arguments concerning the historical 'motor' or dynamics of lifestyles – where do they come from, how are they made and used, how do they change?

TO

See **culture, Fordism, postmodernism, style, subculture**
Further reading Featherstone (1987); Bocock (1992); Giddens (1991); Tomlinson (1990); Myers (1986)

linguistic relativity ⋆ A hypothesis that different languages give rise to different views of the world. ⋆ According to this hypothesis we do not experience the world in a direct and straightforward fashion. On the contrary, the **language** that we use shapes and even creates the conditions for our experience. There is no absolutely neutral and disinterested way of apprehending and representing the world, because the particular language that we habitually use points us towards certain types of observation and predisposes certain choices of interpretation.

This may be partly a question of vocabulary. Thus, different languages carve up areas of experience in different ways. Russian, for example, divides up the colour spectrum with twelve basic colour terms; whereas English segments the same domain with eleven basic terms, using only one basic colour term for 'blue' in place of the two available in Russian. In an Australian aborigine language called Pintupi there are ten discrete expressions for types of hole, many of which can be translated into English only by elaborate paraphrase: for example *katarta* means roughly 'the hole left by a goanna when it has broken the surface after hibernation'.

Languages, however, differ in more than the organization of their respective vocabularies. They also differ in their characteristic ways of forming sentences – in their grammar. The system of tense in one language may be very different from that of another: English grammar, for instance, provides at least two tenses, but Hopi – a North American language – seems to operate without tenses at all. Instead, its verb forms distinguish between what is subjective and what is objective. It seems likely, therefore, that the different grammars of these two languages make available for their speakers quite different senses of time.

On the basis of such evidence, the American linguist B. L. Whorf concluded that

> all observers are not led to the same picture of the universe. . . . Users of markedly different grammars are pointed by their grammars toward different types of observations and different evaluations of externally similar acts of observation, and hence are not equivalent as observers.
>
> (Whorf 1956, p. 214)

Whorf's original formulation of the hypothesis (it is sometimes referred to as the Sapir–Whorf hypothesis in deference to himself and a distinguished anthropological linguist – Edward Sapir – with whom he was working) was published roughly fifty years ago (see Whorf 1940). But controversy has remained strong ever since over its central claims. It is not easy, for example, to provide clear empirical support for linguistic relativity. Critics point to the fact of translation between languages, which should not be possible if one's native language totally constrained one's thought-world.

However, the burgeoning of interest in language, and in linguistic models, as evidenced in movements such as **structuralism** and **post-structuralism**, has given new impetus to forms of the linguistic relativity hypothesis. When a post-structuralist literary critic – such as Catherine Belsey, for instance – argues that a novel is a **discursive** (linguistic) artefact that constructs a reality as much as it mediates it, she is espousing a form of linguistic relativity.

MM

See **discourse, structuralism**

Further reading Whorf (1956); Belsey (1980); Montgomery (1986)

literacy ⋆ The social institution of writing; by extension the social institution of communication by any means other than speech.

⋆ Literacy is not and never has been a personal attribute or **ideologically** inert 'skill', simply to be 'acquired' by individual persons. Neither is it a mere technology, though it does require a means of production both physical (a tool to write with and a material to write on) and social (a recognized notation or alphabet and a way of transmitting the knowledge required to manipulate it).

As a **social institution** literacy is subject to similar kinds of forces to do with its distribution and regulation as are other kinds of institution. Its early history is usually characterized by strict controls as to who had access to it (priesthoods and economic or administrative officials) and what is was used for (sacred and state business).

Modern societies are heavily committed to 'universal' literacy, and use it as an **autonomous** means of communication quite different from that of speech. This has led many observers to seek to account for the peculiarities of modern culture by reference to 'literate consciousness'. First among such critics was Marshall McLuhan (1962). More recently, literacy has become the focus of important debates about the ideological function of education since, it is argued, literacy is a vehicle for the dissemination of both **values** and practices (as well as skills) that may be effective in reproducing **hegemonic** order.

Without having to claim that writing 'caused' the forms of consciousness and through them the social organization of twentieth-century society, it is still possible to study the extent to which literacy carries with it more than just an innocent skill. It is ideologically and politically charged – it can be used as a means of social control or regulation, but also as a progressive weapon in the struggle for emancipation. Above all, however, a literate work-force is a precondition for industrialized production, and the reproduction of a literate work-force requires large-scale state intervention in disseminating the appropriate level, type and content of literacy for this purpose.

JH

See **difference, ideological state apparatuses, institutions, orality, socialization**

lowest common denominator ⋆ A useful term in mathematics where 'lowest' has a literal meaning. ⋆ It should never enter the vocabulary of a student of communication or culture. The phrase is used **metaphorically** by the cultural **elite** to dismiss the tastes of the majority, and to exploit the **objectivity** of mathematics to give a false validation to their own **prejudices**.

JF

mass communication ∗ Usually understood as newspapers, magazines, cinema, television, radio and advertising; sometimes including book publishing (especially popular fiction) and music (the pop industry). ∗

Caution should be exercised with respect to the term itself. The word 'mass' may encourage the unthinking replication of **mass society theory**, while the word 'communication' in this context masks the social and industrial nature of the media, promoting a tendency to think of them as **interpersonal communication**. Since mass communication is neither mass nor communication as normally understood, the term should be seen as something akin to a proper name.

Mass communication is not a concept that can be defined, but a **common sense** category that is used to lump a number of different phenomena together in a non-analytic way. Attempts to define it, however, are plentiful, but they always fail. This is because they are forced to be too restrictive, in which case the definition doesn't do justice to all that we commonly think of as mass communication (it is hard to encompass the diversity of what constitutes print, cinema, radio and television within one definition). Or else they are forced to become too over-extended, in which case the definition ends up applying equally well to something that we don't think of as mass communication at all – like education, religion, or even speech itself.

Having said that, we can proceed with caution. Mass communication is the practice and product of providing leisure **entertainment** and information to an unknown **audience** by means of corporately financed, industrially produced, state-regulated, high technology, privately consumed commodities in the modern print, screen, audio and broadcast **media**.

JH

Further reading   McQuail (1987)

mass society/mass society theory   ⋆ An early twentieth-century model of the social organization of industrial/capitalist societies which characterized them as comprising a vast work-force of atomized, isolated individuals without traditional bonds of locality or kinship, who were alienated from their labour by its repetitive, unskilled tendencies and by their subjection to the vagaries of the wage relationship (the *cash nexus*) and the fluctuations of the market. ⋆ Such **individuals** were entirely at the mercy of (i) totalitarian **ideologies** and **propaganda**; (ii) influence by the mass media (comprising, in this period, the emergent cinema and radio). Mass society theory was an understandable response to the economics and politics of the 1930s, and was neatly summed up in Charles Chaplin's film *Modern Times* (1936). But it has hung on in a **common sense** version which is associated largely with cultural and literary critics for whom industrialization and modern society in general remain a regrettable aberration from **values** and habits which these writers fondly imagine used to prevail before the invention of machines, democracy and the like.

Mass society theory has been refuted by historical evidence, but its continuation as an ideology can be accounted for by attending to the term most often used as the polar opposite of *mass*, namely *elite*. This indicates the politics of mass society theorists – they are advocates of various kinds of cultural **elite** who should be privileged and promoted over the masses, claiming for themselves both exemption from and leadership of the misguided masses. These terms, *mass* and *elite*, are of course convenient 'erasures' or euphemisms for **class**.

Mass society theory has been active in a wide range of media studies, where it tends to produce apocalyptic visions of what the television and cinema are doing to the masses (but never, oddly enough, to the critic). Any time you speculate on what '**effect**' the media have on (other) people, especially if your thoughts turn to notions such as **dependency**, aggression, **narcotization**, brutalization and desensitization, then you are thinking mass society theory. Don't! Go and watch television, and ask yourself why these things aren't happening to you.

JH

See **audience, effects, elite, persuasion**
Further reading Biddiss (1977); Swingewood (1977)

meaning ⋆ The import of any **signification**. The product of **culture**. ⋆ Meaning is a largely untheorized term, although debates about the meaning of meaning are well-known conversation stoppers. In the context of communication studies, it is worth bearing in mind that meaning is the object of study, not a given or self-evident quantum that exists prior to analysis. Hence meaning should not be assumed to reside *in* anything, be it **text**, utterance, programme, activity or behaviour, even though such acts and objects may be understood as meaningful. Meaning is the product or result of communication, so you will doubtless come across it frequently. Meaning has been proposed by Marshall Sahlins (1976) as a common 'third term' – added to material goods (economy) and social relations (politics) – to unify the anthropological study of culture. Meaning *in* economic and political arrangements thus becomes the proper subject of anthropology; and meaning becomes the product *of* culture.

JH

meaning systems ⋆ Parkin (1972) developed this theory to account for the varied responses of groups to their different social conditions. It explains how people make sense of their social world and has been adapted by Hall *et al.* (eds) (1980) to account for the different ways in which people make sense of texts. ⋆ Parkin identified three main meaning systems in western industrial democracies:

174

(1) *The dominant system* This endorses the current structure of social, economic and political relations, and enables people to understand their social location within the existing distribution of **power**, wealth and jobs. It produces in the subordinate **class** deferential or aspirational responses: deferential responses are made by those who accept their position, and aspirational by those who seek to 'improve' it within the same system.

(2) *The subordinate system* This accepts the overall dominant system, but allows particular **groups** the right to demand a better position within it. It produces negotiated responses which frequently attempt to exploit the system to the advantage of a particular group or class within it.

(3) *The radical system* This rejects the dominant system and proposes an alternative one opposed to it. It thus produces oppositional responses.

Let us take people's responses to the wage economy as an example. Those who adopt the dominant meaning system would tend to make sense of their social position by responding subordinately or aspirationally: they take their wages gratefully, or submissively, or else try to boost them by overtime or promotion. The subordinate meaning system is more likely to be adopted by trade unionists, whose response to the wage economy would be to try and negotiate a larger share of the same cake for the same work, for themselves and their members. The radical meaning system, on the other hand, would lead people to oppositional responses that would question the basic principles of the wage economy.

Hall suggests that these socially located meaning systems, which are not mutually exclusive, are the means by which people bring their **social context** to bear upon the decoding of a television (or other mass media) **text**. The systems produce three equivalent codes for the decoding of the text – the dominant **hegemonic**, the negotiated, and the oppositional.

JF

See **preferred reading**
Further reading   Morley (1980, 1992)

175

mediation ⋆ The act of intervening between two parties in order to effect/affect a relationship between them; the act of channelling social knowledge and cultural values through an institutional agency to an audience. ⋆ Mediation is taken to be one of the prime purposes of the mass media: they are the corporate mediators between the various fragmented **groups**, **classes** and hierarchies of a modern society. They themselves use mediators in the form of individual professional presenters – like Trevor MacDonald, Anna Ford, Brian Henderson, Mary Delahunty, Terry Wogan or Bryant Gumble – who personalize the values and public identity of the broadcasting corporation, offering viewers a familiar face and personality with which to identify.

JH

See **accessing, bardic function, cultural reproduction**

medium/media ⋆ Broadly, an intermediate agency that enables communication to take place. More specifically, a technological development that extends the channels, range or speed of communication. ⋆ In the broad sense speech, writing, gestures, facial expressions, dress, acting and dancing can all be seen as media of communication. Each medium is capable of transmitting **codes** along a **channel** or channels. This use of the term is decreasing, and it is increasingly being confined to the technical media, particularly the mass media. Sometimes it is used to refer to the means of communication (for example, in 'print or broadcast media'), but often it refers to the technical forms by which these means are actualized (for example, radio, television, newspapers, books, photographs, films and records). McLuhan used the word in this sense in his famous dictum *The Medium is the Message*. By this he meant that the personal and social consequences of a new technological medium in itself are more significant than the uses to which it is actually put: the existence of television is more significant than the content of its programmes.

Hot and cool media: a distinction by McLuhan. A hot medium extends 'one single sense' in 'high definition', that is a hot medium is filled with data, the **audience** is therefore receptive or passive. A cool medium, by contrast, has low definition and provides limited data, so the audience has to participate, to be active, in order to complete the **message**. A photograph is hot, a cartoon is cool; a film is hot, television is cool (visual definition is higher on the cinema screen than on the television screen), radio is hot (it uses sound as completely as possible), the telephone is cool. McLuhan's categories may be valid for the technical properties of the media, but there must be some doubt about his theory of how they affect audience participation. There is no evidence to suggest that the radio or film audience is less active than the television one.

There is an increasing and unwelcome tendency for the word *media* to be used in the singular in the technical sense.

JF

See **channel, code, mass communication**
Further reading Williams (1976a); McLuhan (1964)

memory ★ An aspect of cognition which refers to the capacity to store and recall past experiences. ★ Such information has to be **encoded** into some hypothetical memory bank, retrieved from that store, and then **decoded**.

There are a number of different types of memory, the briefest of which refers to a virtual **after-image** following a **stimulus**: this has been appropriately labelled by Neisser (1966) as **iconic** memory. It is not quite a state of perception because the image portrays past events. Atkinson and Shiffrin (1971) advance a duplex theory of memory that includes two stores: a short-term memory (STM) that is ill-defined but often includes events experienced within the last few minutes, and a long-term memory (LTM) that stores information processed through STM. Their laboratory-based investigations identified such factors as rehearsal, novelty, intensity and duration of stimuli as being important in affecting the likelihood of retention. However, the duplex theory has problems in accounting for information that is remembered on one occasion but not on another and that does not appear to go through some short-term 'buffer' stage (defined by Miller (1956) as having a limited storage capacity).

Tulving (1972) prefers an alternative distinction: memory that stores chronologically sequenced events, or episodic memory, and memory based on reorganization of information according to meaning and context, or **semantic** memory. When discussing the effects of communication many theorists have identified primacy and *recency* effects, whereby the first or last parts of a **message** are respectively well remembered, and this is thought to be at least partly attributable to interference from other parts of the message. Many **texts** are well suited to taking advantage of primacy and recency. For example, a 30-second television advertisement will often provide much information at the beginning ('this is the product') and at the end ('this is the brand'). The remainder allows for the assimilation of such information, while not providing any interference, but keeping your **attention**. It is unclear as to whether interference affects encoding and storage of the forgotten information, or just the retrieval processes. A useful analogy is the missing book in a library: it has either been stolen or else put back on a different shelf.

A related area of study is that of *mnemonics*, defined as techniques for helping memory at the encoding, decoding and retrieval stages. By reducing complex or lengthy information to an easily remembered code we maximize our chances of retrieving all of the original material. For example, the sentence 'Censorship of machine-made underground news incites crowd agitation through insidiously organized nicety' is more easily remembered if we take the first letters from each word within that statement: the result is 'communication'.

Popular memory goes beyond 'the individual' and refers to the **cultural** construction of a **mythical** past by a social **group** or **nation**. Media forms replay popular memories and may be influential in their popularity and nostalgic appeal.

DS

See **cognition, information processing, language, perception**

Further reading   Gregg (1975, 1986); Lindsay and Norman (1977)

message   * That which is transmitted in the process of communication; the means by which the sender affects the receiver.   *   It is seen as an embryonic **content** that exists before the **encoding** and after the **decoding**; encoding translates it into a **form** in which it can be transmitted, while decoding translates it back to its original state (provided that encoding, decoding and transmission have all worked at maximum efficiency). See **text** for a fuller discussion.

JF

See **sender/receiver, text**

metalanguage ⋆ Literally, a language about language, or more commonly, a way of talking/writing/thinking about texts or speech acts. ⋆ Just as **language** determines our **perception** and interpretation of the world about us, so does metalanguage our perception and interpretation of **texts**: in both cases it is necessary to separate the (meta)language from its **referent** in order to become aware of the arbitrary nature of (meta)language systems and therefore of the fact that other (meta)languages would produce other **meanings**.

Jakobson uses the term *metalingual function* to refer to the function performed by all texts of identifying the language or **codes** that they are using. 'Beanz Meanz Heinz' makes sense only because it identifies itself as using the code of ad-language. 'Lucy in the Sky with Diamonds' makes one kind of sense to those who interpret its metalingual function as saying 'I am poetic language' and another for those for whom the metalingual function says 'I am drug induced discourse'. The metalingual function is a necessary reading aid for the **addressee**.

JF

See **language, functions of**
Further reading Fiske (1982)

metaphor ⋆ Metaphor communicates the unknown by transposing it into terms of the known. ⋆ Thus the metaphor 'The car *beetles* along' assumes that we do not know how the car moves, but do know how a beetle scurries across the floor. The metaphor transposes characteristics of beetles to cars.

Jakobson claims that metaphor and **metonymy** are the two

fundamental modes of communicating meaning. He argues that metaphor is the characteristic mode of poetry. It is also characteristic of advertising where **images** are created out of known cultural **myths** whose characteristics are then transposed on to the unknown product. The Wild West has become a metaphor for a brand of cigarettes, the bright lights of San Francisco for a brand of cosmetics.

Metaphors work **paradigmatically** – they insert the unknown into a new paradigm from which it derives part of its new meaning. In the metaphor 'The ship *ploughed* the sea', the word 'sailed', which is the unstated unknown, is inserted into the paradigm of 'ways of parting solid material' alongside words such as *sliced*, *ripped*, *sawed*, *cut* or *tore*. The reader has, by an act of imagination, to transpose both the general characteristics of the paradigm and the specific characteristics of the chosen unit *ploughed* to give a new meaning to the unknown term 'sailed'.

Metaphors, then, require active, imaginative **decoding**: the reader has to find which characteristics can be meaningfully transposed. This active engagement of the **receiver** is sought by poets who hope that the decoding will provide a parallel imaginative process to the encoding, and by advertisers who hope that the co-operation required will make the receiver more susceptible to the claims of the product.

A *simile* is a type of metaphor in which both the known and the unknown are present: 'The car drove along the road like a beetle scuttling across the floor'. Advertisements and visual metaphors are more like similes in that both terms are normally present.

Connotation tends to work metaphorically – in a photograph of a thatched cottage taken with warm lighting and soft focus, nostalgia is connoted. The lighting is a visual equivalent of the verbal metaphor 'looking through rose-coloured spectacles', and the soft focus is a metaphor of the softheartedness of the emotion.

JF

See **condensation, metonymy, paradigm, sign**

methodology ⋆ The study of techniques used in conducting research within the sciences and social sciences. ⋆ Techniques of data collection, population sampling, analysis of evidence and **experimental** design are commonly referred to. The validity and reliability of evidence used for theorizing and argument thus relies heavily on methodologies deployed for the collection of that information. It can be seen that **empirical** debate centres on the querying of evidence and methodological bias. In communication research some methodologies are more rigorous than others – for example, the construction of information processing **experiments** as compared with analysis of the **unconscious** attempted by **psychoanalytical theorists** and introspectionists. And in some areas of **cultural studies**, the reliability and validity of methodological techniques have been seriously questioned because of assumptions made about **objectivity** and empiricism.

DS

See **empiricism**, **ethnography**, **experiment**, **positivism**, **questionnaire**
Further reading Stempel and Westley (eds) (1981)

metonymy ⋆ Metonymy works by using a part or element of something to stand for the whole. ⋆ Metonymy and **metaphor** are, according to Jakobson, the two fundamental modes of communicating **meaning**. He claims that it is the characteristic mode of the novel, particularly of **realism**. The settings of a realistic television police series act as metonyms for the city as a whole, and our view of the city will change according to the metonyms chosen. New York or London can appear as seedy, ill-lit, decaying, breeding grounds of crime, or as the sophisticated setting for big business depending on the choice of metonym.

News is metonymic: a reported event is interpreted as standing for the whole of the reality of which it is a part. Two or three strikers on a picket line are metonyms of the union side of a dispute; soldiers in a Belfast street are metonyms of the British army in Northern Ireland; a line of police behind riot shields is a metonym of the forces of law and order opposing civil anarchy.

Metonyms work **syntagmatically**: we construct the rest of the 'story' from the part that we have been given, in the same way that we construct the rest of a sentence if a speaker finishes in 'mid-air'. But they tend to work invisibly: metaphors draw attention to themselves by their artificiality and by the imagination required to **decode** them. But metonyms seem so natural that they are easily taken for granted, and we fail to realize that another metonym might give a very different picture of the same whole. A militantly protesting striker and a bored cold striker are both part of the same picket line, but they may be represented as significantly different metonyms.

Myths tend to work metonymically. An image will trigger off a chain of concepts in the same way that a metonym triggers off our construction of the whole of which it is a part.

JF

See **metaphor, signification, syntagm**

minority ⋆ A group that is associated with a lack of power. ⋆ It is misleading to consider minorities as characterized by numbers alone, although of course the fewer the members the more likely the inferior **power base** (but see **elite**). A crucial consideration concerns shared **values**, beliefs and **perceptions** for minority **groups**: if these are not consciously present then that group's existence is psychologically precarious yet sociologically real. It is often through the declaration of grievances that communication increases between members (which allows for further airing of grievances) and a position of solidarity is reached. Minorities will thus move from a position of acceptance to rejection, based on the realization of a weak power base and resentment about such inequality – a point well emphasized by Tajfel (1981) for **race**, and by Spender (1985) for women. Closely allied with the growth of shared identity for minorities is the development of ethnic cultures. In media studies, **stereotyping** has been closely analysed for carrying unfavourable and destructive images of minorities who have little power to change such popular (mis)representations (see Howitt 1982).

Minority can also be linked with minority culture, which Williams (1981) contrasts with mass **culture**. Here the concept becomes closely allied with a superior power base associated with an elite that on the one hand ensures (through patronage) the survival of selected art forms, scientific work and skills, but on the other controls **access** to 'the great tradition'. On occasions we might therefore link minority with high culture, and recognize groups of people who profit from such patronage.

DS

See **consciousness, ethnic, gender, power, prejudice, profession, race, role, stereotype**
Further reading Tajfel (1981); Spender (1985); Williams (1981)

mode of address ⋆ The way those aspects of a **text** or utterance are constructed that establish *relations* between addresser and addressee, as opposed to those which construct *representations*; the way media organizations address their audience or readership.
⋆ Mode of address is straightforward in face-to-face speech; it includes linguistic, para-linguistic and contextual features of an utterance or dialogue that **orientate** each speaker to the other, taking account of their relative intimacy, status, etc., and the **genre** of situation in which the dialogue occurs. You can compare the mode of address appropriate for different **discourse genres** by thinking about describing the *same* event to, say, a friend, a court, your diary, or in a letter home.

Mode of address is an inescapable component of communication; it is therefore always present not only in face-to-face situations but also in the media, where the parties have no personal but only textual contact. Mode of address in these circumstances is also **ideological**; a part of the process of **interpellation**, where the **mass communication** 'hails' or interpellates individuals as the **subject** of its discourse. Put simply, media **texts** invent a fictional image of their preferred **audience's** characteristics, and then address that fictional character.

Commercial radio **broadcasters** in the UK gave a name to the fictional character to whom they address their remarks. She's called Doreen, she lives in Basildon, has a husband (Bill), a short attention span, and while she's not stupid she listens to the radio with only half an ear, so the golden rule is: 'Tell her you're going to tell her; tell her; then tell her you've told her'. Doreen is assumed to have no interest in the politics of the outside world unless they disrupt supplies to her supermarket – here's some advice to trainees on scripting news items:

> If you have information which needs telling to Doreen, be sure you clearly understand what she needs to know and why. 'Hey Doreen – The Sri Lankan Tamils are blockading the island's ports as part of a major strike.' Do you mean that the tea supplies to Doreen are in danger? Then say so!
>
> (National Broadcasting School/CBC Radio)

Mode of address is a matter of high policy for media organizations. This is because it conveys not only their sense of their audience, but their sense of themselves too. Each newspaper or television **channel** wants to set itself apart from the competition and to communicate to potential consumers, advertisers or sponsors what kind of an outfit it is. The same goes for different shows – each current affairs show, for instance, exploits the resources of television mode of address in a different way to distinguish itself from others on the same or competing channels. One show may be populist, another dedicated to investigative reporting, a third to financial and economic news and so on. In each case the differences will be signalled by programme titles and music, style of studio decor, etc., but most importantly by the presenter(s) or **mediators** – their looks and personality, whether or not they are journalists, the style or idiom of their talk, clothing, eye-contact, hair, mutual repartee, and so on. Ratings depend on such **semiotic** minutiae, because it is through them that people will decide whether they are included or excluded by the show's mode of address.

One example of an organization whose mode of address is notoriously its own is the BBC. Perhaps this is because, historically, the BBC appeared to hold itself in much higher esteem than it did its audience. In its **Reithian** period (from 1922 to perhaps as late as the middle 1960s) the BBC carved a unique image for itself in the public mind, largely through its mode of address: formal, upper-class, authoritative, cultured; or, put another way, stuffed-shirt, elitist, arrogant, pompous. This 'house style' permeated BBC practice from presenters' accents ('BBC English') to programming policies, scheduling, **genres**, repertoire. But it was more than a question of **style** – for the BBC it was part of a long-term strategy for survival as a national cultural **institution**, to gain protection from both popular and parliamentary challenges.

JH

model ⋆ The structural representation of a different set of elements that aims to guide analysis of complex and perhaps novel issues. ⋆ The concept of model has been described by Harré (1979) as constituting a central but unstable position within scientific and social scientific enquiry. Models are considered essential for the construction of hypotheses and in suggesting new investigation of old areas because of a reference to situations or processes that may be more easily comprehended. In this sense a model can be an **iconic** representation that reminds one of the real thing – as would a photograph or a doll. Or the model may refer to some ideal type that real versions satisfy only partially, as with some super powerful **hero/heroine**. Other applications, of which there are many, include explanatory modelling, where there is often no exact one-to-one similarity between two corresponding elements within the comparison process. For example, **information processing** models as reviewed by Lindsay and Norman (1977) may refer to computer systems, programs and operations when explaining the **cognitive** bases of communication although no full analogy is intended with all aspects of a computer. Commonly used models in communication include *linear, circular, helical,* **transactional**, **interpersonal** and **intrapersonal**. The danger with the use of models, especially when devised for explanatory rather than descriptive reasons, is that they may be taken too literally. They may then become restrictive to future theorizing because of the acceptance of arbitrarily imposed (but at one time convenient) boundaries.

DS

See **dramaturgy, hypodermic needle model, information processing, psychoanalytical theory, two-step flow model**
Further reading   McQuail and Windahl (1981); McKeown (1982)

moral panic ⋆ An important concept which highlights the processes of interplay between forces of social reaction and control, the mass media and certain forms of deviant activity. ⋆ The term has been introduced into the analysis of the mass media and their capacity to generate social concern by Cohen (1972), who describes the process as one where 'A condition, episode, person, or group of persons emerges to become defined as a threat to societal values and interests' (1972, p. 28; 1980, p. 9). Moral panics then, are those processes whereby members of a society and culture become 'morally sensitized' to the challenges and menace posed to 'their' accepted **values** and ways of life, by the activities of **groups** defined as **deviant**. The process underscores the importance of the mass media in providing, maintaining, and 'policing' the available frameworks and definitions of deviance, which structure both public awareness *of*, and attitudes *towards*, social problems. The term serves also to link this structured public awareness to the **institutional** and other forms of control mobilized to respond to such problems. In its most explicit form a moral panic can be analytically divided into three stages:

(1) The occurrence and **signification** of an initial event, which attracts often dramatic media coverage, and sets in motion often intensive media surveillance and research routines. These are organized and aligned to identify any subsequent events which may be **coded** as similar.

(2) In the wake of initial impact, media coverage starts to work *from* the event in particular, *to* the wider social implications and issues that such an event is defined as raising. Drawing particularly upon **primary definers** and 'accredited witnesses', who represent 'expert' and professional opinion, and possibly 'moral entrepreneurs' who contend in defining the event as symptomatic of wider breakdowns in moral and social fibre and fabric, the media fuel public debate, concern, outrage, and sensitivity. This may be further inflated and intensified by media identification of other events and occurrences that have subsequently taken place (often uncovered by surveillance in (1)). These may, under certain conditions, become defined

and interpreted as the progressive discovery that the problem or event in particular is in fact a part of a widespread and correspondingly more menacing social problem. In this way the initial event becomes constructed as 'the tip of an iceberg', the first 'wave' of a 'flood', an early 'blow' in a developing 'battle', and so on. This spiralling of public attention, and its replay through the media, notably in the forms of news, in itself may lend increased urgency and severity to:

(3) Social control, exercised especially though not always exclusively in the form of state responses to the 'problem' drastically and dramatically revealed. The judicial, legislative and administrative responses and penalties will often be articulated within the definitions and frameworks provided in preceding stages.

The best way to come to terms with this concept is to follow its application through in context. The term and the theory that underpins it also provide an interesting focal area for research.

TO

See **agenda setting, amplification, deviance, labelling, news values, primary definers**

Further reading Cohen (1972); Young (1971) (moral panics and drug-takers); Hall and Jefferson (eds) (1976) (moral panics and youth subcultures); Hall, *et al.* (1978) (moral panics and 'mugging'); Golding and Middleton (1982) (moral panics and 'welfare scroungers'); Weeks (1989) (AIDS and sexuality)

motivation (of the shot) ⋆ The arrangement of props and actions in a film or video shot to suggest the source of **diegetic** features.
⋆ Light is motivated if a window, table–lamp, candle, extraterrestrial being or other source is shown on screen as well as the light that apparently emanates from it. However – and this is the point for analysts – it is extremely rare to find that the scene actually is lit from the motivating source; motivation is a convention designed to promote **naturalism** (verisimilitude).
Motivation is among the **distinctive features** of a **genre**,

contributing to its **aesthetics**. Television soap opera, for instance, has become associated with unmotivated studio–lighting; lots of it, pouring down on the glistening heads of the characters, brightening colours but flattening the scene. Subtly motivated lighting, conversely, is often associated with high–budget drama series, precisely to set such (filmed) shows apart from the 'cheaper' look of studio (video) productions.

Hartley and Montgomery (1985) found the term *motivation* useful to distinguish different kinds of news camerawork. Motivated news filming is where the camera 'defers' to the action and participants, following their movements by panning, re-framing etc. Unmotivated news camerawork, conversely, imposes itself on the scene without reference to what participants are actually doing. Often this is by means of a close-up shot on an apparently insignificant detail, followed by a reframing zoom-out/pan to a wide shot of the main action. Where both motivated and unmotivated news camerawork are co-present in one news item, and applied to opposing parties in an industrial dispute, the argument is that this is a form of visual **bias**, producing an **ideological** preference for those treated 'deferentially'.

JH

Further reading   Hartley and Montgomery (1985); Hartley (1992)

motivation (of the sign)   ★ This term refers to the relationship between the signifier and the signified. ★ The **signifier**, or form of a sign, can be quite independent of its **signified**, or mental concept. The form of the **sign** 'CAT' has no natural connection with our mental concept of the animal. The relationship between the two is determined purely by **convention**. The sign 'CAT' is, therefore, unmotivated or arbitrary. The signifier of a photograph is, on the other hand, highly motivated, for here the form (the appearance) of the sign (the photograph) is largely determined by the nature of the signified. It has to look like a cat. The signifier is not totally determined by the signified, because the photographer can choose the camera angle, distance, focus, and so on. So a photograph is highly motivated, but never totally motivated. In fact, the totally motivated sign is impossible, though the totally unmotivated sign is common.

The form of the signifier then can be determined either by convention (or choice) alone, or by a combination of convention and the nature of the signified; the more highly motivated a sign is, the greater the influence of the signified. Unmotivated signs are called *arbitrary* (though Peirce calls them '**symbols**'); motivated signs are **iconic**.

JF

See **convention, icon, signifier/signified**

multi-accentuality ⋆ A property of signs, consisting in the capacity every sign has to signify more than one meaning, depending on the circumstances of its use. ⋆ The term was coined by Volosinov (1973) as part of an argument which sought to show how the meaning of **signs** is fixed not by the abstract system of language (**langue**), but by the **dialogic** interaction of social relations within which the potential for meaning is fixed.

In principle multi-accentuality is a property of all signs, but in practice most signs are not constantly the object of active struggle. However, the concept remains useful in accounting for such phenomena as **anti-languages** or languages of resistance such as those of slaves in the West Indies in the eighteenth and nineteenth centuries, which are characterized by complete inversions of existing signs and their **values** (thus 'black' is inverted to become the sign for 'good', 'powerful', 'sacred', and so on). Feminism too has demonstrated that apparently inert signs ('he', 'man', 'mankind') are **ideologically** loaded and represent social **power** relations.

JH

See **closure, multi-discursive**

multi-cultural/ism ⋆ The recognition and study of societies as comprising distinct but related cultural traditions and practices; often associated with the different ethnic components of the overall social formation. ★ The recognition of societies as multi-cultural entails two consequences.

First, it entails a rethinking of dominant assumptions about the unity of a culture. 'Britishness' has to be reworked to take account of Welsh, Scottish, Irish, Asian, African, Caribbean, Chinese, Middle Eastern and other settled **ethnic groups**. Such a rework-ing would not take the form of attempts to 'integrate' such groups, since the notion of integration implies that the groups in question are transformed into indistinguishable 'members' of the dominant **culture** without any concomitant adjustments being made to that dominant culture. This is the effect of social policies of incorporation, which multi-cultural analysts have identified as **hegemonic**.

Second, multi-culturalism entails a rethinking of dominant assumptions about the plurality or diversity of a culture. It is not sufficient simply to recognize that there are lots of different types of people and cultural activity, since this neglects the unequal **power** relations between such different groups. Multi-cultural analysis tries to account for different cultural practices in terms of the relations between more or less powerful cultures, rather than as instances of more or less exotic traditions.

JH

See **cultural studies**

multi-discursive ★ A concept we have had to invent while com-piling this book. Concepts are said to be multi-discursive when they can be found with significantly different meanings or conno-tations according to their use within different discourses. ★ The kinds of words that can be described as multi-discursive are those, like **culture**, that depend to a very large extent on their context for their meaning to be clear. However, it remains the case that the word's use in other **discourses** will continue to resonate, as it were, in any one instance. Thus, to use culture in the way the discourse of **cultural studies** does, or as anthropology does, will not silence echoes of the way it is used in the **elitist** discourses of 'high' culture.

This means that multi-discursive concepts differ from those

which hide a lost **metaphor** or archaic usage. For instance, you might say of a band you see on television: 'They're chronic!' It isn't important in this case to know that 'chronic' means 'over time', and that your usage of the word to mean 'seriously deficient in talent' (bad) evolved from the medical use of the term chronic to describe long–term (and hence more serious) illnesses, as in 'chronic bronchitis'. The one usage simply doesn't need the other. With multi–discursive concepts, however, different usages (different discourses) mobilize the same term in different ways concurrently, so that two or more meanings are current at once, and tend to limit, regulate or disrupt each other.

An implication of the notion of multi–discursivity is that meanings are not only context – and user – dependent (not fixed inside words) but that there are active social conflicts going on within the sphere of **signification** in which words come to stand for the relative supremacy of one position over another. Thus particular words may be 'colonized' by a particular **institutionalized** discourse, to the extent that it's hard to use the word at all without 'colluding' with the institution in question. Take the word 'God', and think why the following conversation appears to be a little bit eccentric: 'God is black.' 'No she isn't.'

JH

See **closure, culture, discourse, ideology, multi–accentuality**

mystification ⋆ A term from Marxism that describes the process whereby ideological practices are made to appear natural (that is, with no alternative), when in fact they are culture-specific and therefore arbitrary. ⋆ An important aim of Marxist analysis of **texts** is to demystify them, that is, to expose their arbitrariness and **cultural** specificity and in so doing to posit the (potential) existence of alternatives.

Thus an analysis of a women's magazine which reveals the devices by which it attempts to win women's unwitting consent to their social construction as (i) consumers, for the benefit of advertisers; (ii) nurturers, for the benefit of children and husbands; and (iii) glamour/sex objects, for the benefit of men can be said to 'demystify' the **ideological** practice (or **hegemony**) which makes this social construction of women appear not only natural but also fulfilling, and in women's own interests. The mystification consists (i) of the implication that other definitions of womanhood do not exist (or if they do, they are unnatural), and (ii) of disguising the fact that this construction of women is one that furthers the interests of others (advertisers, men, husbands and children) by consistently misrepresenting it as being in the interests of women themselves. As the media never work independently of other **social institutions**, this mystification is also performed by the social practices enshrined in the family, industry, education and the wider social order.

JF

See **culture, hegemony, ideology**

myth ⋆ A widely and variously used term referring to a culture's way of understanding, expressing and communicating to itself concepts that are important to its self-identity as a culture. ⋆ There are three main uses of the term – the ritual/anthropological, the literary and the semiotic.

The **ritual**/anthropological takes the form of an anonymously composed **narrative** that offers explanations of why the world is as it appears to be, and why people act as they do. It is specific to its own **culture**, though it presents its explanations as universal, or natural. It is a crucial means of turning nature into culture, and thus works also reciprocally as a **naturalizing** agency.

In literary theory, myth becomes a story about, or **image** of, what are seen as eternal, permanent human truths, usually of a spiritual, moral or **aesthetic** kind. It is closely associated with the notion of **archetypal** symbols, that is **symbols** with a transcultural, if not universal, meaning, and belongs to a school that frequently asserts similarities between the social functions of religion and literature. Use of the term is usually the sign of an idealistic, vague and ultimately unsound approach to literature.

The **semiotic** meaning differs markedly from these two. It refers to an unarticulated chain of associated concepts by which members of a culture understand certain topics. It operates non-consciously and **intersubjectively**. It is associative, not narrative; it is culture-specific, not transcultural or universal; it changes over time, rather than being eternal; and it is unarticulated rather than being textually expressed. Its prime function is to make the cultural natural, and it thus shares with other usages the function of naturalization. The semiotic usage, as proposed by Barthes, is discussed more fully under **signification**.

JF

See **culture, intersubjectivity, naturalizing**
Further reading   Fiske (1982)

narcotization ⋆ An American term used to describe a negative effect or 'dysfunction' of the mass media in which **mass communications** are seen as inducing apathy and political inertia among the mass audience. ⋆ Taking its meaning from a 'narcotic' or drug-like **effect**, the term has been used to point to the paradoxical relationship between, on the one hand, *increased* media exposure to information concerning central social and political problems (for example, poverty), and on the other, *decreased* organized social action and involvement to solve those problems. Hence the central suggestion is that the media induce a 'stupor' or lack of activity in the **audience**, people become minimally informed and concerned at the expense of actual involvement. As Lazarsfeld and Merton (1948) have suggested: 'increasing dosages of mass communications may be inadvertently transforming the energies of men from active participation into passive knowledge'.

TO

See **effects, functionalism, hypodermic needle model**
Further reading Schramm and Roberts (eds) (1971)

narrative ⋆ The devices, strategies and conventions governing the organization of a story (fictional or factual) into sequence: 'and then'. ⋆ Narrative can be subdivided – especially into *plot* (A meets B; something happens; order returns) and *narration* ('Once upon a time there was a beautiful princess', or 'Yesterday the President said'). Plot is the irreducible substance of a story while narration is the way that substance is related. It follows that devices such as direct or indirect speech, or using the first person as opposed to third person ('I' as opposed to 's/he') are properties of narrative rather than plot. They can in fact be analysed formally in any story, no matter what its plot is. Narrative analysis has become increasingly common, and more and more sophisticated, in **structuralist** and literary criticism (see Barthes 1977; Propp 1968).

Narrative is a feature of non-fictional stories like broadcast news, where professional **codes** determine certain structures, orders and components of any story (see Hartley 1982). Paradoxically, narrative is implicit in many still **images**, especially those of advertising, where a 'before' and 'after' the actual moment of the photograph is implied within its elements, and we need to recognize this implied passage of time to make sense of the image at all. Similarly, many news photographs rely on an event having just happened or being about to happen, and it is the sense of narrative that makes the photograph newsworthy.

Recently, attention has been focused on the ways we make sense of ourselves and our daily lives by means of narrative strategies: there are structures and well-established forms in which we can render ourselves and our lives *as* narratives (stories). Both **discourse** analysts and cultural historians are active in this interesting new area of study, which indicates that narrative is a pervasive cultural practice.

JH

See **diegesis**
Further reading Donald and Mercer (1982); Woollacott (1982)

narrowcasting ⋆ The sending of messages to distant but defined receivers, for example, by CCTV (Closed Circuit Television) or CB (Citizens' Band) radio. ⋆ (Contrast with **broadcasting**.) By extension it means the sending of **messages** to an **audience**

195

restricted by interest or demand, for example, rather than by technical capability. Minority programmes use narrowcast **codes** to appeal to a defined and limited audience.

JF

See **broadcasting, elaborated code**

nation   ⋆ An 'imagined community' which is understood as distinct and separate from all other nations. 'Nation' is a relational term; like any **sign**, one nation consists in being what the others are not. The concept belongs in fact to the realm of **signification**, not to any external, referential world. Nations have no essential or intrinsic properties; each is a discursive construct whose identity consists in its difference from others. ⋆

'Nation' is often used to mean *nation state* – a sovereign state with its own government, boundaries, defence forces, etc., and symbolic markers of nationhood such as a flag, an anthem, local currency, a head of state, membership of the United Nations and so on. But there are many nations that are not also nation states. Some states encompass more than one nation (e.g., Wales, Scotland and Northern Ireland in the UK). Then there are nations which exceed national frontiers (e.g., until recently the two Germanies) or those incorporated in several other states (e.g., Kurdistan). And there are some nations without any territory at all (Palestine, for instance).

If territory doesn't define a nation, then neither does **race** or **ethnicity**, and neither does **language** or **culture** – most modern nations are multi-racial, multi-lingual and **multi-cultural** to some degree, if not always in official policy. So the dictionary or **common sense** definition of a nation as being a large number of people of common **ethnic** descent, language and history, inhabiting a territory bounded by defined limits, is seriously at odds with the facts.

'Nation', however, refers not to the external world of 'facts' but to a symbolic **referent** – an 'imagined community' (Anderson 1983), which is maintained by a wide variety of **discursive** institutions, ranging from national literatures and languages to national curricula in education. There are of course national inflections in all areas of economic, political, cultural and discursive life; but certain **institutions** play a more prominent and routine role in creating and sustaining an evolving referent for the concept and its subjects. Among the more important of these are the media.

Participation in the nation is 'imagined' because no one can know more than an infinitesimal number of the other citizens of their nation, but it is a 'community' because everyone has complete confidence in the simultaneous co-existence of all the others. This sense of community is built and sustained by the quotidian rhythms of print and electronic media output, along with periodic national ceremonies which are themselves communicated through the media.

With increased migration and mobility, these **symbolic** markers of a nation can be the only common 'heritage' it has. Certainly, such markers are ever more prevalent in the media, a common motif in advertisements, continuity and the like to propose a euphoric unity among groups which otherwise display few common traits. Here, the nation has been appropriated as a 'user-friendly' metaphor through which *multi-national* firms mobilize not citizens but consumers.

JH

Further reading Anderson (1983); Schlesinger (1991); Hartley (1992)

naturalism ★ A term which is often used as a synonym for **realism**. It first became influential in the theatre, where it referred to those plays (especially Ibsen's) which tried to do away with **signs** and replace them with the objects that such signs had stood for. ★ Thus, a play set in a living-room would be staged with a living-room on the stage – aspidistras, chintz curtains and all. Speeches would be written not as staged speeches, but as if they were 'actually happening'. Actors would not represent their characters, but become them (this became codified as 'method' acting). Of course, everyone on stage has to pretend the audience isn't there, since audiences aren't generally to be found in people's living-rooms. So this kind of theatre is voyeuristic from the point of view of the audience, a point of view known as the 'fourth wall', since that is the perspective the audience uses to view the play.

Clearly naturalism was a gift for cinema, and even more for the domesticated medium of television, where the camera and crew replace the audience in the setting, so you don't even have a sense of 'being in the theatre' to put alongside 'being in that person's living-room'. The **ideological** productivity of the naturalist conventions is considerable, because the 'reality' of the objects and interaction represented allows the representation itself to appear as innocent, self-effacing. Our attention is devoted to looking 'through' the screen and into the setting, so that any sense we might make of the drama appears to arise directly from the scene depicted, and not from its **representation**. It comes across more imperatively than something clearly constructed or 'handled' according to recognized **conventions** might do. And that, of course, is the point. Television exploits naturalism on the set to promote the **naturalization** of images/representations on the screen.

JH

naturalizing ⋆ The process of representing the cultural and historical as natural. ⋆ Naturalizing is a **distinctive feature** of ideological **discourses**. The **ideological** productivity of naturalization is that circumstances and meanings that are socially, historically, economically and culturally **determined** (and hence open to change) are 'experienced' as natural – that is, inevitable, timeless, universal, genetic (and hence unarguable).

Naturalization is the prize in modern cultural and **signifying** struggles; class or male supremacy, for example, is expressed as natural, and conversely resistance to that supremacy is represented as unnatural. So socialist and feminist discourses have to contend both with the naturalized discourses that continuously encourage us to understand social relations in ways that reproduce **class** and **gender** inequalities, and with the difficulty of establishing *as* natural (or as not unnatural) their alternative discourses and representations. Naturalizing, then, is a major force in the maintenance of **hegemony**.

JH

See **closure, consensus, hegemony**

nature ⋆ The material world as a whole together with its determining forces; the inherent or essential qualities of an object which determine its form, substance and behaviour. ⋆ Because it is a **multi-discursive** concept which defies attempts to give it a precise **referent**, the term should be used with care in analytical work. At the very least the nature of an object, or the material world of nature, or the word nature itself, should not be taken as self-evident with respect to any qualities, properties or characteristics whatever: these natures are the object of study, not the premisses.

Nature is often contrasted with **culture**; the non-human as opposed to the human. However, this non-human nature is often taken to be an inherent or essential quality of the human itself – as in human nature. In such usages the concept appears ultimately to be a secularization of the category of God – a non-human agency which is beyond our control but which determines our characteristics and behaviour. In this sense, nature is an **ideological** category.

The other main way in which nature is used in analytical **discourses** is as the material properties of an object. Hence the nature of something is contrasted with whatever conceptions of it might be available (the nature of the planet earth is contrasted with conceptions of it as flat). Hence nature in this sense is the proper object of study for science: the attempt to reveal or discover by analysis the 'true' nature (**determining** properties) of an object of study.

JH

negotiation ⋆ A term used in **semiotic** theories of reading or meaning. When a **text** is read, the reader interacts or negotiates with it; this negotiation involves the readers bringing their own cultural experience, their own socially located **meaning systems**, to bear upon the text. ⋆ The meaning of the text that this reading yields is the result of the 'negotiation' between the text and the socially constructed reader – it is therefore potentially unique.

The term *negotiation*, then, implies that the text does not 'have' a meaning, but rather delimits a range of potential meanings: which meaning is realized in a particular reading is determined as much by the reader as by the text. The reader is the point through which socially located meaning systems negotiate with textually located **preferred readings**.

Eco (1981) uses the term *closed* to refer to texts which try, through the way they are structured, to impose their influence upon the negotiation: *open* texts allow the reader a greater and more creative **role** in the negotiation of meaning.

JF

See **closure, meaning systems, preferred reading, text**

new world information order ⋆ A term which has gained currency since the late 1970s and refers to the goal of a series of radical reforms in worldwide cultural relations, demanded in particular by developing nations. ⋆ These reforms seek to counter the dominance of the **global**, **cultural** economy by America and other western nations and their corporations, and to achieve a more democratic global communication system, based on the exchange and 'free flow' of information and other cultural products. These calls for a 'new' world information order have therefore to be understood in the context of the existing, or 'old' historic order, to which they are a response and challenge.

Since the nineteenth century, **power** and control over the international distribution of media technologies and cultural imagery have become highly concentrated in the 'advanced' or 'First World' states, their cultures dominating those of developing nations. These nations, as a result, have become highly dependent upon imported cultural technologies and upon the western news, films and forms of television **entertainment** that they are used to transmit. In many instances it has been argued that these cultural forms act as vehicles for the global dissemination of consumerism and other western values which systematically deny developing nations' control over their own cultural priorities and perspectives as well as **access** to the international arena on their own terms. This series of processes has often been referred to as **cultural imperialism**.

The moves towards a new world information order have been articulated especially by means of a series of UNESCO (United Nations Educational, Scientific and Cultural Organization) conferences held in the early 1980s. These proposed a programme of reforms to break with the inequalities of existing arrangements. In brief the proposals aimed to provide developing states with the material means to preserve and promote their own cultural traditions, industries and identities and the freedom to develop what Mattelart (1984) has referred to as 'alternative audiovisual space'. The aims are to reverse the imbalance in the international flow of information and entertainment, and to narrow the gulf between the information–rich and information–poor societies. The proposals also started to take account of new media technologies, especially developments in satellite **broadcasting**, aiming to guarantee international rights to communication, not solely dependent upon capital and advanced production technologies. Clearly many of these proposals were rejected by the media industries of the developed world, but this has not prevented the concept of the new world information order from gaining considerable international support. The issues it serves to raise are central to an understanding of the politics of international communications and culture.

TO

See **cultural imperialism, nation**
Further reading Smith (1980); UNESCO (1980); Tomlinson (1991); Downing *et al.* (1990); Martin and Heibert (1990)

news values ★ The professional codes used in the selection, construction and presentation of news stories in corporately produced mainstream press and broadcasting. ★ News values are not attributes of individual journalists (as style might be – though even this is usually regulated by a standard 'house style'). News values are a result of the productive needs of industrialized news corporations. People who work for such corporations will display mixed ambitions, allegiances, politics and abilities as **individuals**. Within the corporation they are subjected to an extensive division of labour. Beyond the corporation there are its competitors, and the **occupational ideology** of the journalist and broadcasting **professions**. Within these **contexts** news values operate to produce a standard product out of the contributions of all such people, practices and beliefs.

Nevertheless, news values are an *informal* **code**. This is because they are not justified by reference to the needs of the corporation at all. On the contrary, when they are discussed within the profession (rarely), they are justified by reference (i) to the supposed nature of newsworthy events; and (ii) to the supposed needs/demands of the consumers of news. Of course, neither reporters nor news corporations are supposed to control either events or consumers' demands, so they cannot admit to the operation of a formal, explicit code of news values. Within the trade, then, news values are construed essentially as a *response* to the readership or to the story itself, and many journalists are content to locate the source of this response in their own bodies – reporters are said to have a 'good nose' or a 'gut feeling' for a 'good' story.

Numerous attempts have been made over the years to pin down news values more specifically. But it is hard to collate these into a hard and fast list of **values**, because different studies have approached the whole idea from different standpoints, using different assumptions and terminology. However, the following categories may be helpful – but remember that news values are about news *stories* and not events themselves.

(1) News values prioritize stories about events that are recent, sudden, unambiguous, predictable, relevant and close (to the 'home' **culture/class**/region).

(2) Such events happen all the time without becoming newsworthy. Priority is given to stories about the economy,

governmental politics, industry, foreign affairs of state, domestic affairs – either of conflict or human interest, disasters or sport.

(3) Within such stories, priority is given to personalization, conflict, violence, reference to **elite** nations (USA, USSR, UK, Europe, Japan), reference to elite people, negativity (bad news).

(4) Less agreeable news values can often be shown to be in play, including *metropolitanism* (the world stops beyond London), **racism**, **patriarchy** (news by, for and about men), **naturalization** (representing the cultural/historical as natural), **consensus** (everyone shares the **worldview** of the sub–editor and middle management).

(5) News stories have to appeal to the supposed interests of the readers/viewers, so they must be **commonsensical**, entertaining, dramatic, like fiction (good stories), glamorous, visual, about showbiz, about television.

(6) Stories must be compatible with **institutional** routines, so events must be diary events (party conferences, anniversaries, annual reports, and so on), or already covered in another news outlet, in press releases or in agency reports.

JH

See **code, frame, occupational ideology, profession**
Further reading Cohen and Young (eds) (1981); Chibnall (1977); Hartley (1982); Hall *et al.* (1978)

noise ⋆ A concept from **communication theory** and **information theory**: any interference added to the **signal** between encoder and decoder that makes accurate decoding more difficult; a major source of error. ⋆ There are two main types:

(1) *Mechanical noise* This is noise on the **channel**, for example, static on radio, snow on television, distortion on British Rail station announcements, a stutter or speech impediment.

(2) *Semantic noise* This is interference with the message brought about by dissonance of meaning; this is usually

caused by social or cultural differences between **encoder** and **decoder**. Jargon can be **semantic** noise (it can mean 'Aren't I clever', or 'Isn't my subject difficult?' or 'Aren't I different from you, the layperson?') and this can prevent the intended **message** being accurately decoded. A pompous tone of voice can also be noise.

Noise is combated by **redundancy** and **feedback**, and is one of the factors that limits the capacity of a **channel** to convey **information**.

JF

See **channel, communication theory, feedback, information theory, redundancy, signal**
Further reading Shannon and Weaver (1949); Merril and Lowenstein (1979); Sereno and Mortensen (1970)

non–verbal communication ∗ Communication between people by means other than speech. ∗ Non–verbal communication (NVC) derives from the following major sources:

(1)   eye contact (amount of looking at another person's body and face)
(2)   mouth (especially smiling or grimacing in relation to eye contact)
(3)   posture (for example, sitting forwards or backwards)
(4)   gesture (as with the use of arm movements when talking)
(5)   orientation (of the body to the addressee)
(6)   body distance (as when we stand too close or too far away from others)
(7)   smell (including perfumes)
(8)   skin (including pigmentation, blushing and texture)
(9)   hair (including length, texture and style)
(10) clothes (with particular reference to fashion)

Non–verbal communication is not quite the same as 'body language' because any claim about a **language** must refer to an agreed and identifiable grammar and syntax. NVC is not always so precise or advanced; the vocabulary of non-verbal **signs** is more limited than speech. Even so, it is a mistake to consider NVC as isolated from speech. Instead, some complex interaction is envisaged between word and body **signal**, and one that is not always complementary. Imagine yourself interviewing job applicants. You might not offer employment to a candidate who refuses to look at you, always frowns, hunches both shoulders, sweats a lot, and has a Mohican hair cut – despite the fact that he or she gives thoughtful and interesting replies to your questions. As Argyle (1978) emphasizes, body language or NVC can be an intricate process.

Take eye contact as an example for discussion. Mutual eye contact (where both people look into each other's eyes) can be a sign of liking, but prolonged *gaze* leads to discomfort. Goffman (1969), for example, describes the sustained 'hate stare' as exhibited by bigoted white Americans to blacks. The directed eye contact violates a **code** of looking, where eye contact is frequently broken but returned to, and leads to depersonalization of the victim because an aggressor deliberately breaks the **rules** which the victim adheres to. Eye contact is often enhanced by size of pupils, eyebrow inflection and movement, and smiling. Dilated pupils, intense looking (directed gaze), smiling, and the 'rapid eyebrow flash' are usually associated with sexual attraction.

There are many **cultural** determinants and variations in NVC. Mehrabian (1972), for example, found that patterns of *gesture* differed for Jewish and Italian **groups** within the USA. Similar differences have been observed for body distance, often described as *personal space* (see **proxemics**) and implying the distance preferred by each individual when interacting with others.

No simple predictions about non-verbal behaviour can be made. So much depends on the types of relationships and communication between people. Intimacy and content of conversation must be considered in relation to situations we find ourselves within. It seems that we often seek some kind of balance in communication when speaking with our bodies. The major consideration is that of reciprocation, meaning the answering of another's body questions. Subtle negotiation between participants is envisaged over time. This involves the constant monitoring of, and adjustment to, others' actions: in this way reciprocation is guaranteed. If somebody that we have just met stands too close to us then we tend to back away from them. The other person may then realize that they have offended us and show embarrassment or apology through less eye contact and more blushing. Our reactions to their embarrassment may be similar embarrassment, and so on. Of course all of this will affect verbal communication; it will probably be an altogether disastrous encounter.

DS

See **code, dyad, encounter, facework, interpersonal communication, paralanguage, proxemics**
Further reading Argyle (1978); Mortensen (ed.) (1979); Corner and Hawthorn (eds) (1989); Burton and Dimbleby (1988)

norm/normative ★ Those sets of social rules, standards, and expectations that both generate and regulate social interaction and communication. ★ Norms are identified above all by their morally constraining and binding nature, and are perhaps best viewed as the 'dos and don'ts' of any social situation. They refer to the ways in which we tend to **orientate** ourselves in interaction by reference to what we feel is appropriate, acceptable or generally expected. In this sense norms have been seen not only as negotiated features of interaction, but emphasis has been placed on the ways in which they regulate **individuals** in interaction. This latter emphasis itself stems from a view of society as a constraining external 'normative order' into which individuals are **socialized**.

The concept should therefore be seen as raising a number of related problems and related debates. The extent to which norms may be said to be *universal* or all-embracing within any social **group** or society, forms a useful point of entry into these debates. Think through any two different social situations – for example, interacting with friends at a party, and interacting with strangers on a train. What norms might be common to both scenarios, and which ones might be *specific* to one or the other; do any apparently conflict or contradict? These questions highlight the difficulty of isolating norms from the active **contexts** of interaction, because seemingly diverse and often contradictory norms characterize the social groups, **role** relations and contexts within which we continually interact and participate. A second but related issue concerns the degree to which *all* communication and interaction is structured and determined by norms. One view, for example, would stress the idea that all social conduct is indeed directed towards conforming with the norms and expectations of others. Such a view would maintain that **conformity** and social order are maintained and reinforced by a variety of social controls and penalties, often referred to as *sanctions*. Indeed it is very often through the operation of sanctions that we become aware of norms which commonly do tend to be invisible or taken for granted until broken or transgressed (for example, behaving at a friend's party as if everyone was a stranger on a train). Responses to breaking or ignoring norms range from mild disapproval to outrage, ridicule and a whole battery of formal and informal punishments. However, two major problems confront this view. First, the tendency to suggest that all social activity is governed by norms has been challenged by attending to the creative, relatively unstructured aspects of interaction (see, for example, **symbolic interactionism**), and the ways in which individuals not only conform to but also constantly negotiate and break norms. The second issue at stake here concerns the definition and reinforcement of norms. Do they represent and support particular dominant or powerful groups' interests, activities and values as opposed to others, or do norms represent an underlying social **consensus**, whereby 'society' regulates and reproduces itself?

TO

See **code, conformity, consensus, deviance, institutions, power, rules**

Further reading Bilton *et al.* (1981); Worsley (ed.) (1977); Cuff and Payne (eds) (1979); Browne (1992)

object ★ For Peirce it means that to which the sign refers, its 'designatum'. ★ The difference between Peirce's *object* and Saussure's **signified** is often misunderstood. The object, which may be a thing, event or concept, exists outside the signifying system of which the sign is a unit – it has an independent existence. The **signified** is a mental concept associated with the **signifier** to form a **sign**, and has no existence independent of the sign system of which it is a part.

JF

See **interpretant, referent, sign, signified**

objectivity ★ A scientific approach that is supposedly characterized by statements lacking in bias. ★ Objectivity is a major theme in the natural sciences. The problem for communication studies arises with the emulation of those sciences by theorists interested in the analysis of human behaviour. Assumptions about an external reality which is 'out there' and waiting to be 'discovered' are weakened when we consider intricate links between **language** and **ideology** and the infinite number of **perceptions** about one event.

Attempts at objectivity do, however, have definite advantages. Public access to evidence is encouraged. By looking for consistency of observation and for agreement between investigators much evidence which at first glance appears objective is then exposed as inaccurate and inconclusive. The laboratory **experiment** is perhaps most popular in this respect. Unfortunately, however, much social representation is taken for granted as being fair, real and objective.

Take the example of the Top 40 singles charts. At first glance they appear objective in that they supposedly reflect the best-selling releases for any one week. But it is impossible to monitor all sales. Consequently a sample of music outlets is used. If that list of shops is then leaked to record companies – as happened in the UK during the 1970s – there is the very real possibility of a music company boosting the sales of one release in those sampled shops. Because that release then achieves an inflated position within the charts it may receive more air-play on radio. Any faith in the 'truthfulness' of the Top 40 charts must now be questioned.

Objectivity and **bias** are also terms that frequently occur in discussions of news and **news values**.

DS

See **empiricism, experiment, methodology, perception, positivism, subjectivity**

occupational ideology ⋆ The strategies characteristic of a **profession** or other more or less coherent job category, whereby the practitioners maintain control over access to their mental production, entry into the profession or job, and cohesion within their own ranks as to what their methods, objectives and rewards should be. ⋆

Occupational ideologies are informal **codes**, though they may be backed by **institutional** bodies with quite extensive powers (for example, the British Medical Association). Once initiated, a practitioner of the occupation will be expected to conform to this code in a spontaneous and routine way – it is not so much a **rule** book as a **role** model. Occupational ideologies are characterized by esoteric, specialist or jargon language, which is in fact a **discourse** that both marks and regulates the job. This book may be seen as an unusually frank effort to specify the occupational discourse of communication and cultural studies, though it is clear from this example that simply learning the code does not by itself entail endorsement of the occupation.

Occupational ideologies are also **represented** in non-verbal forms. An interesting instance of this is what Barthes has called 'vestimentary' codes – codes of dress. The professor's gown, lawyer's wig, doctor's stethoscope, scientist's white lab-coat and engineer's boiler suit are markers and exclusion devices as much as they are functional apparel. The same might be said for the business suit and other kinds of clothes that tend to be accepted in certain occupational roles that don't have an official garb.

Clearly occupational ideologies will also include the historically amassed knowledges, **myths** and anecdotes which serve the internal solidarity, working practices and general social/political interests of the **group** in question. Thus they may be understood as both everyday routine actions and the social product of those actions. But one social product may be to **popularize** the ideology: an occupational group may be more successful than others in **naturalizing** its specialist discourse, so that quite esoteric terms of today can be represented and circulated as **common sense** tomorrow.

JH

See **ideology, institutions, profession**

opinion leaders ⋆ Those people who play an influential intermediate role in the transmission of media messages to social groups. The term originates in American studies of the media and voting behaviour (Lazarsfeld *et al*. 1944). ⋆ Opinion leaders usually pay more attention to mass media output than do their peers, and they relay relevant information to persons not directly exposed to media messages. In so doing these leaders actively select and interpret media material, acting as important 'conductors' between media and community; they 'translate' media reality into the experience of local **groups**. The development of the term further marked the decline of the **hypodermic needle model** of media **effects** and its substitution with a **two-step**

flow model that attempted to relate mass media influence to the dynamics and structures of existing social relationships.

TO

See **effects, group, hypodermic needle model, two–step flow model**
Further reading Lazarsfeld *et al.* (1944); Katz and Lazarsfeld (1955); McQuail and Windahl (1981)

orality ⋆ That which characterizes speech; a culture characterized by the primacy of speech over other forms of signification. ⋆ Usually opposed to **literacy**, orality refers to those aspects of a culture's way of life that are attributable to its investment in the resources of spoken **language**. These may include formal ways of organizing thought (**myth**) or knowledge (magic); or they may be associated with **rhetorical** and other systems for fixing and transmitting sense.

The idea that oral cultures are fundamentally different from literate ones at the level of social and individual consciousness is associated with Marshall McLuhan, and may be followed up in Ong (1982). The analysis of oral systems of thought has occupied social anthropologists for years, and is perhaps best approached via the work of Lévi-Strauss (see Leach 1976 and Sturrock 1979), whose structural method revolutionized western thinking about 'primitive' myths, analysing them as a form of reasoning appropriate to oral societies.

Despite its official promotion and pervasive presence in industrial societies, literacy nevertheless has to coexist with an abiding orality in certain crucial cultural spheres – perhaps the most obvious of which is the early **socialization** of infants.

JH

See **literacy**

211

orientalism ⋆ The historical construction of eastern cultures and people as 'foreign', often alien or exotic objects of western scrutiny or contemplation. ⋆ The concept is associated with the influential work of Edward Said, who has identified orientalism as a key feature of western attitudes and writing about the orient from the eighteenth century onwards. Orientalism is best understood as a **discourse** which both assumes and promotes a sense of fundamental **difference** between a western or occidental 'us' and an oriental 'them' – the cultures and people of eastern, Asiatic origins and traditions. Grounded in particular ideological assumptions held by western writers, scholars, civil servants and politicians, the discourse of orientalism has been embodied historically in the complex social and political practices which western societies have employed to dominate and gain authority over eastern, oriental cultures.

Orientalism should not be understood as crude **racism** or jingoism although these may draw upon related values or assumptions. In Said's terms, it refers to those forms of communicative practice, such as serious travel writing or journalism, academic or political accounts, which seek to present **objective** analysis of eastern phenomena to western audiences. A characteristic of these accounts is their tendency to dehumanize the oriental, presenting a fixed, unchanging **other**, lacking **subjectivity** or internal variation and condensed in binary opposition to western consciousness and culture. In these and other forms, Said argues that the discourse of orientalism ultimately reveals less about the characteristics of the eastern countries to which it refers than about the **consciousness** and **culture** of western **groups** which have looked at them, studied them and sought to exercise rule over them. As a historical set of ideas for making sense of the 'unfamiliar' – the orient – they reveal much about the preoccupations and structures of 'our world' – western European culture. Orientalism has emerged as a significant theme in recent discussions of reporting the Middle East, including the Gulf War and Islam and in the analysis of contemporary travel and tourism writing.

TO

Further reading   Said (1978); Mills (1991)

orientation ⋆ A property of signs within an utterance or other signifying performance or text; the way they are organized to express the relationship between the addresser and the addressee. ⋆

Semiotics has shown that no **sign** 'has' a fixed or intrinsic meaning which it conveys, but rather that signs gain their capacity for **signification** from the systematic structure of the sign system of which each is recognized as a differentiated element. Hence the abstract system (**langue**) generates the concrete utterance (**parole**). However, every utterance is *internally organized* not only according to the rules of the langue, but also as a manifestation of a social relationship between speaker and hearer – the signs are oriented towards these parties' relative stance towards each other.

At the level of **dyadic** speech, this phenomenon is simple and uncontroversial – what you say and how you say it depends on your relationship towards the person you're addressing. S/he may be more or less powerful than you, or more or less well known to you, for example. But the property of orientation is characteristic of all utterances, including those of written, printed or broadcast form in which the **addresser** doesn't know who the **addressee** is, and vice versa. Here the implications of the concept become clear. Orientation is a property of the utterance itself, and not of the intentions or experience of the actual parties to it 'outside' it. Hence verbal performances and **texts** can be analysed to disclose their orientation – they manifest signs of the implied or **preferred reader**/hearer, and of the position from which the utterance is addressed. It follows that in this context the addresser and addressee are not persons, but are themselves textual phenomena.

JH

See **dialogic, preferred reading**

other: significant and generalized other ⋆ Symbolic entity located outside of the self and associated with one or more other individuals. ⋆ Proposed by Mead (1934), the concept of other is particularly relevant to **symbolic interactionist** perspectives, where the emphasis is placed on communication between the self and others (and assimilation of others within the self). Such communication will not always take place within face-to-face encounters. Others can be real people or fictional characters.

Perhaps the starting-point for perceived others is when the child differentiates self from not-self. That vast category of not-self will then be gradually subdivided according to **learned** differences between others. Eventually the other will refer to participants engaging, or with the ability to engage in, symbolic interaction. Furthermore, some others appear to behave in consistent ways and to show specific expectations about the self's behaviour.

Many theorists have shown particular interest in emerging relations between the self and the significant other within childhood. The rewarding and punishing actions of adult figures affect **socialization**, **language** development, and **motivation**. In **psychoanalysis**, for example, the focus is upon whether significant others frustrate or satisfy the infant. In the first instance they may be judged good or bad, but this might then set a path for subsequent assessment of other people and of the self. Indeed the significant other, through criticism of the self, provides the basis for appraisal, reflection and conscience. Increased experience of language and symbolic activity involving others leads to the realization about the significant other being representative of some larger **group**. It is thus argued that there may be a progression from the recognition of significant others to the constellation of generalized others.

Although the concept of other has proved invaluable when discussing socialization and the experiences of **interaction**, it can also be criticized on a number of counts. At the most extreme level it becomes part of a social **behaviourist** argument where others totally shape, control and condition the self via reward and punishment. At a more mundane level, little evidence has suggested at which point in life the significant is augmented by the generalized. The interrelationships between significant and gener-

214

alized others continue throughout life, although they are rarely identified.

DS

See **primary group, symbolic interactionism**
Further reading Schellenberg (1978); Cuff and Payne (eds) (1979); Laing (1969)

P

paradigm ⋆ A set of units from which one may be chosen to combine with units from other paradigms to form a **syntagm** (that is, a combination of units into a signifying whole). ⋆ The paradigmatic dimension of language is that of choice, the syntagmatic that of combination. Saussurian linguistics argues that all **languages** and **codes** are built upon these two dimensions. The alphabet is a paradigm, and letters chosen from it may be combined to form written words (syntagms). A man's wardrobe holds a number of paradigms for instance – one each for shirts, ties, socks – which are combined into a syntagm (his dress for the day). A road sign is a syntagm formed from units from two paradigms (the shape of the sign, and the symbol in the middle).

A paradigm, then, is a set of units which have an overall generic similarity: within the set each unit must be significantly distinguished from the others: the meaning of the unit chosen is defined by its relationship to the others in the paradigm that were not. In the lay paradigm of 'farm animals', the unit *cow* stands for a farm animal distinguished from *horse*, *pig* and *sheep*, but in the farmer's paradigm it means something different because it is distinguished from *heifer*, *steer* and *bullock*.

Paradigms are generally shared among members of a **culture**: they come within the area of **langue**. Syntagms can be unique combinations created for the occasion. They are examples of **parole**.

JF

See **choice, commutation test, metaphor, syntagm**
Further reading Fiske (1982)

paralanguage ⋆ Communication based on vocal but non-verbal utterances. ⋆ The most commonly identified types of paralanguage can be listed:

(1) pitch (low–high key intonation, as with bass–soprano)
(2) rate (frequency and regularity of sound, as with a slow, hesitant delivery compared with a manic, speedy speech)
(3) timbre (tone and quality of sound, as with gravel–sonerous voice ranges)
(4) volume (intensity of sound, from a whisper to a scream or shout)

It is useful to consider interface between linguistic and paralinguistic processes in terms of relations between *what* is said when compared with *how* it is said.

DS

See **language, non-verbal communication**
Further reading Myers and Myers (1976)

parole ⋆ In Saussurian linguistics, the activity of speaking. ⋆ The term was used by Saussure to separate out those variable and accidental aspects of speech that were to be excluded from the focus of linguistic enquiry. As such, parole needs to be understood in relation to its contrasting term, **langue**. Parole amounts to individual instances of speaking; langue to the abstract system that underlies it. Although what people actually do when speaking may be of interest to the physiologist or the behavioural psychologist, it cannot form the basis of linguistic study, because – for Saussure – it was subject to too much random fluctuation. Instead, linguistics should focus on the underlying sets of rules and conventions that make parole possible and guarantee its intelligibility.

There is none the less a close and complementary relationship between langue and parole. Parole may be seen as a continual implementation of the underlying system constituted in the langue; but conversely the continual practice of speaking affirms and adjusts the langue, moulding it gradually into a different form. No one individual can control or shape the langue; but generations of speakers can and do alter it from one historically specific state to another.

Like many of the terms originally developed in Saussure's lectures between 1906 and 1911, langue and parole achieved new currency during the 1960s and 1970s with the emergence of semiology as the study of sign systems. In this study a particular film or fashion garment could be seen as an individual instance of parole against the backdrop of the underlying system of film language or fashion codes. One difficulty with this application of the term is that it was much more difficult to think of ways in which film as a system of **signification** was available for study except through its parole whereas language was more generally available through introspection because of its mental basis.

MM

See **code, competence, langue, performance**
Further reading Saussure (1974); Culler (1976); Montgomery (1986)

participant observation ∗ A technique or process designed to collect information within a non-laboratory context that is at least partially determined by the observer's presence. ∗ Participant observation is therefore a **methodology** for social research. Its great advantage is that it allows for observation of **groups** with the self as a member of the group. Its main disadvantages are that the participant may impose his or her **values** on the observation process, and that if the *participant observer* fails to declare his or her true identity, the ethical problem of deliberate deception arises. One classic example is the virtual infiltration of a spiritual group that had predicted the end of the world on 21 December 1954 and the recording of the devotees' conversations when that date had safely passed (Festinger 1957). In order to collect such information the researchers had to pose as converted group members who sincerely believed in their leader's premonition.

By contrast, *field observation* ensures contact with the group but without necessary acceptance of group membership. Many examples of field observation are found in the discipline of social anthropology, where a close community will be described by an outsider who is none the less tolerated. Participant observation has also found some favour in recent **cultural studies** (see Willis 1978). Accusations concerning **objectivity** (namely that participant observation is invalid because the author observes only those things that s/he wants to observe), are frequent whenever transcribed interactions are provided by field or participant observers. This is especially the case when such observation is contrasted with the more controlled and **empirical** context of **experiment**.

DS

See **ethnography, methodology, objectivity**
Further reading Festinger (1957); Willis (1978); Shimanoff (1980); Aronson (1988).

patriarchy ∗ The structural, systematic and historical domination and exploitation of women by men. ∗ In its original usage, this term referred rather narrowly to specific types of tribe, **group**, family or household that were characterized by a dominant male ruler, the patriarch, who assumed decisive powers of control over the group and its social relations. In the case of family and household groups, the patriarch combined the **power** of the father with that of dominant male member. The concept is now more widely and generally used to refer to the total social organization of **gender** relations, **institutions** and social processes which produce and reproduce women as socially, politically and sexually subordinate to men.

Several key issues are worth stressing here. The first concerns the importance of recognizing patriarchy as a *system*. In other words, our own **individual** and **subjective** senses of **gender** identity, of being a woman or being a man – and what this might mean – are ultimately derived within historical structures of a system which gives power to men over women. As many feminist writers have argued, patriarchy is not simply a system of **differences** between men and women, these differences are organized in a structured relation of subordination and domination, which is historically reproduced from generation to generation.

Such a system has been profoundly **naturalized** as one of the prime conditions of its historical existence. As a result, it is often held that the social positions and powers of men and women are biologically **determined**: for instance, that it is 'natural' for men to dominate and assert, 'natural' for women to be passive or emotional. Here it is important to **foreground** the distinction between sex and gender. Sexual differences refer to basic physiological distinctions between males and females that are largely genetically determined. Gender differences between masculinity and femininity are, however, **culturally determined** and their forms may vary considerably from one cultural context to another. We are **socialized** into distinctive patterns and relations of gender identity according to the cultural rules and codes of our social and historical situation. This process is not naturally determined, and patriarchy accounts for the fact that in most known societies and cultures, men have more power and authority than women, and exercise power over women. Some writers would suggest that male oppression of women has been a feature of all human societies. Against this, others have argued that patriarchy emerged under specific material and political conditions. However, both perspectives would agree that in the development of capitalism, changes in the mode of production served to extend and legitimate the power of men in significant ways. For example, the reorganization of the labour force under capitalism denied equal participation by women who became restricted to undervalued and unpaid forms of labour in the domestic sphere of the family. The emergence of the capitalist state consolidated and legitimized the power of male householders over 'their property', which encompassed not only the dwelling place but also women and children living in it. As a result, many writers suggest that women in capitalist countries are 'doubly disadvantaged' by the structures and interrelations between the patriarchal and capitalist systems.

The activity of producing and sustaining a concerted critique of patriarchy in all its forms has been the enterprise of the women's movement and feminism. This struggle aims to construct radically new relations between men and women and to transform the social relations of production and political power. This challenge has had to confront the ways in which patriarchial relations are produced and reproduced in communication, cultural and institutional processes. The study of **language** (Spender 1985; Mills 1990) and media **representations** (Root 1984), for example, have provided important focal points for work of this kind.

TO

See **culture, gender, power**
Further reading   French (1986); Hearn (1987)

perception   ⋆ Initial consciousness of sensory activity; a process implying awareness and interpretation of surrounding **stimuli** or events. ⋆ Perception differs from **sensation** in that the latter refers to a more passive process that involves the triggering of sense receptors, whereas perception means the active selection and making sense of material from the total immediate world.

Perception also differs from **attention**. The latter term refers to a state of clearness or heightened sensitivity that operates beyond a broader perceptual base. Perception provides a foundation for information – already selected after sensation – that supports and directs subsequent monitoring. With perception much depends on previous knowledge, **experience** and **memory** as regards how any configuration may be understood. It is an oversimplification to think of perception as the process through which our senses give us information about the world. The process is not as simple as this.

Philosophical quests for any definition of **objective** reality continually refer to the basis of our knowledge, or evidence, about the world: perceptions vary greatly between **individuals** and **cultures** – perhaps because of **language** differences. This

221

raises the question of accuracy about one interpretation as compared with another. One conclusion is that all knowledge is essentially uncertain or even illusory because all answers are based on differing evidence that stems from varied meanings imposed by differing language boundaries. Such a discussion inevitably leads to the appraisal of **meaning**, structure, **image, sign** and **symbol** and becomes central to the analysis of communication.

Much psychological theory and research utilizing laboratory and **cross cultural** analysis has been concerned with individual differences in perception. For example, **behaviourist** and neo-behaviourist theorists have emphasized the importance of learning processes in the formation of perceptions: varying interpretations are therefore attributable to differences in the contexts of the perceiver's culture. Detailed perceptual research includes the study of visual illusions and ambiguous stimuli (stare at the figure for a few minutes – can you see two cubes or one?) and also speech perception.

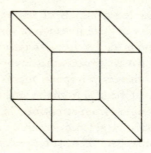

DS

See **consciousness, language, memory, motivation (of the sign), objectivity, subliminal**
Further reading Neisser (1976); Gregory, Lindsay and Norman (1977); Corner and Hawthorn (1989); Roth and Frisby (1986)

performance ★ The semiotics of self. ★ The concept of performance has gained ground in recent **cultural** analysis; it encompasses both **institutionalized**, professional performances (drama, **ritual**), and a non-psychologistic approach to individual people's self-presentation and interaction.

The appeal of performance as a general analytic category is twofold. First, its very generality: the term has been applied not only to what actors and other professionals do but also to the 'performance' of unrehearsed cultural practices in everyday life, the actions of **audiences**, spectators and readers not least among them. Although performances in everyday life will differ markedly from big-deal theatrical or media performances, there are sufficient connections to make comparison worthwhile. You can analyse the differences between fictional and public performance (drama and politics); between acting conventions (**naturalistic** and ritualistic); between media (cinema and television); between **genres** (soap opera and Shakespeare) and so on.

Second, the concept of performance directs the analyst's attention not to the internal psychological state or even the behaviour of a given player, but to formal, rule-governed actions which are appropriate to the given performative genre. If you start looking at ordinary **encounters** in this way, from doctor–patient interviews to telephone calls, it is clear that there are performative protocols in play that require skill and creativity in the manipulation of space, movement, voice, timing, turn-taking, gesture, costume, and the rest of the repertoire of enactment.

A specialist use of the term has arisen in Chomskian linguistics, where verbal performance is contrasted with linguistic **competence** (see following entry).

JH

See **dramaturgy, facework**

performance, linguistic ⋆ Actual verbal behaviour. ⋆ The term is used by the American linguist Chomsky to designate the activity of speaking as opposed to the knowledge that underlies it. Performance, as described by Chomsky, cannot be the focus of linguistic enquiry because everyday verbal behaviour is marred by false starts, slips of the tongue, unfinished sentences and grammatical errors. These performance errors provide an unreliable basis for systematic linguistic description, since, as data, they are – in Chomsky's terms – *degenerate*. Accordingly, Chomsky argued, the focus of linguistic description should not be the actual behaviour but the tacit knowledge and intuitions that enable us to distinguish between 'errors' and well-formed, grammatical utterances. This emphasis on **competence** enabled Chomsky to stress the mental and cognitive basis of language as a universal human capacity. It did lead, however, to a corresponding neglect of the particulars of everyday speech which were left wholly to cognate disciplines such as sociology (more particularly **conversation analysis**), ethnography and socio-linguistics. What is striking about much of the work undertaken in these areas is the way in which it suggests a systematic basis for many of the features (such as false starts or self-corrections) that Chomsky wished to exclude from consideration as random errors in production. This has led some commentators to reject his distinction or to replace it with another such as that between *communicative competence* and *grammatical competence*.

MM

See **competence, langue, parole**
Further reading Chomsky (1965); Hymes (1974)

persuasion ⋆ The intentional influence of opinions, beliefs, values or attitudes by an external agency. ⋆ Intentional persuasion on the part of advertisers, political parties, military forces, and religious **institutions** has been well discussed by Merton (1946), Brown (1972) and Dyer (1982). Much sociological analysis has focused on media control by powerful **elites** in society, who may then construct, manipulate, or **censor** information which ultimately mystifies a true state of affairs and presents favourable **images** of their own controlling positions and interests.

Whilst psychological studies have also shown an awareness about the political and commercial bases of persuasion, the major concern has been in analysing and explaining how persuasion works. It is important to note that such research has also provided strategic advice for many persuasion campaigns. In the 1960s and 1970s this was often linked with public information **campaigns**: for instance, attempts to counter **racial prejudice**, achieve the fluoridization of water and increase the use of seat belts (see Aronson (ed.) 1988).

Whilst such social and health campaigns continue (especially with reference to AIDS, and to ecological awareness), more clandestine applications have been in the marketing of political parties in order to persuade voters (Atkinson 1984). This raises a crucial query: can state support for selected issues establish priorities in persuasion campaigns which then override and outperform the standards and ethics of most commercially based persuasion techniques?

An inevitable part of persuasion involves attitude change: the process whereby existing **attitudes** are altered, modified or completely replaced by different ones towards the same objects or events. Debate centres on the validity and permanence of possible attitude change brought about by, for example, the mass media. As Brown (1972) emphasizes, advertising within the media represents a good platform for discussion of attitude change because 'the needs it satisfies are either so superficial to be trivial or so deep seated as to be universal' (p. 190).

The suggestion here is that media can change attitudes towards peripheral issues but may not be so powerful an influence on centrally held ones. To illustrate, an advertisement about washing-up liquid may well influence our next choice of brand for that product. However, it would be far more difficult to claim that a party political broadcast influences our voting behaviour within a general election.

DS

See **campaign, conformity, propaganda, subliminal, conformity**
Further reading Freedman *et al*. (1981); Brown (1972); Dyer (1982); Atkinson (1984); Packard (1970); DeFleur and Ball-Rokeach (1982); Aronson (ed.) (1988); Roloff and Miller (eds) (1980)

phatic communication   ⋆ Communication whose aim is to maintain and strengthen social relationships rather than to pass **information**, or produce original or creative **texts**. ⋆   It is

redundant, its form is determined by social and textual **conventions**, and it relies upon a common social and cultural experience.

Much casual conversation is phatic, most folk art is phatic, politeness is phatic. Most **popular culture** has an important phatic function, as have the styles of dress, special language and musical taste of **subcultures** such as punks or hippies. Phatic communication helps bind cultures and communities together because it is their means of expressing their commonality of taste, expectations and experience, and therefore of identifying and affirming their cultural membership. Jakobson describes the phatic function of a **message** as being **oriented** towards the **channel**, that is the function of establishing and maintaining contact with the **addressee**.

JF

See **convention, redundancy**

phonemic/phonetic ⋆ A useful conceptual distinction between two kinds of elements in a signifying system – one capable of generating meaning, the other not. ⋆ The terms are borrowed from linguistics, but are applicable to any sign system. In linguistics, a *phoneme* is one of a limited number of sounds (in English there are about forty of them) which are *recognized* as part of the system of such sounds. Verbal utterance is based on the selection and combination of groups of these phonemes in a rule-governed order.

Phonetic, on the other hand, describes the sounds *actually made* by a speaker. The point about this is twofold:

(1)   Each speaker will use her or his physiological, regional, contextual and other resources to produce *a unique* version of the generally recognized phoneme. No one says 'I' in quite the same way as anyone else, but everyone in a speech community will recognize the phoneme 'I' when used by a native speaker.

(2)   All languages recognize as 'the same' phoneme sounds that are actually different. For instance, the 'k' sound in the spoken words 'kin' and 'ink' *sound* 'the same' to the

speaker and the hearer. But they are *actually* different sounds, produced in slightly different parts of the mouth. Try it.

The conceptual point about this is again twofold:

(1) If we paid attention to the sounds we all *actually* make rather than the ones that are *recognized by the language* there's little chance of us being able to make sense of anything – there are too many differences.

(2) The power of **language** (as opposed to actuality) is so great that it's difficult for us to perceive anything outside its recognized elements: you may flatly disagree that the 'k' sounds differ – but an oscilloscope would spot it.

There's no mystery about this property of language. Following Saussure, we can say that phonemes are abstract, they belong to **langue**, whereas phonetics are concrete, they belong to **parole**.

JH

See **difference, phonology**
Further reading Hawkes (1977)

phonology ✶ The branch of linguistics devoted to studying the sound patterns of a **language**. ✶ The human vocal organs are capable of producing an extremely rich array of different sounds. Each language, however, draws for communicative effect upon only a small portion of this total range. Phonology examines which particular units of possible sound constitute the basic meaningful set for any one language. It does so in the first instance by building up contrasting pairs of sound on the principle that for any one language certain sounds will cause changes in the meaning of words, whereas other sounds will not. In English if we change the initial sound of /pig/ from /p/ to /b/ we end up changing one word into another – changing *pig* to *big*. By using this test, known as the minimal pairs test, it is possible to discover which sound substitutions cause a difference in meaning. Each change in meaning isolates a new element of the basic sound

227

structure of the language, each element being known as a **pho-neme**. Thus the minimal pair

pig versus *big* isolates the phonemes /p/ and /b/
pig versus *pin* isolates the phonemes /g/ and /n/
ten versus *den* isolates the phonemes /t/ and /d/
rip versus *lip* isolates the phonemes /r/ and /l/

and so on. The total inventory of phonemes built up with this method is *language-specific*. The contrast between /r/ and /l/ in English, for instance, is not matched by an identical contrast in **dialects** of Chinese.

Phonological analysis is to be distinguished from **phonetic** analysis where the emphasis is on the description and classification of speech sounds independently of meaning.

MM

See **phonemic/phonetic**

pidgin ⋆ A pidgin is a synthetic, simplified **language** of a type which sometimes develops between **groups** who lack a language in common, in order to facilitate contact between them.
⋆ Many recorded examples of pidgins involve contact between an invading European colonial or mercantile power, and indigenous communities. Initially the pidgin serves primarily for contact between the groups for quite specialized purposes such as trade. In these circumstances the pidgin borrows key vocabulary items from the language of the invading power to cover crucial areas of **meaning** such as number or livestock. This borrowed vocabulary is used with a highly simplified grammar in which word order is fixed, inflections are dropped, fewer prepositions are used, and so on. Pronunciation is likely to owe much to local sound patterns.

However, it is possible for the restricted purposes of the original pidgin to become extended, even after the withdrawal of the colonial power, if the pidgin proves useful for communication between local communities, especially where these communities speak mutually unintelligible languages. In Cameroon on the west coast of Africa there are at least two hundred vernacular languages for a population of less than eight million. Although French and English are maintained as official languages, there also exists an important link language – Cameroon Pidgin English – which is common amongst all sectors of the population, is widely distributed amongst the two hundred **ethnic** groups, and has been spoken in the area for at least 150 years. Under such conditions quite significant developments can take place within the pidgin, increasing its complexity, extending the functions to which it is put, including its use for written communication.

MM

See **creole**
Further reading Mulhauser (1986); Todd (1984)

pleasure ⋆ Until the 1980s, a relatively neglected concept in communication and cultural studies, usually defined (by reference to the psychological sensations of the individual) as the anticipation or enjoyment of that which is felt to be desirable or gratifying. Recently more attention has been paid to the social, **ideological** and **discursive** aspects of pleasure. ⋆ This was partly in response to a criticism of much **structuralist** and **semiotic** analysis as being too concerned with texts as rational, logical structures and with reading as an act of information **decoding**. Such analysis neglects the importance of desire, repression, and so on in the enjoyment of **texts**, and of the regulation of pleasure as a socially exchanged commodity (**entertainment**).

Recent cultural analysis has tried, therefore, to specify how and by what kinds of device texts promote different kinds of pleasure; and how pleasure is **institutionalized**, as it were, into socially available forms. Such analysis has focused attention on the extent to which pleasure is subject to cultural policing: certain forms are 'acceptable' in public, others are literally unspeakable and come to be seen as pleasurable largely because of their clandestine quality.

The relation between **language** and the **unconscious** has been shown to be one of the determinants of pleasure – even in such apparently desexualized activities as watching television or cinema (especially the latter) there is an element of **voyeurism** from which the pleasure may derive. But such pleasure is also

229

textual, a product of the relation between the viewer and the text's specific **representations**.

Beyond the interplay between pleasure and sexuality, the most important attempts to theorize the social reproduction of pleasure have been undertaken by feminist writers. They have drawn attention to the way in which advertisers and film-makers attempt to sexualize their messages by representing them as women – but the pleasure of desire so promoted is not without its problems for any women who may be watching.

JH

Further reading Mercer (1982); Culler (1983); Coward (1984); Fiske (1989a, 1989b)

pluralism/liberal pluralism ∗ A theoretical perspective concerning the sources, distribution and structure of power and power relations in advanced western societies. ∗ This perspective is defined by its emphasis upon the increasingly *diffused* distribution of **power** among and between a variety (or *plurality*) of constantly competing independent interest **groups** and **elites**. As such it must be seen against other theories of power: for example, Marxist or classical elite theories, where emphasis is generally placed on the high and relatively constant if not inevitable **concentration** of power in the hands of cohesive ruling **classes** or elites.

Growing out of a long tradition of liberal democratic political philosophy, pluralism, particularly in the context of postwar USA, has become a dominant perspective informing and directing many studies and debates concerning power and processes of social change in their widest economic, political and cultural forms. The crucial feature of modern industrial societies for pluralists (for example, Dahl 1961) is their movement towards a progressively differentiated and diverse structure. The consequence of such a process being the emergence of a 'plurality' of correspondingly divergent interests and groups, demanding and competing for access and control within all political and institutional arenas.

The characteristic feature of pluralist analysis is the fragmented and decentralized view of power it proposes, tending to play down conflict and power in competitive relations.

At the general level this thesis has promoted a great deal of **empirical** research and critical response. It has been contested in the analysis of specific social, economic and political **institutions** and their operations. Studies of the ownership and control of mass media institutions and processes of cultural production, and their relations to wider economic and political structures, have formed an important recent focus for debate.

TO

See **concentration, institution, power**
Further reading   Bilton *et al.* (1981); Lukes (1974)

polysemic   ⋆ A property of all signs; the property of being capable of signifying multiple meanings. ⋆

JH

See **multi-accentuality, multi-discursive**

popular/popular culture   ⋆ Of people in general; for people in general; well liked by people in general. ⋆ 'Popular' is usually synonymous with 'good' in ordinary conversation, but this is an inversion of its earlier pejorative connotations. In its original form, popular was used to distinguish the mass of the people (not 'people in general') from the titled, wealthy or educated **classes**. Not surprisingly, since most writers on the subject were either members or clients of the latter three classes, its synonyms were gross, base, vile, riff-raff, common, low, vulgar, plebeian, cheap (*OED*).

From these inauspicious beginnings the term has to some extent been 'decolonized', principally through its usage in democratic politics in and since the nineteenth century. However, it still retains sufficient traces of its history to be a **multi-accentual** term: the popularity of something may be taken either as an indication of its positive or of its negative value, depending on your alignment to 'the people'.

Thus the concept is not exempt from politics, which has in fact

231

dogged its usage within the sphere of cultural analysis. The popularity (ubiquitousness) of the mass media in particular has resulted in a recurring ambiguity in both academic and public debate about whether the products of the media are good because they're popular, or bad because they're popular (the 'more means worse' idea).

The ambiguity is not simply a matter of the personal prejudices of the critic. It is implicit in the position of those people and products that can be described as popular. The ambiguity has two aspects. First, there is ambiguity about the extent to which popular culture is *imposed on* people in general (by media corporations or state agencies), or *derived from* their own **experiences**, tastes, habits, and so on. Second, there is ambiguity about the extent to which popular culture is merely an expression of a powerless and subordinate class position, or an **autonomous** and potentially liberating source of alternative ways of seeing and doing that can be opposed to dominant or official culture.

These ambiguities have an important bearing on the study of *popular culture*, since they make it very hard to specify an easily agreed object of study. What 'counts' as popular culture depends to some extent on whether you're interested in what **meanings** are produced *by* or *for* 'the people', and whether you take these meanings as evidence of 'what the public wants' or of 'what the public gets'. Further, the study of popular culture requires some attention to cultures other than popular – especially what is known as *high culture*. However, discussion centred on **differences** between popular and high culture has traditionally focused on matters of taste and artistic merit. For instance, there is an implicit valuation in distinctions such as those between 'serious' and 'pop' music, which are frequently **institutionalized** in the form of entire radio networks (like Radio 3 and Radio 1 in the United Kingdom); or between creative genius (high culture) and commercial consumption (popular). These distinctions appear at first to be derived from the qualities of the works associated with each type: Mozart writes 'better' music than a chart-topping pop group, and moreover Mozart's music is not tied to time, nation or class – it is seen as an expression of human genius in general. In short, the accepted (or at least the established) evaluations of different cultural products are **naturalized**: accounted for as intrinsic properties of the product and not as a result of their assignation to different cultural categories.

What is at stake in the attempt to specify popular culture is the status of these naturalized evaluations. For they may themselves be explained as an **ideological** strategy whereby **class** relations (supremacy and subordination) may be 'lived' as natural differences. In fact the study of popular culture cannot get very far without some attempt to relate the social production and reproduction of meanings to the economic and political divisions and antagonisms of class.

The recognition of a relation between class and culture has led on to further issues. First, attention has broadened beyond its original focus on such obviously cultural artefacts as **texts**, to include practices, **lifestyles** and 'lived culture' – especially in the ethnographic study of **subcultures**. Second, there has been a rediscovery of 'cultural politics', often associated with the work of Gramsci (1971) and his concepts of **hegemony** and the 'national-popular'. Finally, attention to class has led on to consideration of the complex relations that exist between this and, especially, **gender** and **ethnic** relations.

JH

See **class, culture, cultural studies, ideology, subculture**
Further reading the Open University course *Popular Culture* (U203) together with its associated readers and broadcasts (1982); Turner (1990); McGuigan (1992); Fiske (1989a, 1989b)

positivism/logical positivism ⋆ An ideology of science first proposed to deal with the phenomena and actions of the natural physical world, and particularly associated with nineteenth-century physics. The term was taken over by **analogy** into the study of people and society ('the social sciences') where it survived long after its original proponents abandoned it. ⋆

Logical positivism is characterized by a total concern with observable evidence, and a refusal to discuss matters that cannot be publicly verified. It is thus essentially **empirical** in outlook and is opposed to any approach which claims to go beyond

233

observable evidence. For positivists, **objectivity** and public verification are crucial, and they refuse to discuss introspective, private or existential events. This, together with an emphasis on defining objects in terms of the observable operations that they perform, leads to a hard-line scientific approach that would have difficulty in, for example, contributing to the discussion of imagery or orders of **signification** as referred to in **semiology**.

Positivism has had much influence on the development of **experimental** research, with particular reference to **behaviourism** and the rejection of introspectionism. The actual positive (+) connotation appears far removed from its aims and objectives, especially when no contrasting negativism (−) can be readily identified.

DS

See **behaviourism, empiricism, experiment, objectivity**

postmodernism ⋆ A portmanteau term encompassing a variety of developments in intellectual culture, the arts and the fashion industry in the 1970s and 1980s. ⋆ Among the characteristic gestures of postmodernist thinking is a refusal of the 'totalizing' or 'essentialist' tendencies of earlier theoretical systems, especially classic Marxism, with their claims to referential truth, scientificity, and belief in progress. Postmodernism, on the contrary, is committed to modes of thinking and representation which emphasize fragmentations, discontinuities and incommensurable aspects of a given object, from intellectual systems to architecture.

Postmodernist analysis is often marked by forms of writing that are more literary, certainly more self-reflexive, than is common in critical writing – the critic as self-conscious creator of new meanings upon the ground of the object of study, showing that object no special respect. It prefers montage to perspective, intertextuality to referentiality, 'bits-as-bits' to unified totalities. It delights in excess, play, carnival, asymmetry, even mess, and in the emancipation of meanings from their bondage to mere lumpenreality.

Theorists of postmodernism include Jean Baudrillard, Gilles Deleuze and Félix Guattari, Fredric Jameson, Paul Virilio, Dick Hebdige, Jean François Lyotard, among others; a list whose maleness has not gone unnoticed (see Probyn 1987), but which may immediately be countered by reading the exemplary essay by Meaghan Morris (1988) which moves easily among postmodernism's sense of multiple mobilities, bodily, temporal and textual, without ever claiming postmodernist status for itself.

JH

Further reading   Foster (ed.) (1985); Harvey (1989); Clarke (1991); Featherstone (ed.) (1988)

power   ∗ The means by which certain individuals and groups are able to dominate others, to carry through and realize their own particular aims and interests even in the face of opposition and resistance. ∗   The term refers principally to the *sources*, *means* and *relations* of dominance, control and subordination, as they are enacted in historically specific social processes and situations. Power may be purely *coercive*, involving directly punitive physical force in order to impose and maintain dominance. Or it may be the product of the differential access to, and distribution of, fundamental resources in society; resources in both the material sense of property, wealth, technology or raw materials, and symbolic forms, such as knowledge, **literacy**, science, and other types of **cultural capital**.

While sometimes thought of as restricted to the public domain of politics, in its **institutional** and organizational forms, power is potentially or actually in play or contest in *all* social relationships and moments of interaction, structuring and demarcating the interrelations between **individuals** and **groups**. Because of this centrality, power and power relations provide a fundamental set of problems and focal points for both the situated analysis of interaction and communication, and their wider structural locations and determinants. The study of power and power relations, therefore, is both indivisible from and serves as a basis for the study of communication.

Power is not always mobilized or experienced in directly

235

repressive, coercive ways. It may be seen as the exercise or experience of *authority*, and held to be *legitimate*. *Authority* refers to the **institutionalization** of power relations, whereby groups or individuals become **socialized** or accustomed to obeying and conforming to certain **rules**, orders or regulations. The degree to which power is transformed into authority will depend upon its apparent legitimacy, and unless an authority can claim legitimacy successfully, it must constantly reconfirm its power by direct coercive means. *Legitimation* refers to those processes whereby the possession and exercise of power and authority are mobilized and constructed as 'right' or 'just' guaranteed by its own 'natural' moral superiority and 'taken for granted' inevitability.

While the term *control* is often used in a general sense to describe the practices and aims of the powerful, *social control* is often more precisely employed to refer to socially generalized authority, forms of negative or corrective social regulation (which appear 'disembodied'). Where power is positively defined, implying rule and dominance contested and exerted through conflict and struggle between individuals, groups or social **classes**; social control often implies a **consensually** authoritative social order, whereby society regulates itself. The interrelations between power and social control have been particularly contested and subject to debate in the analysis of those social processes that operate both to produce and to prevent conduct and activity defined or labelled as **deviant**.

TO

See **class, conformity, consensus, deviance, hegemony, ideology, institutions, stratification**
Further reading Berger and Berger (1976); Worsley (ed.) (1977); Bilton *et al.* (1981); Lukes (1974); Cuff and Payne (eds) (1979)

pragmatics ⋆ The study of the interpretation of utterances and more specifically how the context of situation influences their meaning. ⋆ Traditionally the study of meaning has focused upon the meaning of words or sentences as if meaning inhered within the linguistic expression itself and was ultimately determined by the linguistic system. Pragmatics, however, emphasizes the role of context in determining meaning. In fact, of course, it has long been recognized that linguistic items such as **deictics** and other *indexical expressions* depend for their meaning on the context of situation. In particular, deictics such as the personal pronouns 'I', 'YOU' and indexical expressions such as 'tomorrow' all depend for their meaning on the circumstances in which they are uttered. Thus, the precise meaning of 'I'll visit you tomorrow' will vary depending upon who actually is speaking to whom, and on when the utterance takes place.

But in any case, even apart from deixis, many words have multiple senses. Even a simple item such as 'coach' has several senses, including 'a mode of transport' and 'someone who trains people in a particular sport'. Its use, therefore, in an utterance such as 'Look out for the coach' is potentially ambiguous, and we rely upon context to select the relevant sense.

Pragmatic issues, however, go far beyond issues of word meaning to include consideration of complicated kinds of contextual effect where the meaning of an utterance is much more than what is literally said. If in a review of an opera we read that 'Mr Jones sang a series of notes which corresponded to those of an aria from *Rigoletto*' we infer that he sang badly, *even though the utterance does not actually say so*. Similarly if while driving in a strange town we ask someone 'Is there anywhere we can get petrol round here?' and they reply 'There's a garage just round the corner' we assume that it's the type of garage that sells petrol (not that it's one for parking your car) and that it's open. These kinds of inferences that go beyond the literal meaning of what is said are known as **implicatures**.

A further kind of contextual effect relates to the notion of **speech act**. *Directives*, for instance, are a commonly occurring type of speech act designed to get someone to do something. An utterance such as 'Play the piano, John' is likely to be a directive whatever the circumstances of its occurrence. But utterances such as 'Would you mind playing the piano, John?', 'Can you play the piano, John?', 'The piano, John', etc. may or may not prove to be directives depending on the context of situation. If a teacher in a music lesson says to a pupil, 'Can you play the piano, John?', with the piano waiting for someone to play it, then it is most likely to be heard as a directive. If, on the other hand, a group of acquaintances are discussing what instruments they can play and one asks of another 'Can you play the piano, John?' then s/he would most likely be heard as requesting information rather than making a directive. In this way, what an utterance is heard as doing (in other words, what speech act it is performing) can vary according to its context of situation.

The aim of pragmatics is in the first place to describe these various kinds of contextual effect; but more significantly it aims to explain how language users actually make sense of each others' utterances in the face of the various kinds of indeterminancy and ambiguity outlined above. The contribution of pragmatics to communication studies is potentially considerable, though as yet unrealized, since it goes to the heart of some of the most troubling issues surrounding **text** and interpretation (e.g., 'Where is meaning – in the text; or in the context?'). At the same time, however, pragmatics has become closely associated more recently with the interests of cognitive science and the study of artificial intelligence. Such links tend to produce a strong emphasis on the supposed rationality of communicators, and on the universality of the interpretative procedures which they adopt, so that much work remains to be done on the socially structured distribution and organization of pragmatic knowledge and procedures.

MM

See **context of situation, conversation analysis, discourse language, meaning, semantics, speech act**
Further reading Levinson (1983); Leech (1983)

preferred reading ∗ A **text** is open to a number of potential readings, but normally 'prefers' one (or, occasionally, more). ∗ Analysing the internal structure of the text can identify this preference.

Texts, according to Eco (1981), can be open or closed. A *closed text* has one reading strongly preferred over others: an *open text* requires a number of readings to be made simultaneously for its full 'richness' or 'texture' to be appreciated (to use literary critical terms). Open texts tend to be high brow, high culture, whereas closed texts tend to the more popular, mass culture. Most mass media texts are closed in so far as they prefer a particular reading.

Alternative readings to the preferred one usually derive from differences between the social positions and/or the cultural experience of the **author** and the **reader**, or between *reader* and *reader*. Eco uses the theory of **aberrant decoding** to account for this, but Hall and Morley produce subtler and more sophisticated accounts based on Parkin's (1972) theory of **meaning systems**. Hall *et al.* (eds) (1980) proposed three main types of decodings or readings of television texts which correspond to the reader's response to his or her social condition, not to the structure of the text. These are:

(1) The *dominant-hegemonic* which accepts the text 'full and straight' according to the assumptions of the encoder. This is the preferred reading, and corresponds to Parkin's dominant meaning system.
(2) *The negotiated reading* which acknowledges the legitimacy of the dominant codes, but adapts the reading to the specific social condition of the reader. This corresponds to Parkin's subordinate meaning system.
(3) *The oppositional reading* which produces a radical decoding that is radically opposed to the preferred reading, because it derives from an alternative, oppositional meaning system. The radical meaning system in Parkin's terminology.

As an illustration, we might take potential readings of a series of advertisements portraying women as sex objects, clothes horses or mother figures. A preferred reading according to the dominant-hegemonic code is to accept and agree with this portrayal as natural, accurate and attractive. A negotiated reading may be produced by a middle-class career woman who broadly accepts the preferred reading, but 'for others, not for me!'. She reserves the right to produce her own reading of the ads which corresponds to her social condition as an independent woman. An oppositional reading might be produced by a feminist as insulting, degrading, restricting and proof of men's exploitation of women. The first reading could be produced by women who would buy the products, the second by women who might, if it suited their purposes, and the third by women who would not.

Underlying this theory is a definition of reading as the generation of meaning that occurs when the structures of the text meet with the socially located meaning systems or **discourses** of the reader. The text can prefer one reading, but the reader always has the resources of his or her meaning systems to produce his or her 'own' reading. Morley (1980) demonstrated this when he took a broadcast of *Nationwide*, a current affairs programme, to a number of very different types of **audience**, and studied the variety of readings they produced. However, in an illuminating postscript to this study, Morley (1981) noted a series of key tensions surrounding the concept and its use in research. These concerned the extent to which the preferred reading was to be understood as a principal property of the *text* in question, or the *reader* of that text, or of the *analyst* studying text–reader interaction. This tension has sparked a good deal of research and debate in the later 1980s and into the 1990s; much of this has sought to understand the reader in context, and to specify more precisely the cultural conditions under which people construct their 'private' readings of given texts. The great majority of this work has concentrated upon television programmes in the domestic context of the home, and the tendency has been to counteract earlier emphasis on purely textual **power** or **determination**.

JF/TO

See **closure, code, cultural capital, discourse, ideology, meaning systems, negotiation, popular culture**
Further reading Morley (1989, 1992); Turner (1990); Fiske (1987, 1989a, 1989b) Moores (1992)

prejudice ★ Predisposed aggression or other negative dispositions to a **group** of people that has been **stereotyped** according to simple characteristics based on incomplete information. ★ This definition concentrates on the negative aspects of prejudice and does not refer to all predispositions towards any category of objects or events.

Targets for hostility and victims of prejudice vary from society to society and **culture** to culture. Often they are associated with a lack of **power**, which in turn decreases the likelihood of effective retaliation. Some of the most obvious social groups that bear the brunt of prejudice include Asians (regardless of whether they are, for example, Hindu, Moslem or Sikh), Afro-Carbbieans, women, gays and unemployed youth. Less obvious but none the less effective stigma towards people may depend on accent, style of dress, type of employment, mental health and fatness.

Discrimination (with regard to **race** relations 'ethnic hostility' or 'cleansing' has euphemistically replaced this word) implies the acting out of prejudiced attitudes. However, some studies have shown that discrimination does not always follow on from prejudice, and that much depends on social **context**. Explanations of prejudice are many and varied, as is the extent of prejudice held by individuals within and between groups. Bogardus (1928) concluded that some people will accept a so-called ethnic minority into their employment but not into close kinship by marriage, whereas others will not even accept that group as visitors or citizens of their country.

Frustration and aggression have often been posited as the causes of prejudice: if the individual's path to a goal is blocked and the obstacle is too powerful to overcome then subsequent aggression will be displaced and redirected towards a more vulnerable target. Other theorists suggest that conformity is as important an explanation of prejudice: negative evaluations of selected groups may be culturally located and an inherent part of socialization. Yet others have tried to define an authoritarian personality that is more likely to be prejudiced because of a dogmatic thinking style (see Adorno *et al*. 1950, Rokeach 1960 for further discussion).

The analysis of prejudice remains a diverse and complex area, but one that is essential to the description and explanation of intergroup relations as formulated by direct or indirect contact within any social system. In the study of communication much recent interest has been expressed in the role of **media** when locating racism (see Hartman and Husband 1974, Hall *et al*. 1978)

241

and sexism (see Manstead and McCullouch 1981) within a wider social and cultural context.

DS

See **attitude, conformity, displacement, minority, nation, projection, race, stereotype**
Further reading Cottle (1978); Centre for Contemporary Cultural Studies (1982); Billig (1982); Husband (ed.) (1987); Davey (1983); Aronson (ed.) (1988)

primary definers ⋆ Those sources of information, usually official, that generate, control and establish initial definitions of particular events, situations and issues. ⋆ Examples would include state and governmental **institutions**, courts, police, political parties, commercial agencies and pressure groups, professional and trade union bodies and so on. The routine activity of news production is heavily dependent upon and directed towards these official and accredited sources and their representatives. As a consequence, a good deal of news coverage tends to reproduce and translate the interpretative frameworks and definitions generated by primary definers, and in such a way the media usually operate as secondary definers. Chibnall (1977) has argued that these control agencies usually recognize three broad goals in their dealings with news media:

(1) They are concerned very often to protect the public reputation and **image** of the control agency.
(2) They may aim to facilitate directly the work of the control agency, in for example controlling and apprehending **deviants**.
(3) They have an interest in promoting the particular aims, **ideologies** and interests of members of the control agency.

Primary definers, both directly and indirectly, therefore play an important and strategic part in processes of controlling and managing social information. While the institutional and professional imperatives of 'balance' and '**impartiality**' or '**access**' require that the news media should within certain limits elicit

242

alternative definitions or viewpoints, these generally follow later, and are required to respond within the **discourse** constructed and established by the primary definers. In the USA the term 'advocate' is often used to describe this function.

TO

See **agenda setting, ideology, labelling theory, moral panic**
Further reading Chibnall (1977); Hall and Jefferson (eds) (1976); Hall *et al.* (eds) (1978); Murdock (1981); Golding and Middleton (1982); Schudson (1991)

primary group ★ A group characterized by frequent contact between a limited number of people. ★ The study of primary groups is usually directed towards the family, childhood and adolescent peer **groups**. This is unfortunate because adult primary groups, for example in the work–place, have been seriously neglected.

Face–to–face contact is an essential feature of primary groups, together with the formation of intimate relationships. The primary group is viewed as the major agency for **socialization**, and as constituting a fusion of selves which in turn transcend any one person. Such groups provide the **individual** with initial **experience** of social being.

Two major disciplines have discussed primary groups. Social psychological interest has tended to concentrate on **non–verbal communication** and **dyadic** interaction. Sociological interest has centred around **cultural** acquisition and the communication of **values** within societies. Both approaches encounter problems because of some implicit secondary group: a far more nebulous and ill–defined collective based on a presumed lack of intimacy, interaction or shared values.

DS

See **dyad, group, interpersonal communication, socialization**

production/consumption

production ★ The act or result of the socially organized transformation of materials into a new but previously determined form. ★ Production is traditionally opposed to a converse term, **consumption**.

243

consumption ⋆ The act or fact of using up the products or yield of any industry in the support of any process. ⋆

Production and consumption are terms borrowed from political economy, and they are now widely used (often uncritically) to describe the parties to and the transactions of communication. Thus **meanings**, media output, **texts**, and so on are said to be produced and consumed. Media **professionals** are seen as industrial producers while **audiences** or **readers** are seen as the consumers of meaning.

The industrial metaphor is useful and suggestive as far as it goes, but there is a danger of taking it too literally. This is especially the case with consumption, which as a concept implies the using up of a finished product by an individual. Meanings and communication, however, are not consumed as finished products. The consumption of messages, therefore, is simultaneously an act of production of meanings.

Production is a term you will encounter frequently in Marxist social theory, where it is often qualified in one of a number of ways: see **base**.

JH

See **authorship, class, cultural production, cultural reproduction, culture**

Further reading   Bennett (1979); Wolff (1981)

profession/professionalism/professionalization ⋆ It is difficult to think of professions apart from in the descriptive sense of their medical, legal and other generally high-status occupations. ⋆   The term carries a jumble of meanings and values, from efficiency to wealth; from prestige through altruism to public service. There have been two major analytical approaches to the study of professions, and the associated practices of *professionalism*.

One approach, associated especially with the **functionalist** school of social theory, attempts to define them by isolating certain characteristics of occupations or occupational **roles** regarded as professional. These commonly include:

(1)   specialized *skills*, based on theoretical non-**common sense** knowledge;

(2) these are gained through extensive, often intensive *education*;

(3) which makes possible *regulation of occupational entry*, often in the name of 'the profession';

(4) which also regulates entrants' conduct by a *code of ethics*;

(5) which tend to stress *public service*, as opposed to self-interest.

Underlying this list of 'professional criteria' (and the difficulties in operationalizing them) is the assumption that the professions are unique in terms of both their relevance to the core values of society (justice and health, for example), and the special mutual relationship that exists between the professional practitioner and the client.

Alternatively, recent approaches have argued for a redefinition of professions and professionalism. As Johnson (1972) argues: 'a profession is not, then, an occupation, but a means of controlling an occupation'. In other words, professions are about **power**, they are distinctive as occupations, precisely in terms of their high degree of power and control, which is employed ultimately to benefit the practitioner (and profession), rather than the client (or public). Professional knowledge and practice serves first as the guarantee for an unequal power relationship between practitioner and client, while also serving as an important basis for claims for **autonomy** and reward for the practitioner. In these terms, professions become much less a static descriptive or intrinsic category, and more part of wider power relations and conflicts, the changing outcome of a historically specific occupational contest for professional power, status and reward. Significantly, most professions since the late nineteenth century have had to accede to, and increasingly contend with, state regulation (and many occupations have since claimed professional status). While all professionals are in varying degrees authoritative communicators, the term will be encountered particularly in the context of the production of mass media texts. *Media professionals*, **broadcasters**, journalists, and so on, may well be characterized by all or at least a combination of some of the factors listed in the first approach above. They also work in complex institutional and

245

organizational **contexts** which subject them to a variety of controls and regulations. Recent studies of media organizations (see further reading below) have stressed the importance of professionalism as an **occupational ideology** and set of strategies for negotiating, controlling and combatting these constraints and pressures. At the heart of the study of the mass media lies the relationship between the potentially closed culture of professional values, conventions and practices, which shape and encode mass communications, and their wider social and cultural contexts and determinants.

TO

See **news values, occupational ideology, power**
Further reading   Johnson (1972, 1973); Bilton *et al.* (1981); Elliott (1977); McQuail (1975)

projection   ⋆ Projection literally implies a throwing outwards or forwards; it refers to a process or technique by which ideas, images and desires are imposed on an external environment. ⋆ Whilst the most obvious use of projection involves technology and cinema, the concept has also proved to be popular in the study of **psychoanalysis**. Freud recognized that projection denies unpleasant accusation of the self and projects such accusation on to other people. This has been discussed by Adorno *et al.* (1950) when investigating **prejudice** and the concept of authoritarianism: prejudiced individuals attribute their own motives and characteristics to out**groups** while failing to recognize the same aspects as applied to their ingroup.

DS

See **defence mechanism, displacement, identification, prejudice, psychoanalytical theory**
Further reading   Adorno *et al.* (1950); Stafford–Clarke (1967)

propaganda   ⋆ The intentional control, manipulation and communication of information and imagery in order to achieve certain political objectives. ⋆ The word propaganda should be used very carefully. The intentional aspect of so-called propaganda is often obscure. The use of Shakespeare's *Merchant of Venice* within English and drama syllabuses, for example, are not usually described as intentional propaganda even though it is an anti-semitic **text**. Similarly, a political objective does not mean an objective of a political party. Instead propaganda may stem from some dominant **ideological** stance located within **social institutions**. By way of illustration, money-lending for profit has been prohibited by some societies and yet few schools ever question the ethics of western banking when calculating interest charges on hypothetical bank loans in maths classes. Even then it would be wrong to equate education with propaganda simply because educational institutions are (with many wealthy exceptions) associated with state control: propaganda tells people *what* to think whereas education is, ideally, more concerned with the *how* of thinking. Having said this, you will of course notice many occasions where the two overlap.

Because of the close links between ideology and propaganda it is perhaps more accurate to locate propaganda*s* within *social structure*. One form of propaganda (for example, the elucidation of the writings of Marx) may then be contrasted with another (for example, capitalism) in a deliberate and counteractive way. The most common historical association of the term is with times of war or national crisis. In these situations mass media are mobilized in often emotive, large-scale and systematic attempts to promote certain opinions and **attitudes** with regard to particular issues. Propaganda is therefore best viewed as an historically specific form of mass **persuasion** (involving the production and transmission of specifically structured texts and **messages**) designed to produce or encourage certain **responses** in the mass **audience**.

This close relationship between the ways in which the texts are structured, and the political objectives and goals for which they are employed, is the central feature of propaganda. The power to fabricate, withhold or manipulate media information and public opinion solely to recruit support for a political party, cause or policy directly contradicts the political ethos of liberal democratic societies. Not surprisingly, it tends to be viewed negatively and is associated with totalitarian states. This should not deflect attention from instances of propaganda that have occurred, and that continue to occur, within democratic **contexts**.

DS

See **campaign, consciousness, ideology, mystification, persuasion**
Further reading   Brown (1972); Foulkes (1983)

proxemics   ⋆ The study of the significance of distance, orientation and space relations in interpersonal communication. ⋆ It is a complicated area, and Argyle (1987) identifies proximity as only one of a number of socially significant relations within **non-verbal communication** processes; the others include gesture, posture, facial expression and general appearance. **Cultural** differences in preferred proximity within **dyads** have been claimed: for example, Swedes and Scots are supposed to stand at further distances than do Latin Americans or Arabs. Much may depend on the content and topic of **interaction** of course, with closer distances and contact being selected for more intimate discussion.

Of interest is the suggestion that just as preferred proximity varies between situations, some type of body territory or *personal space* can be identified: literally an area of space that surrounds the body, and which should not be invaded by others unless express permission is given. Personal space increases with **power** and **status** of the individual. This may be because of that person's demands and preferences. It may also be because of other people's fears and expectations. In this way interactants are assumed constantly to negotiate proxemic relations. As Goffman (1963) recognizes, in more densely populated city conditions any set of proxemic **rules** would often be violated, which may then result in a virtual depersonalization. This might perhaps explain the marked lack of eye contact or attention to others in such conditions as underground trains during the rush-hour or a crowded lift.

DS

See **interpersonal communication, non-verbal communication**

Further reading   Argyle (1987); Hall (1973); Aronson (ed.) (1988)

psychoanalytical theory ⋆ A theoretical perspective, originally formulated by Freud, concerning internal psychic **structures** and the complex relations between them. ⋆ The communication system arising out of such a psychic matrix is of especial importance for the analysis of **intrapersonal communication, motivation, socialization** and development. Freud was particularly interested in the treatment of neuroses, initially prompted by the realization that many of his patients' physical complaints did not in fact have any physiological bases but instead stemmed from psychological origins.

By using free association (which replaced hypnosis) and interpretation of patients' remembered life histories Freud constructed an elaborate **model** of the psychological functioning of the human psyche and the relations that people develop with the external world. At the heart of psychoanalytical theory is the simple assumption that drives, desires and wants are geared towards satisfaction and therefore **motivation** is primarily viewed as hedonistic or pleasure-seeking. Frustration arises out of blocked motives, producing pain and self-criticism, which in turn poses problems for our pleasure-seeking selves.

Ingeniously, Freud suggests that such experience is eliminated from **consciousness** via repression into the **unconscious** or translation into more distanced events – for example, by **projection** or **symbolism** (as in dreams). The unconscious thus refers to an unorganized part of the psychic apparatus and leads to the formation of what Freud labelled *das es* or id. Control of the id is allocated to consciousness, or ego, while the eventual internalization of **others** through **socialization** plus gradual awareness of personal shortcomings leads to the formation of a more critical conscience, or super-ego.

Freudian-based psychoanalytical theory has been criticized for being reductionist and emotional and for being obsessed with sexual impulse. However, it should be remembered that such theory has undoubtedly contributed much to the investigation of **sign**, **symbol** and **image**. Freud also inspired later theorists in their construction of more elaborate models. Carl Jung, for example, advanced *analytical psychology* and Alfred Adler proposed *individual psychology*, both of them being students of psychoanalysis who for at least some parts of their lives were closely associated with Freud.

More recently, psychoanalysis has been further popularized through the writing of Jacques Lacan. His insistence on the linguistic structures associated with the unconscious has proved highly influential in **cultural studies**. The analysis of sexuality and sexism within social relations has also attracted much feminist interest – but with a thorough reworking of some nineteenth-century ideas (see Mitchell 1974).

DS

See **archetype, catharsis, consciousness, defence mechanism, displacement, projection, subconscious, symbol, unconscious, voyeur**
Further reading Billig (1982); Badcock (1980); Mitchell (1974); Stafford–Clarke (1967); Reppen (ed.) (1985); Gallop (1982)

public and private spheres ⋆ A way of describing the separation in modern **cultures** between the 'closed' worlds of the personal, biographical and domestic and the 'open' spaces of work, politics, mass media and of wider **institutional** affairs. ⋆ The origins and dynamics of modern divisions between these dual worlds of culture and **consciousness** are rooted in nineteenth- and twentieth-century changes in the industrial process and their redefinition of the relations between 'home' and 'work'. The politics of the concepts, as applied to culture and communication, have in recent times concerned two distinct issues. First, feminist and other writers have drawn attention to the **gendered** divisions of labour and forms of power which have been prompted and naturalized by this dimension. Second, recent studies of **mass communication** have argued for the importance of retaining a *public sphere* – open and accessible to all – as a key component of modern, participatory, democratic life.

TO

See **institutions, public service broadcasting**
Further reading   Garnham (1986); Bonner *et al*. (eds) (1992)

public service broadcasting   ⋆ The provision of radio and television **channels** as public goods rather than private commodities. This has entailed their organization as national cultural **institutions** dedicated to extending public resources of information, **representation** and **entertainment**. ⋆ The history of the development of broadcasting systems in many **nation** states has been profoundly influenced by **discourses** of public service, either in the form of state monopoly or more latterly as a significant public element within a mixed system, most commonly allowing competition with commercial variants of radio and television broadcasting. In the UK context, the 'core' components of public service broadcasting (PSB) have tended to include the following principles. First, as a public service, broadcasting should be universally available to all citizens and attempt to cater for diversity as well as unity within the national **culture** and its communities. Second, the service should be financed and accountable via a simple system of public sponsorship, which allows for the insulation of broadcasters from the vested interests of governments, political parties, commercial or corporate power. Finally, the services provided should be of good 'quality' (a key term in recent debates) and responsive to the needs of all groups in modern culture regardless of their **power**, status or influence.

In historical terms, it is important to note some key tensions and shifts in the ethos and practices associated with PSB (see Kumar 1977). In the UK, long-established criticisms of cultural **elitism** and paternalism have been accompanied in more recent times by a market-based, deregulatory critique of the inefficiencies of large-scale public service provision and its inabilities to deliver popular programming, in tune with the multiple demands of **audiences** in the modern period. This phase has also coincided with the emergence of new multi-channel media technologies and products such as cable, satellite and video which have added weight to the challenge to the old rigidities and **hegemony** of many national broadcasting systems. As a result of this and other forms of fragmentation, many contemporary writers have suggested that PSB is a monolithic concept which has outlived its historical moment and its relevance. Against this, and in the light of experience of tendencies within deregulated systems, some recent assessments of PSB have sought to restate the importance, in modern mass democracies, of equality of **access** to a shared public, broadcast culture. From this point of view, the erosion of this facility is understood as a political weakening of an important historical right of citizenship as well as an index of modern social and cultural fragmentation.

TO

See **broadcasting, deregulation, public sphere, Reithian**
Further reading Scannell (1989, 1990); Kumar (1977); MacCabe and Stewart (ed.) (1986); Schlesinger (1987); Hood (1986)

questionnaire ★ A series of questions designed to collect information about people's **attitudes**, **values**, opinions or beliefs with regard to a particular topic. ★ Questionnaires can be written or verbal, and they can incorporate questions about one or a number of subjects.

Answers can be totally unstructured in the sense that participants are asked simply to write whatever they want to for their reply. Or they can be more structured when the respondent selects one of a number of alternative answers provided (this is sometimes called a *multiple-choice* technique). Questions can be direct when their intentions are fairly obvious, or they can be indirect when their objective is more disguised and difficult to recognize.

Questionnaires should be balanced so that they contain an even distribution of questions requiring yes and no answers for scoring on a particular subject. For example, if testing for an **audience's** attitudes towards **violence** on television, a questionnaire should have 50 per cent of statements agreeing with the claim that there is too much violence, and 50 per cent of statements disagreeing with the suggestion that there is too much violence. Similarly, question order should be varied as the questionnaire is administered, because the wording and/or answer for one question can affect a subsequent reply. Another crucial variable involves sample size and representativeness, with sampling being defined as the selection of a limited but representative number from a larger population. Obviously if the sample is too small, or **biased** in some way, then any conclusions based on that questionnaire and applied to the general population that the sample purportedly represents are rendered seriously suspect.

The above factors should be continually remembered when discussing the validity of audience surveys within mass media analysis, social psychology and market research. There are many unfortunate occasions when questionnaires have been poorly designed or executed, where the proportion of people not co-operating is not provided, where questions have been badly constructed and are unnecessarily obscure, and where freedom to answer has been too limited.

DS

See **attitudes, methodology, objectivity**
Further reading Stempel and Westley (eds) (1981); Shimanoff (1980); de Vaus (1986); Fink and Kosecoff (1985)

R

race ✶ A social category of people who are supposedly distinguished by inherited and invariable characteristics. ✶ Whereas race can at first glance be viewed as an innocent description of what certain people look like, it carries a hidden **agenda** about their '**nature**', how they behave and are expected to behave. Racist **ideologies** therefore they claim that essential genetic and psychological characteristics define a population which has little choice in the matter, and as such is **stereotyped**. It is this kind of recognition that provides Tajfel's (1981) distinction between human **groups** (which have choice) and social categories (which do not). It should be emphasized that this is a profoundly unsatisfactory form of classification in social science, yet one that is popularly referred to in everyday speech. To illustrate the conceptual confusions, consider the phrase 'the human race' as a generic term referring to all man- and womankind. Then consider the anthropological distinction between the human races – such as Caucasian, Negroid and Mongoloid. Furthermore, refer to the term **ethnic** – this often assumes the further addition of cultural characteristics for a group of people (for further discussion of these issues see Van den Berghe 1967). It is thus somewhat confusing when Celts or Jews are popularly referred to as racial groups (despite an absence of physically inherited criteria), when Asians are also popularly defined as a race in Britain (but not in, for example, India or Pakistan), and when women and men are excluded from categories of race despite their physical differences. Ultimately we have to identify an unofficial package of ideas and assumptions that go with race: that a racial group has historical legacies associated with a geographically defined area and culture of origin, and that usually such groups can be identified by skin colour. The stage is therefore set for xenophobia and bigotry because such people are seen as 'different' and 'foreign' (immigrant). As emphasized by Husband (1987) and Billig (1976), this label of 'different' can quickly be transformed to 'inferior' – especially when in the past certain authors (most notably Eysenck and Jensen) have argued for links between race and intelligence.

If arguments are proposed concerning racial inferiority, it must therefore follow that certain races are superior – herein lies the essence of **institutionalized** racist **ideology** which is often built on the assumption of a hierarchy of groups which range from sub- to super-human. Observers and interpreters of racism have been somewhat bemused by the recurring equation of superior race = dominant social order within society or the world order. Racism is thus seen as an institutionalized policy of **prejudice** and discrimination which is directed towards minorities characterized by colour and other forms of supposed **difference** by more powerful and established groups. Lawrence (1982) dissects **common sense** notions of race which support racism, and exposes the inherent contradictions of such dominant values and beliefs. Ultimately he reminds the reader about the inevitability of racist thought when the roots of common sense ideology are analysed.

Modern-day stereotypes and prejudices are undoubtedly linked with historical and institutional assumptions and practices. The great problem is that little progress seems to be made against racist ideologies – a point forcefully made by Hartman and Husband (1974) and Husband (ed.) (1987) as regards **representation** in media organizations and productions. Indeed the only time when powerful agencies appear to take notice of the politics of race is when violent action is observed, often a response to closure of all other legitimate channels of protest – rioting being the obvious example here (Tumber 1982; Gilroy 1987). Such responses represent a move from acceptance of inferiority and degradation to a position of rejection (associated with such diverse themes as **anti-language**, social mobility, exit from primary group, or exploration of cultural heritage).

Concern about preservation of law and order has finally placed race on training agendas for professions and occupations associated with face-to-face communication in society – most notably the police. Given the institutional form of ideologies of race, however, the extent to which educational programmes change more deep-seated values and attitudes, or whether they are nothing more than superficial window dressing should be questioned. If the latter is the case and society is viewed not as pluralist but as merely paying lip service to changing race inequalities then in the context of the UK, Gilroy's statement – 'there ain't no black in the union jack' is to be believed. There is no such thing as 'race' – but there is racism.

DS

See **class, consciousness, ethnic, group, minority, myth, nation, orientalism, power, prejudice, stereotype**
Further reading Gilroy (1987); Husband (ed.) (1987); Tajfel (1981); Van den Berghe (1967); Centre for Contemporary Cultural Studies (1982); Donald and Rattansi (eds) (1992); Van Dijk (1991)

realism ⋆ The use of representational devices (**signs, conventions, narrative** strategies, and so on) to depict or portray a physical, social or moral universe which is held to exist objectively beyond its representation by such means, and which is thus the arbiter of the truth of the representation. ⋆ Realism is often used almost interchangeably with other terms, like **naturalism** or *verisimilitude*, which were established in art/literary theories in the nineteenth century. In such usage, the concept often refers merely to the extent to which representational details resemble or concur with the knowledge of the object (which may be an emotion, theme or idea as well as a thing) that we already have. We won't find a circus scene set in ancient Rome 'realistic' if we spot a gladiator wearing a wristwatch – but we tend not to be upset by the fact that he's speaking English. Thus realism of this kind is above all **conventional** – we learn to recognize a fictive world as 'real' by means of certain devices.

Frequently the concept of realism is implicitly or explicitly contrasted with others. In philosophy, for instance, it is opposed to *idealism*, but it may be contrasted with fantasy, sentimentalism, the far-fetched, and so on. In these cases, realism tends to be used to describe not just **denotational** authenticity (verisimilitude), but attention to the grubbier or less edifying aspects of life. Here it is useful to remember that realism is a **multi-discursive** concept – it is also to be found in philosophy and politics. In political **rhetoric**, realism is often used to justify expedient policies which don't follow established moral principles. In **representations** too, the concept of realism can be used to justify attempts to break free of the conventions which tend to over-discipline an art form or medium once it has become routine.

This 'progressive' notion of realism was prevalent in the nineteenth century, and it gave rise to one of the more specialized (theorized) usages of the concept, deriving principally from the work of the Marxist literary theorist Lukács. He maintained that certain writers – Balzac and Dickens for instance – were able to escape their own personal class **prejudices** and **ideologies** in their writings, and represent the social totality of a **class** society. Realism in this context is a quality of writing or other representation which gets under the surface of ideology to reveal the 'true' relations between people and their source in class struggles. It follows that it is possible for representations to be realistic in this formulation without having to obey the demands of naturalism or verisimilitude. Conversely, representations can be naturalistic and full of verisimilitude without being recognized as realism. The distinction between realism and naturalism/verisimilitude in this case is not so much a property of a given text as of an ideology – it is the perceived 'truth to life' that qualifies a work for realism, and of course what 'truth to life' amounts to depends on what you're looking for. So realism as a critical concept is also the site of ideological struggle between different critical positions.

It is at this point that we can see that the concept of realism as used in the analysis of representations has lost little of its original (philosophical) force. That is, it still relies on an ideological commitment to an objective, external, reality (whether of time-less universal abstract notions like 'human nature', or of historical but objective facts like class struggle). Whatever it is, the status of external reality is privileged over its representation in whatever medium; our attention is directed *through* the representation to the 'truth' beyond.

In order to combat this tendency, and to assert instead that timeless notions and objective facts alike are all products of the discursive strategies that seem to 'reveal' them, recent **structuralist** and **semiotic** work has concentrated not so much on the 'what' as the 'how' of realism. This is also in response to realism's establishment as a routine in the screen media especially. Nowadays it is hard to find a television or film **genre** that doesn't have some claim to it. Within this kind of analysis, realism is seen as a signifying practice characteristic of bourgeois representations (but with a claim on all classes). It is, literally, made of devices such as characterization, **narration** and **mode of address**, which are reproduced over and over again in various guises. Thus, while realism itself seeks to suppress the act of representation in order to propose its version of truth as *the* truth, the analysis of realism turns the tables on it by restoring the act of representation to primacy and showing how realism is an effect not of 'life' but of **texts**.

JH

Further reading   Bennett *et al*. (eds) (1981a); Belsey (1980); Donald and Mercer (1982); Fiske (1987)

reality   ⋆ The sense or product of **discourse**. ⋆

JH

redundancy   ⋆ Predictability structured into a message or text, in order to facilitate accurate decoding or to strengthen social bonds – or both. ⋆   Redundancy aids accurate **decoding** in a number of ways:

    (1) It is used to overcome **noise** on the **channel**: to counteract static on radio we spell key words, and frequently increase the redundancy again by giving alphabetic checks to each letter – A for apple, S for sugar.

(2) It is used as a means of error detection and correction: because **language** is about 50 per cent redundant (or 50 per cent predictable) I know that 'seperate' is an error and I can correct it to 'separate' and thus prevent the error from affecting the communication. If there were no redundancy in language we would not be able to decipher bad handwriting, or understand broad accents, or ignore spelling mistakes.

(3) It helps overcome problems associated with the **audience**: the encoder will build more redundancy into the **message** if s/he predicts that the audience is not strongly motivated towards what s/he has to say, or if s/he knows that the message is aimed at a large, heterogeneous audience with a variety of backgrounds and motivations. Thus popular art is more redundant than highbrow art, and an ad for a chocolate bar is more redundant than a technical ad in a specialist journal.

(4) It helps overcome deficiencies of the medium: a lecture should be more redundant than a book, because the reader can create redundancy by reading a point again, whereas a listener cannot. Visual aids, which use one medium to duplicate or support another, are also ways of creating redundancy to facilitate accurate decoding.

These four functions are all essentially technical and derive from Shannon and Weaver's (1949) process **model**: they are most relevant when the prime aim of the message is to communicate **information**. But there are functions of redundancy that are social rather than technical, and that come into their own when the aim of the communication is **phatic**.

Redundancy strengthens social bonds in messages that are highly **conventional** and thus highly predictable. Saying 'Hello' when we meet someone may be totally redundant, but it strengthens or maintains our relationship. The refrain of a folk song is redundant, and singing it communally is a way of asserting our membership of the **group** or **subculture**. Popular television programmes like police series are predictable and redundant because they rely on the common tastes, expectations and experience of members of the culture that they serve. Enjoying a popular programme therefore, is an indirect way of expressing commonality with the millions of others who are also watching it: this expression frequently becomes direct when we discuss a programme with friends or workmates in order to confirm the shared tastes and experiences of the group to which we belong. Saying 'Hello', singing the refrain of a folk song, and participating in popular culture by the sharing of tastes and expectations with others are all examples of **phatic communication** whose aim is to strengthen social bonds, not to pass information.

But whether redundancy is working within informational or phatic communication, it is always evidence of a concern for the **receiver** or audience. The sender of messages with high redundancy, or the producer of popular **texts**, think more about their audiences than about themselves, or the uniqueness of what they have to say. They are concerned to establish commonality with their audience, rather than difference from it – they do not wish to emphasize their own expertise, originality, uniqueness or individual difference. Redundancy, therefore, plays an important, positive **role** in communication, and the lay meaning of 'something unnecessary' must be erased from our thinking.

JF

See **convention, elaborated and restricted codes, phatic communication**

reference ∗ Ogden and Richards's term for the mental image produced by the sign or symbol, and by the user's experience of its referent. ∗ It corresponds to Peirce's **interpretant**. Ogden and Richards's triangle of meaning models the relationship of **referent**, reference and symbol like this:

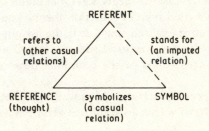

Note that Ogden and Richards's term '**symbol**' refers to what is now more commonly called a **sign**.

JF

See **interpretant** (for Peirce's corresponding model), **referent**

referent ⋆ Ogden and Richards's term for that to which a **sign** refers, or its denotative meaning. ⋆ It corresponds to Peirce's term **object**, and is defined in opposition to **reference**.

All theories and definitions of signs include the concept that signs must stand for something other than themselves, and other than the people using them: this is their *referent* or *object*. Sometimes we meet terms like 'external reality' or 'pre-cultural reality' which raise all sorts of questions about the nature of reality and whether we can apprehend it except through a sign system. The term *referent* manages to avoid this problem area by restricting its definition to 'that to which the sign refers'.

JF

See **reference**

reflection theory (mirror metaphor) ⋆ Any doctrine proposing that the object of study can have its form, substance or actions explained in terms of a form, substance or agency outside it. ⋆ In practice there are two common manifestations of reflection theory relevant to communication. The first is the doctrine that media **representations** and **discourses** reflect an already-existing and self-evident **reality** that exists independently of its representation in discourses including those of the media. This version of reflection theory is, of course, usually encountered as a negative: that the media don't, but ought to, reflect such a reality. The second type of reflection theory you might come across is a more specialized one – it is the assumption in some Marxist analysis that cultural and communicative practices and forms are reflections of the economic **base** of the society in question.

Reflection theory is rarely stated explicitly; in both variants it is usually reproduced within an argument as an unstated **model** or assumption which can remain uninspected because it is an 'obvious' kind of knowledge. The **metaphor** of reflection is in fact so **naturalized** that it is easy to use it unwittingly – even when you are aware of the dangers of taking the mirror metaphor literally.

JH

register ⋆ Stylistic variation in language according to its **context of situation** ⋆ The selection of words and structures by the language-user is strongly influenced by features of the situation. Indeed, utterances typically carry the imprint of their context so markedly and we are so attuned to contextual variation that we can often infer features of the original context of situation from quite fragmentary, isolated linguistic examples. For instance, most readers will feel confident that they can reconstruct the original context of situation for the following examples:

(1) 'I'm going to give you a prescription for the pain.'
(2) 'New Tubifast. The tubular dressing retention bandage. No sticking. No tying. No pinning.'

And so it will come as no surprise to hear that (1) is from a doctor–patient interview; and (2) is from a magazine advertisement. What is more difficult to explain is how we recognize the original context in each case. Why, for example is (1) not from an exchange in a pharmacy; and why is (2) not from a discussion between two nurses in casualty?

The finetuning that goes on between language and its context of situation operates along three independent parameters. First, the activity or topic on which the talk is based influences the kind of language used, particularly in the selection of vocabulary. Second, the nature of the social relationship will affect the language: talk between friends, for instance, is likely to avoid formal expressions, unless for ironic effect. And finally the medium of communication adopted – whether face-to-face speech, written text, telephone, dictaphone or whatever – will affect the way utterances are formed. These three parameters are known as *field*, *tenor* and *mode*, respectively. Collectively they shape the register of a particular **text**.

MM

See **context of situation, genre**
Further reading Halliday (1978); Montgomery (1986)

Reithian ✳ A term describing that set of cultural values, goals and practices embodied in the **public service broadcasting** ethos and policy established within the BBC during its formative years under the leadership of its first Director General, Lord John Reith. ✳ Most if not all studies of British **broadcasting** and the BBC have stressed the powerful historical legacy of Reith's leadership and his particular blueprint for a model public broadcasting service (see, for example, Burns 1977). In essence Reith's conception of the social role of broadcasting emphasized the idea of an autonomous, non-commercial, national service embodied in an **institution** somewhat akin to the Church, a service dedicated to the maintenance of the highest possible standards in shaping public taste by the provision of information, education and entertainment. The translation of this ideal into institutionalized **professional** broadcast practice, initially in the context of radio and later television, has attracted two major critical responses.

The first highlights the problem of the **autonomy** of the BBC, particularly from political intervention and control. Studies of the BBC's **role** in particular national crises, from the General Strike of 1926 onwards, have concluded that autonomy has not always been realized or maintained in practice (see, for example, Tracey 1977). Second, critics have pointed to the uncomfortable paradox in Reith's dedication to the highest cultural standards, arguing that the BBC represented and reproduced a narrow set of **elitist** standards and **values**, rather than serving the diverse needs of the British public as a whole. Any use of the term therefore needs to recognize and take into account these problems, and to consider the historical transformation of the Reithian ethos.

TO

See **autonomy, broadcasting, deregulation, elite, public service broadcasting**

Further reading   Burns (1977); Tracey (1977); Curran and Seaton (1991); MacCabe and Stewart (eds) (1986)

representation   ⋆ Representation is the social process of representing; representations are the products of the social process of representing. The term refers, therefore, both to the process and to the product of making **signs** stand for their **meanings**. ⋆   It is a useful concept because it unifies what appears at first sight to be an unconnected diversity of conceptual bits and pieces. Representation is the process of putting into concrete forms (that is, different **signifiers**) an abstract **ideological** concept: so you can look out for representations of women, workers, Wales; or of the family, love, war; or of individualism, industry, class, and so on.

Representation is the social process of making sense within all available **signifying** systems: speech, writing, print, video, film, tape, and so on. So if you're looking for representations of sexuality, for example, you'd soon discover that its representation is organized and regulated across different media, and within different **discourses**. It is represented both *as* and *in* pornography, but also in advertising, cinema, literature, various established discourses in speech, and in official and authoritative discourses such as legislation and educational practices. It soon becomes clear that sex has no 'natural being' that is represented uniformly in all these **forms** and discourses. For instance (to take a clear example), in total **institutions** like mental hospitals, prisons, public schools and armed forces it occurs in practice that homosexual sexual activity is regarded as less 'scandalous' than heterosexual sexual activity, even though the latter is overwhelmingly represented elsewhere as the **norm** and the natural and the only acceptable kind. Further, what is represented as sexual differs from form to form, time to time; and representations themselves also change. Hence, the concept of representation allows full force to the notion of re-presentation; the reworking and bringing into view of signifiers for the 'same' signified.

The term also has a political connotation, retained from its use in parliamentary **rhetoric**, where it refers to the fiction of democratic representation – where professionalized leaderships act socially (take **power**) on behalf of others whom they are said to represent. This usage should be allowed to echo noisily in the term's **semiotic** application, since it indicates how far any one representation 'stands for' the many others that might be used.

JH

response ⋆ A reaction to a **stimulus** which may be internally (inside the body) or externally (outside the body) located. In media studies the term is often used to refer to behaviour of an **audience** that results from interpreted **message** characteristics emanating from **channel** and **sender**. ⋆ The first interpretation refers extensively to learning theory, **behaviourism**, and **experimental** control whereas the second refers more to social psychology, **group** interaction, market research and **questionnaire** surveys.

DS

See **behaviourism**
Further reading Walker (1975)

rhetoric ⋆ The practice of using **language** to persuade or influence others and the language that results from this practice. The formal study of oratory, exposition, **persuasion**. ⋆ Rhetoric was a formal branch of learning in medieval Europe; one of the seven liberal arts or sciences, the others being grammar, logic (dialectics), then arithmetic, geometry, astronomy and music. It fell into serious disrepute and did not survive the Reformation. Rhetorical figures have survived, however, along with certain rhetorical terms (**metaphor**, for example) which have achieved the status of ordinary language.

Since **structuralism** began to disclose how much of what we know and **experience** is structured by the **sign** systems we inhabit and encounter, there has been a noticeable revival of interest in rhetoric. There are two good reasons for this. First, rhetoric as a branch of learning requires us to attend to the sign system itself (whether verbal or visual), and to concentrate on the devices and strategies that operate in **texts** themselves – it offers a well-established and elaborate set of terms and classifications we can use to see how sense is made, not by reference to imponderables like **authorial** intentions or 'truth to life' but by reference to actual **discourses**.

Second, if rhetoric didn't already exist it would no doubt have to be invented, since so many of the various forms of cultural production we're surrounded by are themselves highly rhetorical. Publicity, advertising, newspapers, television, academic books, government statements, and so on, all exploit rhetorical figures to tempt us to see things their way. If we have available a means to unpick these strategies we can begin to take a more critical and less intimidated stance towards them.

JH

Further reading Dyer (1982), chs 7 and 8, for a modern application of rhetorical analysis to advertising; Ong (1982), pp. 108–12, for an account of its history

ritual ★ Organized symbolic practices and ceremonial activities which serve to define and represent the social and cultural significance of particular occasions, events or changes. ★ The study of ritual has been a prominent focus for anthropologists, whose analysis of religious and magical rituals in pre-industrial **cultures** has been particularly influential.

Such studies have often distinguished between two main aspects of ritual. The first relates to what Van Gennep (originally published 1909: 1977) has termed *rites de passage*, those celebrations and ceremonies that mark socially defined changes in the lives of **individuals** and **groups**. Birthdays, marriages and many other changes in status or kinship relations, legal or social position are examples of occasions sequenced and signified by this form of ritual activity. Such rituals, then, **symbolize** the cultural recognition of transition and represent changes from one social stage, or state, to another. Mair (1972) suggests that they are often the meeting point for rituals of symbolic initiation, segregation and integration, whereby a 'new' social identity is gained or conferred. Berger (1973) suggests that they operate in both modern and pre-industrial societies to 'transform the individual event into a typical case, just as they transform the individual biography into an episode in the history of the society' (p. 62). In this way *rites de passage* mark and punctuate the passage of time and express the transitional rhythm of a group, community or society. This may be ritually expressed predominantly through representations of changes in nature, as in harvest festivals, celebrations for rain or growing seasons, or in ritual celebrations of particular historical events, such as Christmas, Independence Day, New Year and so on.

Such rituals, however, not only mark time (and hence serve to construct and confirm a sense of individual and collective identity, of cultural and historical location and transition), they also often operate to ensure success, security or a defined state of well-being for the individual or social group concerned. This second major aspect of rituals concerns the ways in which they function to procure symbolic (often supernatural) intervention and assistance in achieving certain desired objectives. Worsley (1957), for example, in his study of cargo cults in Melanesia, demonstrates how particular cult rituals (apparently irrational to the outsider) served to express and represent a form of symbolic response and expression to the experience of rapid social and cultural change through colonization. In this way much anthropological evidence points to the intensification of ritual activity in situations of social instability, or when the 'normality' of individuals or a community is perceived as threatened in some way.

The term has been rather unevenly developed from this anthropological base, although it has clearly entered the analysis of modern industrial cultures, their institutions and forms of social interaction. As a result it is often used in a more general and secular sense to refer to sets of recurrent rule-governed practices which are of symbolic significance for either individuals or particular social groups. In this sense the term may face the problem of over-inclusion, it becomes 'stretched' to the point where it is difficult to distinguish activities that are *not* in some way ritualized. Some useful examples of its recent use in the study of culture and communication are provided below.

TO

See **culture, institutions, non–verbal communication, ritual condensation**

Further reading   Bocock (1974); Leach (1976); Mair (1972); Turner (1974)

Examples   Goffman (1967); Elliott (1980); Marsh *et al.* (1978); Hall and Jefferson (eds) (1976)

ritual condensation   * A kind of cultural reasoning process, wherein abstract ideas, **myths** and so on, are projected on to the external world in a condensed form, in which form they can be subjected to test and modification, or to affirmation and celebration, by being enacted in **rituals** which enable the abstract ideas to be grasped in concrete but active ways. *

The notion of ritual condensation comes from anthropology, where it is used to show how abstract notions like good versus bad come to be condensed into simple material or natural forms – white versus black, for example. In this condensed form, the process and product of human reasoning can be shared socially and understood as objective. As Leach (1976) points out, you can do more complex calculations more easily with a calculator or with pencil and paper than you can with mental arithmetic; similarly cultures think their way through abstract problems more easily with artefacts than with 'mentifacts'.

One way in which ritual condensations may be active in modern cultures is through the medium of television. Within its everyday fare of action series and drama serials, television **condenses** abstract, impersonal ideas into concrete **forms**, and 'thinks through' their implications in the form of dramas between characters in situations. Characters rarely make sense merely as conflicting personalities, they are also **representations** of abstract oppositions – good:evil, normal:deviant, efficient:inefficient, nature:culture, individual:institution, active:passive, and so on. These condensed abstractions can then be **ritualized** in the form

269

of dramatic conflict or **violence**, so that a bar–room brawl becomes, in effect, a 'calculating machine' by means of which the abstract ideas can be 'thought through' in an ordered and logical way, and the outcome of the brawl corresponds to the QED of a mathematical theorem.

JH

See **bardic function, binary opposition, condensation, discourse, ritual**
Further reading Leach (1976); Fiske and Hartley (1978)

role/roles ⋆ Socially defined positions and patterns of behaviour which are characterized by specific sets of rules, norms and expectations which serve to orientate and regulate the interaction, conduct and practices of individuals in social situations. ⋆ We often think of roles in the theatrical or dramatic sense, as referring to those parts played or performed by actors or actresses in a play or drama. In the study of social and cultural relations, roles, by extension of this theatrical idea, refer to all the different 'parts' that may be 'played' by **individuals** (actors and actresses) as they **interact** (perform) in different **contexts** (scenes and acts) within a particular society (the overall drama, play or theatre). Both on and off stage, individuals occupying certain positions or roles within society are expected to 'act' and behave in certain predictable ways, to follow and **conform** to certain **rules** and **norms** that seem to exist independently of the particular individuals involved. We are **socialized** into these sets of expectations, often taking for granted the ways in which they define and classify the social world into seemingly endless and obvious relations between men, women, bakers, brothers, politicians, friends, and so on. The central point here is that roles always exist in relation to other roles: the occupational role of doctor, for example, implies and relates to the roles of patient, nurse and consultant, different roles which carry different expectations and degrees of **power** and **status**.

Like actors, people play many different and changing roles throughout life, and at any one point in time are involved in a multiplicity of different roles and role relations. As a student, for example, you may also be female, a friend, a union member, a cousin, sometimes a guest, a car driver, a customer, and so on. Not all of these roles can be played at the same time – significantly they may sometimes contradict, leading to 'role conflict' – and neither are they all equal or identical. Anthropological studies of roles and 'role systems' in different **cultures**, for example, have distinguished between roles that are socially *ascribed* to individuals at birth, or by virtue of age or kinship position, and roles that are socially *achieved* with access dependent upon individual performance, competition and qualification (Linton 1963).

While the term is commonly used in discussions and descriptions of social interaction and communication, its analytical value and explanatory power have been questioned. Too often it assumes a static, **consensual**, over-determining and over-simplified view of social relations, thereby neglecting both individuals and structures of power and inequality.

DS

See **dramaturgy, institutions, norm/normative, performance, rules, interaction**
Further reading Worsley (ed.) (1977); Banton (1965); Bilton *et al.* (1981)

rules ⋆ The means by which all social and cultural relations are in varying degrees constituted, guided and regulated. ⋆ In this broad sense, the discussion and study of rules serves as a useful way into a number of debates and problems that are central to communication studies. Rules may be defined at a number of different levels, and in terms of a variety of functions. An initial point to consider must be the extent to which *all* social and communicative activity is rule-governed. The immediate difficulty here is that in **interaction** we are not constantly aware of rules and their operations. We recognize *explicit* rules, particularly in as much as they have direct consequences for regulating our own aims and actions, much more easily than we do *implicit* or 'ground' rules which may be said to constitute the wider boundaries and frameworks of that interaction.

Cicourel (1964) calls those of the latter type 'basic rules' and emphasizes their predominantly unspoken and unexamined nature, and the way in which they operate to define the world as 'taken for granted'. However precariously, they construct and mediate collective and individual senses of 'normality', ordering and marking out how we expect and predict the world to be. In this sense, rules at the *implicit* level can be seen as important elements of the largely hidden social and cultural **codes** which enable people and groups to relate, communicate and interact in socially meaningful and predictable ways. As a strategy for their exposure, many discussions of *implicit* rules draw an **analogy** between aspects of 'real life' situations or social encounters, and games. It is easier to appreciate the sense in which games are constituted, or made possible by their rule structures. Any game (by definition) is impossible without its 'map' of rules that serves to define the frameworks and 'spaces' (spatial, temporal or strategic) within which players must or may, move, act and interrelate. Players involved in a particular game constantly recognize and negotiate *explicit* rules, the formal regulations governing what you specifically can or cannot do under certain circumstances. Under-pinning these are levels of implicitly taken-for-granted rules, which even the players themselves rarely call into question or examine (for example the rule that a football pitch has a goal at either end is seldom questioned). In this way, Brittan (1973) argues, 'Games, as played consciously, are merely a symbolic formalization of basic social process' (pp. 130–1).

In many instances of social interaction and communication, because we are experienced or practised 'players', we tend to accept implicitly the rules defining the 'game'. None the less they are there, marking out boundaries and organizing by including and excluding, **encoding** and **decoding**, **orientating** and relating. The main reason that we do not constantly think of ourselves as acting in relation to implicit rules for the majority of the time is because they have been internalized, made implicit through **socialization**. In a sense they become part of ourselves, our habits, beliefs and convictions about how things should normally be done.

Explicit rules on the other hand do tend to be recognized; they are usually directive and regulate social interaction in a more

272

prescriptive and visible way than their implicit counterparts. It may be useful to think of them as varying in degrees of openness and **closure** (open and closed forms). The most obvious concrete examples of rules are closed and imperative, such as formally coded regulations, orders and prohibitions. These explicitly dictate what is expected and demanded in certain contexts (no jeans; no smoking; no talking; drive on the right; essays to be handed in by Friday; and so on). They usually carry formal sanctions or penalties for **deviance** or disregard. Open forms of explicit rules allow more fully for individual independence, negotiation or discretion. They do not strongly prescribe or dictate one narrow course or option; rather they offer a range or choice of possible and permissible ways of **conforming**. These are closer to **norms** or **conventions**, and examples would typically include reference to how things are normally done (dress smartly; drive carefully; eat politely; speak correctly; and so on).

Rules therefore operate at a variety of shifting levels and in differing forms. An important point to bear in mind is that they are always **context**-specific. That is, they are part of a particular situation, **(sub)culture**, historical period, and so on. It is equally vital to recognize that we are always potentially faced with the option of 'breaking out', or deviating from rules. In general terms rules become more apparent and visible when they are broken, although individuals who break any rules run the risk of facing a variety of sanctions or penalties.

Given their centrality in social and cultural relations it should not be surprising that rules are subject to considerable theoretical contest and debate. For example, **consensus** perspectives tend to stress their integrative (constitutive) social function, interpreting the existence of rules as evidence for the fundamentally shared and organized unity of social life. Against this view, conflict perspectives emphasize regulation and control, and the ways in which rules imply power relations between at a basic level groups of *rulers*, and groups who are more or less successfully *ruled*. In this sense rules are central to the ways in which forms of dominance (and by extension forms of subordination) are achieved, defined and reproduced. In both of these perspectives the study of rules within interaction and communication is inseparable from wider theories of social and cultural process and structure. They are both to some extent countered by the **symbolic interactionist** emphasis upon rules as constantly (re)negotiated elements of creative situated contexts, always 'up for grabs' and potentially unstable.

TO

See **code, conformity, consensus, convention, deviance, norm/normative, power, simulation**

Further reading Douglas (ed.) (1973); Worsley (ed.) (1977); Brittan (1973)

rumour ⋆ Unofficial and unaccredited **discourses**; the end result of unverified information that has developed over a number of stages within a communication system. ⋆ As information is passed on at each stage, some distortion in accuracy often occurs. With rumour the essential feature is that the **receiver** of information is unaware of the inaccuracy and thus attempts to **transmit** such a version to the next link within a social network. After a number of such distortions the product may of course be markedly different from the original source. The selective loss of information over time can be attributed to **cognitive** processes associated with **perception**, *attention*, **memory** and the construction of **schemata**.

The growth of *media* communications enhances such an effect and has modified the more traditional interpretation of rumour as always involving face-to-face contact between people. One example concerns the continual reporting of pending breakups of British Royal marriages in the late 1980s and early 1990s. A number of rumours followed the same pattern: unofficial statements concerning possible romance which were then amplified through newspaper coverage and followed by official denial. What began at the face-to-face level ended up as official regulation at the societal level. Because of the near-simultaneous transmission of information associated with some mass media it may even be the case that the reporting of rumour as fact actually legitimizes such information and leads to it becoming part of the verbal or literary heritage of a community. Such a legitimization process defies the typically short life-span of rumour, secures inaccurate information within history, and likens rumour to folk-tale.

DS

See **cognition, media, memory, schemata**
Further reading Hunter (1964); Evans (ed.) (1969); Shibutami (1966)

S

schema/schemata ⋆ A schema (sometimes called scheme), plural schemata (or schemes), may best be viewed as a **model** (Baddeley 1976) or as a mini–system (Phillips 1981) by which we internalize, structure and make sense of an event. ⋆ The term is used to explain how established ways of understanding, or ways of structuring *experience*, are used to make sense of new situations. The new is made to fit the pattern of the familiar.

This would explain the distortion of novel information so that it fits in with existing expectations: a useful account of information loss or distortion within communication processes. With reference to **cognitive** development, Piaget has referred to schemata as **symbolic** representations that are assimilated within an intellectual framework. For example, a child might assimilate the **sign** 'pram' and this then provides a future understanding or reference point for other restricting yet mobile objects.

Ultimately, complementary schemata may be organized into some coherent structure or mental map. As such, they may be modified or replaced as more and more events and relationships are assimilated and acted upon, or as cognitive structuring becomes more advanced.

DS

See **cognition, memory**
Further reading Phillips (1981); Neisser (1976)

semantics ⋆ The study of meaning from a linguistic perspective.
⋆ Semantics aims to analyse and explain how meanings are
expressed in language. Current enquiry seems to be organized
around three important distinctions.

(1) Sense versus reference The meaning of a linguistic expression – a word, for instance – can be treated in terms of its
connection with extra-linguistic reality. Thus, the meaning of the
word 'chair' lies in its capacity to refer outwards from the language to objects like the one on which you may be sitting as you
read this entry. From a different perspective, however, the meaning of a word can be considered in terms of its relationship to
other words in the language. Thus, the meaning of the word
'chair' lies in its relationship with other words such as 'furniture',
'table', 'seat', 'bench', etc. A famous example of the distinction
between sense and **reference** is the way in which objectively the
same planet – Venus – can be referred to equally appropriately as
'the morning star' and 'the evening star', since it has the capacity
to shine brightly in both the morning sky and the evening sky.
Consequently, the two expressions 'the morning star' and 'the
evening star' have an identical **referent**, although the sense of
each expression is of course quite different. More attention in
semantics has been given to the area of sense relations than to that
of reference, in line with Wittgenstein's dictum: 'the meaning of a
word is its use in the language'.

But ignoring either side of the contrast between sense and
reference tends to lead to unbalanced theories of meaning and this
can have consequences that go beyond the domains of linguistic
theory. It is worth noting, for instance, that rival **aesthetic**
theories can be divided into two camps depending upon whether
they tend to favour one or other side of the distinction between
reference and sense: **realist** theories favour art that appears to
mirror or **reflect** reality in as direct a way as possible; other more
Formalist theories, however, stress the **conventionality** of artistic **representation** and see art, and more particularly literature, as
a continual experiment with meaning (or 'sense'). Contemporary
literary theory tends to be very strong on the conventional bases
of meaning, so much so that at times it seems to deny the
possibility of any reality at all outside language. At the very least,

it insists that reality is not **mediated** to us directly, but is constructed through acts of meaning, so that we have no direct access to it outside of language. One pitfall of this position is that it can lead to a species of idealism in which reality is spoken into existence through language, and arguments about interpretation become avowedly **subjective**, to the exclusion of **culture** and history as material process.

In modern semantics sense relations have been treated in terms of the following major relationships that words can have with each other.

(1) *Synonomy*: expressions which can be used in identical ways are considered synonymous; by which criterion an expression such as *to ponder* is held to be synonymous with *to meditate*, or *loutish* is held to be synonymous with *uncouth*.

(2) *Antonymy*: expressions which reverse the meaning of each other in some way are considered to be antonymous. Thus, the pairs *woman/man*, *fast/slow*, *up/down*, *good/bad* and so on all express relations of antonymy.

(3) *Hyponomy*: expressions may also operate in hierachical relations of meaning where the meaning of one expression includes that of another. Thus, the expression *dog* is a hyponym of the expression *animal*, the latter being a superordinate term for a range of co–hyponyms with *dog*, such as *cat, monkey, giraffe, rabbit*, and so on. *Dog* itself, of course, is a superordinate term for another range of hyponyms such as *terrier, hound, retriever*, etc.

Synonymy, antonymy and *hyponomy* consist, therefore, of differing kinds of sense relations possible within the vocabulary of a language. They provide a way of conceptualizing the construction of meaning as it goes on within the linguistic system. In this respect it is worth emphasizing that they display linguistic and not 'real–world' classification. There is no reason in the real world why terms for animals should be organized in the particular types of sense relation adopted in English, as becomes immediately apparent when comparisons in particular areas of meaning are made between languages. According to Whorf (1956), the Hopi tribe of North America, for example, used one word *masaytaka* to designate all flying objects except birds. Thus, they actually designated an insect, an aeroplane and an aviator by the same word, whereas English provides quite separate lexical items.

(2) Word meaning versus sentence meaning　Other approaches to the meaning of words involve notions such as semantic features and **collocation**. Whatever approach is adopted, however, it does not seem possible to account for the meaning of a sentence merely by building upwards from the individual words that make it up. Otherwise 'Man bites dog' would mean the same thing as 'Dog bites man'. None the less, it seems possible that there may be parallels between the kind of sense relation we have described between words and those that exist between sentences. A sense relation such as synonymy, for instance, may be considered to hold not only between individual words but between whole sentences. Thus 'Sidney sold the book to Sheila' may be considered to be synonymous with 'Sheila bought the book from Sidney' and the same kind of relation can be claimed between 'The police arrested the miners' and 'The miners were arrested by the police'. Other kinds of relationship that can hold between sentences are those of **entailment** and *presupposition*. *Entailment* is a relation whereby, given two sentences A and B, A semantically entails B if under all conditions in which A is true, B is also true. Thus, a sentence such as 'Achilles killed Hector' entails 'Hector is dead'. In these cases B follows from A as a logical consequence. If it is true that Achilles killed Hector, then Hector must as a logical consequence be dead. *Presuppositional* relations are somewhat different. Basically, whereas negation will alter a sentence's entailments, it will leave presuppositions in place. Consider the sentence (i) 'Sidney managed to stop in time'. From this we may infer both that (ii) 'Sidney stopped in time' and also that (iii) 'Sidney tried to stop in time'. These inferred sentences, however, do not behave in quite the same way. Sentence (ii) 'Sidney stopped in time' is a logical consequence of sentence (i) – an entailment – and it does not survive under the negation of (i) – 'Sidney did not manage to stop in time'. Sentence (iii), however, is a presupposition; and whilst the original entailment now no

longer holds, the presupposition that 'Sidney tried to stop in time' still survives intact.

These kinds of distinctions are important for the analysis of meaning in all kinds of discourse. **Ideological** claims, for instance, are often promoted implicitly rather than explicitly, covertly rather than overtly; and they often need to be recovered from the presuppositions or entailments of a discourse rather than from its surface assertions. Thus, when a Ministry of Defence pamphlet urged that 'Britain must do everything in its power . . . to deter Russia from further acts of aggression', various unargued propositions were merely presupposed; notably, for example: (i) 'Britain has power' and (ii) 'Russia is committing acts of aggression'.

(3) Text versus context The third major area of inquiry and debate is addressed to issues such as how much of meaning is created and carried by the linguistic system and how much and in what way it is determined by crucial characteristics of the context in which any utterance is grounded. Indeed, some aspects of meaning previously considered to be semantic – i.e. part of the linguistic system itself – are now being treated as part of **pragmatics**.

The history of linguistics during the last sixty years can be read in terms of a continual deferral of the study of meaning. Indeed, the progression during this time has been very much from the smaller units of linguistic organization, such as the **phoneme** to the larger, such as the *sentence* or **text**; it has also been a progression from substance (**phonology**) to significance (semantics). **Meaning**, however, has at last come centre stage, and the last ten years has seen an immense burgeoning of work in both semantics and pragmatics. Meaning, of course, cannot be other than the ultimate goal of linguistic enquiry; and findings in this area undoubtedly have important consequences for associated areas of scholarship such as media studies, literary criticism, interpretive sociology, or **cognitive** science, in all of which issues of meaning are often at the centre of debate.

MM

See **collocation, discourse, multi-accentuality, pragmatics, semiotics, speech act**
Further reading   Lyons (1981)

semiotics/semiology   ★ The study of the social production of meaning from sign systems. ★   Semiotics isn't so much an academic discipline as a theoretical approach and its associated methods of analysis. It has not become widely institutionalized as a 'subject'.

An indication of semiotics' provisional and marginal status is that it is still usually defined in the terms first proposed by its so-called 'father', the Swiss linguist Ferdinand de Saussure. He suggested a 'science that studies the life of signs within society', in a book published in 1916. The suggestion was taken up principally by the French **structuralist** Roland Barthes, who was chiefly responsible for popularizing and extending semiotics in the 1960s.

Semiotics as an intellectual enterprise endeavours to reveal and analyse the extent to which **meanings** are produced out of the structural relations that exist within any **sign** system, and not from the external reality they seem so naturally to depict. Since it is committed to the notion of systematic relations operating in abstract structures (that is, structures that cannot be observed directly, like **language**), semiotics has a tendency towards abstraction, formalism and lack of historical grounding. However, since it is equally committed to the *social* production of meaning (language cannot be invented by individuals) semiotics has always sought to relate the production of meanings to other kinds of social production and to social relations.

Semiotics as a method takes its terminology from linguistics and uses spoken language as the prime example of a sign system. However, its growth and success is not so much in the analysis of speech as of other sign systems, especially literature, cinema, publicity, photography and television. In fact semiotics has become associated largely with the increasingly serious study of various forms of **popular culture**. It has been especially useful in this context, since popular culture was previously a very neglected field in academic study, and such attention as it did receive was often either highly derogatory or else a limited side branch of American **empirical** sociology. Semiotics does not, in principle at least, approach popular culture with prior notions of artistic or moral merit by which to judge a given **text** (an approach common in certain kinds of literary criticism) and unlike empirical sociology it is able to deal with the single text rather than with large-scale patterns.

Thus semiotics is in the first place text-centred, since it is devoted to analysing how **meaning systems** produce meanings via texts. But as it has developed, greater attention has been paid to the role of the **reader** in realizing or producing meanings out of textual resources in an interactive way. Thus semiotics began by showing how texts were structured reworkings of the signs, **codes**, and so on of their particular sign systems, and how these structures generated **myths**, **connotations**, and so on. It went on to demonstrate how such textual structures and devices as point-of-view, **mode of address** or **preferred reading** proposed or even fixed a position from which sense could be made by a reader – the positioning of the **subject**. At this point it became clear that 'actual' readers might not necessarily occupy the position proposed for them by **ideological** texts and **discourses**, and further that hitherto too much attention had been paid to the **cognitive** or rational activities involved in reading, and not sufficient to the **pleasure** and desire involved. Thus semiotics was forced to take account of the social processes in which texts are encountered, and of the role of pleasure in these social processes.

Clearly such issues as these are not the exclusive preserve of semiotics, and there has in fact been a fruitful cross-fertilization between it and other intellectual enterprises, notably **psychoanalytical theory**, Marxism, feminism and various sociological approaches.

The distinctive feature of semiotics remains, however, its attempt to specify in general and in detail how meaning is socially produced (not individually created), and subject to **power** relations and struggles just like other kinds of social production. When it turns its attention to the individual reader, this should not be understood as a return to the free-floating abstract **individual** but rather the individual/subject whose individuality is largely a product of the ideological discourses and signifying practices which s/he inhabits or encounters in social relations.

JH

See **cultural studies, structuralism**
Further reading Culler (1976, 1983); Hawkes (1977); Fiske (1982)

sender/receiver ★ Broadly, the key points at the beginning and end of the linear process model of communication, though in some models they may be preceded by terms like *source*, and followed by ones like *reaction*. ★ The terms *sender* and *receiver* are the most general ones, easily understood by the layperson, but within their area of meaning we will come across a number of more specific terms. The most common of these are:

Encoder/decoder Using these terms can imply that we think of the **message** as having an abstract existence to which encoding gives a concrete **form** that can be transmitted. Decoding can then restore it to its original abstract content or meaning. This is the implication of their use within the process school. But these terms (or more commonly their verbal forms *encoding* and *decoding*) are also used in the **semiotic**, linguistic school. Here they imply that a **text** is composed of a number of codes which are derived from other texts and cultural products: encoders and decoders who share broadly similar **codes** (as a result of broadly similar **cultural experience**) will generate broadly similar meanings in the text, but those with different cultural experience, and thus different codes, may find their meanings differ significantly.

Addresser/addressee These terms are used by Jakobson, a linguist, and they imply a relationship between the two parties, within which certain **modes of address** are appropriate. An addresser has an **orientation** towards the addressee that affects the form and function of the message.

Transmitter/receiver These are pieces of technology used to extend human powers of transmission and thus the range of **communication**, but are sometimes used in the process school to refer to human beings.

Author/reader Those involved in the semiotic act of encoding and decoding (see above). The reader is as creative as the author, as both bring to the **text** their cultural experience via the codes that they use. The author may, through textual means, try to impose his or her 'authority' on the reader (that is, may guide him/her to a **preferred reading**), but can never do so absolutely. The reader is where the **signifying** system of the text intersects with the **value** system of the culture, and reading is the generation of meaning that results.

JF

sense/sense relations ⋆ The communicative value assumed by a word or expression by virtue of its place within a linguistic system. ⋆ The precise **value** of a word or expression may be explored in terms of its sense relations with other words in the system. Particular kinds of sense relation include those of *antonymy*, *synonymy*, and *hyponomy* (see **semantics**), which are relations of opposite meaning, identical meaning and included meaning, respectively. All words and expressions, of course, are capable of sustaining multiple senses, though context usually works to highlight one sense and exclude others.

MM
See **meaning, multi–accentuality, polysemic, pragmatics, semantics**
Further reading Lyons (1981)

sign ⋆ A sign has three essential characteristics: it must have a physical form, it must refer to something other than itself, and it must be used and recognized by people as a sign. ⋆ Barthes gives the example of a rose: a rose is normally just a flower, but if a young man presents it to his girl friend it becomes a sign, for it refers to his romantic passion, and she recognizes that it does.

Signs, and the ways they are organized into **codes** or languages, are the basis of any study of communication. They can have a variety of **forms**, such as words, gestures, photographs or architectural features. **Semiotics**, which is the study of signs, codes and culture, is concerned to establish the essential features of signs, and the ways they work in social life.

Saussure divides a sign into its two constituent elements – the **signifier** (its physical form as perceived by our senses), and the **signified** (the mental concept of what it refers to). Peirce thinks that there are three types of signs – **icons, indexes** and **symbols**. Both these early authorities have had a considerable influence over later work in this area.

Saussure stresses that a sign can properly be understood only in relation to other signs in the same code or system: its meaning is determined partly by other signs which it is not. The significance of a bowler hat is clear only when we say it is not a topper, and not a trilby. The sign BOY is understood as not-MAN or not-GIRL, and MAN as not-ANIMAL, or not-GOD. As a linguist, Saussure is primarily interested in the relation of signs to each other within a code, and in the relationship of signifer to signified within a sign. He is less interested in the relationship of a sign to its **referential** reality (which he calls **signification**).

Peirce, on the other hand, gives this relationship at least as much emphasis as others. He, like his followers Ogden and Richards, takes the viewpoint of a philosopher, and believes that a sign can be studied only in relationship to two other elements which we can simplify into the terms *mind* and *referential reality*. His terms for them are, respectively, the **interpretant** and the **object**; Ogden and Richards's terms are the **reference** and the **referent**.

JF

See **signification, signifier, symbol**

signal ⋆ In communication theory, the physical form that the message is given in order to be transmitted: the term does not refer to the content or meaning, but only to the physical existence or form of the message. ⋆

JF

signification ⋆ For Saussure, the relationship of a **sign** or sign system to its referential reality. ⋆ Barthes makes much more of the concept, and uses it to refer to the way that signs work in a **culture**: he adds the dimension of cultural **values** to Saussure's use of the term.

Barthes identifies two *orders of signification*: the first is that of *denotation* (which is what Saussure calls 'signification'), the second is that of *connotation* and *myth* and occurs when the first order meanings of the sign meet the values and established **discourses** of the culture.

The first order of signification: denotation   This refers to the simple or literal relationship of a sign to its **referent**. It assumes that this relationship is **objective** and value-free – for all their differences, the words 'horse', 'steed' and 'nag' all denote the same animal. The mechanical/chemical action of a camera in producing an image of what it is pointed at is denotation. The concept is generally of use only for analytical purposes; in practice there is no such thing as an objective, value-free order of signification except in such highly specialized languages as that of mathematics: $4 + 8 = 12$ is a purely denotative statement.

The second order of signification: connotation   This occurs when the denotative meaning of the sign is made to stand for the value-system of the culture or the person using it. It then produces associative, expressive, **attitudinal** or evaluative shades of meaning. In photography the mechanical/chemical process produces denotative meanings, but the human intervention in the choice of features such as focus, framing and lighting produces the connotative. Connotation, then, is determined by the form of the signifier: changing the signifier while keeping the same signified on the first order is the way to control the connotative meanings. Examples are: two photographs of the same girl, one in sharp focus, the other in soft; the same word spoken in different tones of voice, or printed in different typefaces; or the choice between 'horse', 'nag' and 'steed'. Connotation works through style and tone, and is concerned with the *how* rather than the *what* of communication.

The second order of signification: myth   Barthes's rather specialized use of the term **myth** refers to a chain of concepts widely accepted throughout a culture, by which its members conceptualize or understand a particular topic or part of their social experience. Thus our *myth* of the countryside, for example, consists of a chain of concepts such as it is good, it is natural, it is spiritually refreshing, it is peaceful, it is beautiful, it is a place for leisure and recuperation. Conversely, our *myth* of the city contains concepts such as unnaturalness, constriction, work, tension, stress. These myths are arbitrary with respect to their referents, and culture-specific. In the eighteenth century, for example, the city was *mythologized* as good, civilized, urbane, polite; the countryside as bad, uncivilized, rude, primitive. A typical twentieth-century advertisement shows a happy family picnicking in a meadow beside a stream, with their car parked in the background. The mother is preparing the meal, the father and son are kicking a football, and the daughter is picking flowers. The ad acts as a trigger to activate our *myths* of countryside, family, sex **roles**, work-and-leisure, and so on. To understand this ad we must bring to it our 'ways of conceptualizing' these topics (or our myths): if we do not have these myths, the ad will mean something different to us, or may not mean very much at all. The term *myth*, then, is not to be used in the layperson's sense of a 'false belief', but in the anthropological sense of 'a culture's way of conceptualizing an abstract topic'. Myths are conceptual and operate on the plane of the signified; connotations are evaluative, emotive and operate on the plane of the signifier.

Signification and ideology: the third order Fiske and Hartley (1978) suggest that the connotations and myths of a culture are the manifest signs of its **ideology**. The way that the varied connotations and myths fit together to form a coherent pattern or sense of wholeness, that is, the way they 'make sense', is evidence of an underlying invisible, organizing principle – ideology. Barthes identifies a similar relationship when he calls connotators (the signifiers of connotation) 'the **rhetoric** of ideology'; Fiske and Hartley suggest that it may be helpful to think of ideology as the third order of signification.

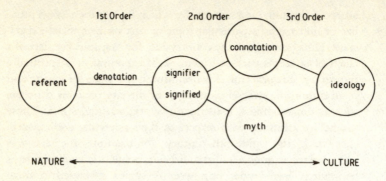

See **code, ideology, intersubjectivity, signifier/signified**

signifier/signified ⋆ The pair of concepts which together constitute a **sign** according to Saussure. He models them thus:

The signifier is the physical form of the sign as we perceive it
through our senses – the sound of a word or the appearance of a
photograph. The signified is the user's mental concept of what the
sign refers to. ⋆ The relationship between the two can be either
arbitrary or **iconic**. In the arbitrary sign there is no necessary
relationship between the signifier and the signified: the signifier
takes the form it does by **convention** or agreement among its
users. In the iconic sign, the nature of the signified influences the
form of the signifier: the signifier looks or sounds like its signified
(see **motivation (of the sign)**).

It is important to realize that these two terms are used for
analytical convenience only: a sign cannot actually be split into
signifier and signified any more than a coin can be split into heads
and tails. Saussure believed that the arbitrary nature of verbal
language is the main reason for its complexity, subtlety and
ability to perform a wide range of functions.

JF

See **motivation (of the sign), sign, signification**

simulation/game ⋆ A process which involves a working representation of reality for the purpose of learning by doing. ⋆ Strictly speaking, simulation can easily refer to other concepts such as **model** and **experiment** because they also set up artificial worlds of activity which are supposed to mirror reality. For communication and cultural studies the concern is with using simulations and games as a methodological device that proves useful for experiential learning. This involves a student-centred approach which aims for practical learning and exploration of a number of issues associated with communication. These approaches have rapidly gained in popularity within both secondary and tertiary education and complement (and even replace) more traditional 'chalk and talk' teaching techniques (see Jones 1985; Marshall and Williams 1986; Crookall and Saunders (eds) 1989). The concept of *game* can be used synonymously with *simulation* because both involve the negotiation of rules and roles within make-believe contexts, and often with some element of competition involved. When a distinction can be made, it usually involves the identification of winning and losing players in games, whereas simulations involve participants who may co-operate as well as compete.

Media simulations and games are one area for illustration. For example, Front Page (Jones 1986) asks participants to make up the front page of a daily newspaper from fictitious stories already provided. What's News (Gamson 1984) involves a similar editing process but this time for televised news, and with real stories. At the end of the exercise it is possible to compare the finished product with the actual news programme broadcast by one of the USA's television networks. Another area of relevance is that of **role** play (van Ments 1983), which illustrates aspects of interpersonal communication and conflict between and within groups. The most powerful example is Starpower (Shirts 1971), which allows one particular group to change the rules of play half way through – invariably it does this to its own advantage, a process that mirrors patterns of dominance, discrimination and **power** relations within many social contexts.

Care should be taken with such activities, because the game element associated with competition and winning can very easily victimize people or set up hostility within groups. Indeed, the frequent criticism of simulation gaming – that it is make-believe and therefore irrelevant – is often rejected because such artificiality is forgotten once people become involved. It is up to the organizer or facilitator (rather than 'teacher') to ensure that a thorough discussion of events takes place after the exercise finishes – what is technically called *debriefing*. This is the most serious failing of many exercises: not enough time is devoted to analysis of what happened because of poor planning or because participants got carried away with the activity and could not stop. Successful debriefing, however, will include discussion of theoretical themes associated with the discovery, changing and breaking of rules, codes of conduct, and even of self-identity associated with the playing of a part in role play situations. Conceptual issues will also be explored: with the previously mentioned media simulations, typical issues in debriefing would include **stereotyping**, sensationalism, editing, **censorship**, **agenda setting** and **amplification** (see Dyer 1982). The great advantage, therefore, is that simulations provide practical experience which can then be drawn on to illustrate and explore mainstream issues in communication studies. As Williams (1976b) says, one great problem is that certain educational authorities – what we might call 'pedagogic dinosaurs' – can prevent such application because of a traditional resistance to adults learning through play.

DS

See **dramaturgy, experience, experiment, methodology, role**

Further reading Crookall and Saunders (eds) (1989); Williams (1976b); Jones (1986)

socialization ∗ A central concept, which in its widest application refers to all those complex and multi-faceted processes and interactions that transform the human organism into an active participating member of a society. ∗ In short the term refers to the ways in which we both become and are made social; White (1977), for example, suggests that it describes the 'long and complicated process of learning to live in society' (p. 1). While many writers would agree on this general definition, the study of socialization is better viewed as a site for a number of problems and issues which are themselves the product of clashes between differing conceptions of the structure of societies, the nature of social and cultural relations, and the individual subject. The initial question to consider here is what **individuals**, or **groups**, are socialized *into*. This can be posed in a number of ways. First, what at birth do we or people enter *into*, into what **cultures**, sets of **values**, **rules**, **ideologies** and social conditions are we socialized, a process often referred to as **cultural transmission**? Second, either as a result or in reaction to this what do we *become*? This issue is interwoven with debates concerning the origins and development of our **subjectivity**, our sense of self and **individual** identity. These questions themselves serve to raise a further set of problems concerning the 'how' of socialization – how and by what agencies is such a process achieved? Is the process to be viewed as guided by an almost mechanical pre-defined social logic, which slots individual 'cogs' into the 'great machine' of society, or should we be more concerned to examine the negotiated development of self-consciousness and identity through ongoing **interaction** and the acquisition of **language**?

The intuitive, taken-for-granted view of socialization is that it essentially concerns children and childhood; it is a form of early 'total training' or 'moulding' that all children undergo. This view has in many ways underpinned traditional sociological and psychological approaches. It is however important to note the deterministic, machine-like, one-way process it often implies. Children, by definition immature and unregulated, posing as Campbell (1975) has noted 'immense, incalculable threats to the social order', are transformed into mature, competent and regulated social adults by means of a programmed system of instructions, rewards and punishments. Children are 'empty vessels', waiting to be filled by the social and cultural reservoirs of their society. If they are not 'filled' or socialized properly, so the argument goes, a defective or **deviant** product will result. This orthodox view of socialization has become increasingly criticized, contested and amended in recent years.

Primarily, the issue is one of **determination** and social

continuity. Wrong (1961) has indicated that the orthodox **functionalist** view has tended to overplay the conservative function of socialization. He forcefully rejects the notion of 'society' preserving and reproducing 'itself', by simply and unproblematically 'fitting' individuals into pre-defined social **roles**. Terming this an 'oversocialized' view, he further suggests that it cannot adequately account for social change or individual variety. Developing out of this criticism is the issue of the *active* participation of the individual. **Symbolic interactionists**, such as Mead and Schutz, have argued that the individual involved in socialization is an active participant, increasingly capable of negotiating and redefining the boundaries and rules of the learning situation. This implies a considerable move from the passive 'absorption' **model** that has characterized traditional views of parent–child, teacher–child relationships.

A further logical move from this model is implicit in recent work. Within the orthodox view socialization is a process that gradually stops as the subject passes from childhood through youth to adulthood. The function of education has in many ways been identified as crucial, and finishing school is equated with the end of or at least a significant break in the process. Two questions are important here: should socialization be seen as a finite process, ending in advanced industrial societies in the late teens, or is it in fact a lifelong process, present in all interaction new and old, familiar and unfamiliar? Berger and Luckmann (1971), for example, have distinguished between primary and secondary forms of socialization, but in their discussion they note that 'socialization is never total, never finished' (p. 157). Second, this issue in turn raises the problem of the relationship between early childhood socialization, and subsequent **experience**. To what extent are basic unalterable traits of behaviour and thought established in childhood? While this has been commonly claimed, work by Goffman (1968), for example, has demonstrated that certain processes of *resocialization* into occupations or institutional settings like prisons or mental asylums may drastically challenge and alter the individual's identity and sense of self.

Finally, most contemporary approaches consider the issue of **power** relations, suggesting that questions of inequality and social control have very often been eclipsed within orthodox approaches by assumed **consensus**. In this sense not only socialization, but also the whole concept of childhood and youth has undergone critical reexamination (Aries 1962; Murdock and McCron 1976). More specifically, relations between socializers and socialized – parents, teachers, children, and so on – have been placed in the context of **class** and **gender** relations. This emphasis has considerably redefined the functions of socialization in terms of the social and **cultural reproduction** of specific sets of values, ideas and activities that uphold and maintain social class, gender and other relations, hence serving to perpetuate the inequalities and ideologies that stem from them.

Socialization therefore is a term that needs careful consideration. Its implications may be usefully thought through in the context of these debates and differences of interpretation; it poses some fundamental problems.

TO

See **class, cultural reproduction, gender**
Further reading White (1977); Halliday (1978); White and Mufti (eds) (1979); Berger and Berger (1976); Bernstein (1971)

speech act ⋆ The action performed by an utterance as part of an interaction. ⋆ The concept developed out of the work of the philosopher J. L. Austin who demonstrated that many utterances are significant not so much in terms of what they say, but rather in terms of what they do. Indeed, in the case of many utterances it makes more sense to ask 'what is this utterance trying to do?' than to ask 'is what it says true or false?' – as may be seen if we consider the following fairly unremarkable examples of everyday utterances:

'I bet he won't turn up.'
'Stop here on the left.'
'Hello.'
'Please keep your seat belts fastened.'
'Okay.'
'Sod off' (or words to that effect).

'I now declare the Garden Festival open.'

These utterances exemplify a whole range of speech acts, including those of *betting*, *commanding*, *greeting*, *requesting an action*, *acknowledging*, *insulting*, and so on. None of them is limited to asserting some kind of propositional truth. This kind of observation led Austin to the conclusion that stating or asserting (in ways that can be judged true or false) is only one of many kinds of action (or speech act) that **language** makes possible – actions as diverse as warning, promising, naming, exemplifying, commenting, challenging, and so on. Significantly, for many of these actions it is difficult to envisage how else they might be performed except in words. Since Austin's pioneering work, most attention has been devoted to trying to identify a determinate range of speech acts and also to specifying precisely the recognition criteria for the most common speech acts such as questions or commands.

The concept is an important one for communication and cultural studies partly as a way of countering simplistic linear flow models of communication that see it simply in terms of 'information transfer' or 'exchanging ideas'; it has also been influential in studies of social interaction by providing an analytic tool for a variety of research traditions ranging from **discourse analysis** to ethnography of communication.

MM

See **discourse, language, functions of, pragmatics**
Further reading Austin (1962); Montgomery (1986); Searle (1969)

speech community ⋆ A group of people who share a common language or linguistic variety. A speech community in the strongest sense will also display common ways of using the shared language and common attitudes towards it within a given society. ⋆ The term is important for highlighting the way in which **language** exists not just as an abstract system, codified in grammar books and dictionaries; it is integral to everyday social life and belongs ultimately to its community of users. It is they who make and remake it in their everyday **encounters**.

At the same time it is a term beset with difficulties. In the first place the reference to 'speech' recalls earlier societies based on face-to-face contact, and this seems inappropriate to societies where print and electronic means of communication have opened up a whole range of mediated transactions that don't rely on speech. Some linguists now use the term *language community* instead.

In the second place, the reference to 'community' seems something of a misnomer under late capitalism. This is not just a question of the division of labour. In the case of UK society, for example, it is now more clear than ever that gross inequalities of material advantage continue to accumulate around the divisions of **ethnicity**, **gender**, **class** and region. And if the society displays not only diversity but also fundamental division, then verbal practices themselves will not just be held in common, but will come to operate actively in opposition to each other.

MM

See **anti-language, standard language**
Further reading Montgomery (1986)

speech event ⋆ A culturally salient event, with well defined boundaries, which rests upon the performance of some established and recognizable verbal routine. ⋆ Examples of speech events would be events such as a 'lecture' a 'job interview', a 'quiz programme', a 'sermon', a 'classroom lesson', an 'after–dinner speech', and so on. Speech events typically have a recognizable beginning, middle, and end, so that members of the **culture** (or more particularly the **speech community**) can clearly identify moments of transition into and out of them. This is important because the salient speech events of a speech community each require potentially different kinds of participant behaviour. The same participants in the same setting may switch from one repertoire of verbal practices to another as they move from one speech event to another. A teacher and pupils in a classroom, for example, may be talking amongst themselves just prior to a lesson: but once the lesson begins (and this will be marked overtly by the teacher in some way) the rules governing who speaks to whom, when and how, change in character. Shouting out, and swearing, for example, which may be appropriate verbal behaviour for some speech events, are considered inappropriate for most classroom lessons.

The concept is particularly important in socio-linguistics and the ethnography of communication, where it is referred to in more recent treatments as *communicative event*.

MM

See **genre, register, speech act**
Further reading Sackville-Troike (1982)

standard language ⋆ A dialect that has assumed ascendancy within a language community to such an extent that its internal rules become the standard of correctness for the whole community. ⋆ A standard language tends to have abrogated more prestige and authority to itself than the varieties with which it competes, principally because it usually emerges from the **dialect** of the dominant group. The emergence of a standard language is often related to the process of nation building; and just as nations are imaginary communities within the social sphere, so standard languages are imaginary systems within the linguistic sphere – not many of us actually speak the standard, though most of us either think that we do or believe that we should. Their imaginary nature is suppressed by elaborate processes of codification in prescriptive grammar books, guides to usage, and dictionaries. All these help to give the standard a spurious air of reality, perhaps with a greater degree of success than that achieved in the UK by the Queen's televised speech at Christmas, which attempts to convince us that we all belong to one nation (or Commonwealth).

MM

See **dialect, register, variety**
Further reading Milroy and Milroy (1987); Leith (1983)

star/stardom ⋆ Individuals who, as a consequence of their public performances on screen and in other media, become known and regarded as significant **symbols**, within and across cultural groups. ⋆ Stars are modern, secular icons, public embodiments of ideals and **values** which result from their fictionalized appearances and performances on – and off – stage and screen. Part of the **power** or fascination for stars, as Monaco (1977) notes, is the fact that they appear as 'ordinary people . . . made strangely important'. Conventionally we are encouraged to understand stars as exceptional not just because they are widely circulated images from film and other media. Their position and distinction is usually firmly anchored in definitions of their individual, unique talents and the **generic** forms they work within. Some critical studies of stardom have suggested that it serves to endorse **individualism** and promote the 'cult of the individual' in modern times. To date, the most significant mass medium for the manufacture of stardom has been film, operating within and across national and international contexts. The most powerful cinematic **institution** involved in this, the 'star system', is associated especially with the Hollywood studio industry in pre- and postwar years.

The study of stars as **cultural** phenomena has sought to encompass three related strands. First, to understand stars as agents and commodities, used to promote films and other merchandise and to mobilize audiences for cinematic and other forms of profitability. Second, stars, both in the characters and performances they play, and in their reported, 'disclosed', 'private' lives, act to condense and represent certain ideals of behaviour, action, **style**, sentiment, etc. In this context they operate as **powerful signs**, **images** or types within cultural **codes** and process. Finally, some attention has more recently been given to the star–**audience** relationship. Stars are popular because they are regarded with some form of active esteem and invested with cultural value. They resonate within particular **lifestyles** and **subcultures** and are subject to differential forms of identification dependent upon **gender** or sexuality for example.

Stardom is generally associated with twentieth–century, modern historical conditions and with cinema. Some writers have noted recent developments, whereby forms of stardom are now widely associated with music, sport, television and other popular cultural fields. An interesting dimension in this debate concerns recent studies of the 'media personality' as a distinct modern but related phenomenon. The paradigm instance here has been that of the 'television personality', which is held to signal a post-cinematic shift in modern culture. The requirements of **broadcasting** and the broadcasters' need to relate, with a human face and persona, to ranges of diverse everyday domestic settings contrast quite sharply with the cultural relations of the film star and cinema in the 1940s and 1950s. The significance of these shifts and their implications provides an important and continuing area for research and analysis.

TO

See **audience, stereotype, voyeurism**
Further reading Dyer (1979a, 1987); Ellis (1982); Langer (1981); Lewis (ed.) (1992)

status ⋆ Prestige associated with divisions of labour located within a variety of social contexts. ⋆ Status becomes much more meaningful if it is compared with other **role** positions within the same situation. Inferior and superior **others** locate the person within a competitive hierarchy. Usually the person is not alone with a status position; instead we can identify status **groups** that are differentiated from one another in terms of **power**, role playing and ability to act out roles.

Much depends on upward or downward social mobility of the individual: prestige takes into account past events and future prospects as well as the present **context**. It might be argued, for example, that young generals who used to be corporals achieve higher status than old generals who went straight into an officer rank on leaving Sandhurst.

The concept of status, as first introduced by Max Weber, contributes much to our understanding of **stratification** within society. It also extends any discussion of **class** and class as perceived by those people within various status groups. For example, to allocate a working-class label to an unpaid mother who is the daughter of a lord and wife of a plumber would be odd unless complemented by a discussion of the specific circumstances of that woman.

Status does not come from our own evaluations about ourselves, but is instead prescribed by a social organization. It may thus remain a **value** judgement that does not always coincide with the person's **perception** of his or her self. Furthermore, status is always associated with social context: if the latter changes, so may the amount of prestige given to that individual. After all, a change in social context often implies a change in surrounding others as well. Yet in much sociological literature the described status groups appear to be remarkably enduring despite a variety of work and leisure activities for members of those groups.

TO

See **power, role, stratification**

status conferral ⋆ The ability of media coverage to bestow prestige upon, and generally legitimize the authority of persons, **groups**, **institutions**, events or issues. A term used largely in American **functionalist** analyses of the social role of the mass media. ⋆ One of several interrelated social functions, the term implies that the media confer **status**, or raise the social standing of those subjects receiving favourable attention in their coverage. As Lazarsfeld and Merton (1948) have suggested: 'The audiences of mass media apparently subscribe to the circular belief: "If you really matter, you will be at the focus of mass attention and if you *are* at the focus of mass attention, then surely you must really matter" ' (pp. 561–2).

TO

See **functionalism, power, status**
Further reading Wright (1975); Schramm and Roberts (eds) (1971)

stereotype/stereotyping ⋆ The social classification of particular groups and people as often highly simplified and generalized signs, which implicitly or explicitly represent a set of values, judgements and assumptions concerning their behaviour, characteristics or history. * Initially introduced from the language of printing into that of the social sciences by Lippmann (originally published 1922; 1965), the concept has been developed particularly in social psychology, occupying a central place in the study of **cognitive** processes, **attitudes** and **prejudice** (see Tajfel 1963, and Cauthen 1971).

Stereotyping in much of this work has been defined as a particular extension of the fundamental cognitive process of categorization, whereby we impose structure and make sense of events, objects and **experience**. This process in itself requires the simplification and organization of diverse and complex ranges of phenomena into general, **labelled** categories. In so doing attention is focused on certain similar identifying characteristics or **distinctive features**, as opposed to many other differences. Stereotypes, however, not only identify general categories of people: **national** populations (e.g., the Irish), **races** (e.g., the Latin race), **classes** (e.g., the working class), **genders** (i.e. men or women), occupations (e.g., accountants) and **deviant** groups (e.g., drug-takers), etc., they are distinctive in the way that they carry *undifferentiated judgements* about their referents. Whilst they may vary widely in terms of their emotional appeal and intensity, they generally represent underlying power relations, tensions or conflicts (i.e. the 'stupid' Irish, the 'excitable' Latins, the 'cloth-cap' image, the 'dumb' blonde, the 'boring' accountant, the 'evil' junkie and so on). In short, they operate to define and identify groups of people as generally alike in certain ways – as committed to particular values, motivated by similar goals, having a common personality, make-up and so on. In this way stereotypes encourage an *intuitive belief* in their own underlying assumptions, and play a central role in organizing **common sense discourse**.

The degree to which they are believed in, tacitly accepted or rejected and countered, has promoted a great deal of research in social psychology. Recent work in cultural studies has turned to their social and political circulation and significance in the mass media, notably in the context of media representations of race, women, political and industrial relations, and forms of deviance.

Such studies have, for example, pointed to the ways in which the **conventions** and **codes** of news production encourage particular forms of stereotyping as a logical outcome of their orientation within a particular institutional context and set of professional **news values**. The search for 'extraordinariness' (cited as 'the primary or cardinal news value' by Hall *et al*. 1978, p. 53) and subsequent tendencies towards exaggeration and dramatization are capable not only of generating stereotypes, but also of giving or denying legitimacy to those commonly in circulation. Crucially this recent attention has brought together the concept of stereotype with theories of **ideology** and **hegemony**.

Despite its simple appeal, the term is a difficult and demanding one which raises some important problems, and serves as a useful point for discussion.

TO

See **attitude**, **labelling theory**, **nation**, **prejudice**, **race**
Further reading Perkins (1979); Hartmann and Husband (1974); Aronson (ed.) (1988); Cohen and Young (eds) (1981); Tajfel (1981); Eiser (1986); Forgas (1985); Dyer (1979b); Barker (1989)

stratification/social stratification ⋆ Refers to the hierarchical structure and ranked organization of societies, particularly to those ways in which they are socially divided into relatively permanent groups distinguishable by their *unequal access* to resources, power and privilege. ⋆ While the term implies an *analogy* between societies and rock formations, composed and divided into different layers or *strata*, it is important to recognize that social formations differ markedly from their more fixed and static geological counterparts. Social stratification essentially concerns both the nature and basis of relations of dominance and subordination, superiority and inferiority that demarcate and characterize social **groups** and their interrelationships. To say that all societies are in some ways stratified is however not to suggest that they are all identical or unchanging, as both historically and **cross culturally** societies exhibit different forms or systems of social stratification. In order to come to terms with these differences it is important to note the different sources or dimensions of stratification.

In many instances social relations between groups within

societies are governed by **objective** economic or material criteria. One's position and **power** in a feudal society, for example, would be largely dictated by birth into either a land or estate-owning group, or birth as a serf or landless labourer. Similarly the ownership or non-ownership of wealth fundamentally divides many modern societies into different social **classes**. However, stratification may also operate in non-directly economic forms, as in the case of **status** differences determined on the basis of age, **gender**, **race** or caste divisions. The importance of stratification lies in the ways in which it structures relationships between groups and **individuals**. These relations are fundamental to, and form a prime focus for, the study of communication.

TO

See **class, culture, power, status**
Further reading Bilton *et al.* (1981); Worsley (ed.) (1977)

structuralism ⋆ An intellectual enterprise characterized by attention to the systems, relations and forms – the structures – that make meaning possible in any cultural activity or artefact. ⋆ It is associated with a number of French writers who became influential in and after the 1960s.

Structuralism is not an *interpretative* approach to **meaning**. Unlike certain well-established kinds of literary and cultural criticism, it does not seek to reveal the hidden, essential or intrinsic meaning of a **text** or artefact. On the contrary, structuralists refuse the very idea of essential or intrinsic meaning, together with the notion that individual texts or individual people are the source of the meanings they generate. Structuralism is an analytical or *theoretical* enterprise, dedicated to the systematic elaboration of the **rules** and constraints that work, like the rules of a **language**, to make the generation of meanings possible in the first place.

Thus early structuralism was distinguished by the use of Saussurian linguistics and its terminology: especially the notions of **signifier** and **signified**; **langue** and **parole**; **synchronic** and **diachronic**; **paradigm** and **syntagm**. These and other distinctive features of a language structure were used to show how disparate and apparently unorganized phenomena were actually instances of the same structural patterns and relations just as all the different things that can be said in speech depend on the rules and constraints of **langue**. Further, structuralism was dedicated to showing how such structures were to be found in all kinds of cultural activity. Thus there are structuralist analyses of architecture, fashion, food, kinship networks and the unconscious, as well as of the more obvious signifying 'systems' of cinema, television and literature.

The most prominent names in structuralism are Roland Barthes (criticism) and Claude Lévi-Strauss (anthropology). Other influential writers who were associated with the enterprise are Louis Althusser (Marxist theory), Jacques Lacan (psychoanalysis) and Michel Foucault (studies of sexuality, madness and incarceration in terms of theories of power, discourse and knowledge); see Sturrock (ed.) (1979).

During the 1970s structuralism underwent a transformation. This was partly due to the proliferation of different positions within the enterprise, which eventually became too diverse to be understood as a unitary approach. It was also brought about by the unease which some of structuralism's original proponents began to express that it was becoming itself the very type of intellectual orthodoxy that it was originally set up to challenge. The outcome of this transformation was to produce at least three rather different fields of study:

(1) *Semiotics* which had hitherto been synonymous with structuralism but which became established as a major strand within the study of **popular culture**.

(2) *Deconstruction* which is overwhelmingly a mode of literary analysis, derived from the writings of Jacques Derrida. Derrida, a philosopher, showed how the philosophical assumptions that underlie writings are not by any means the guarantors of their meaning – on the contrary, the **discourses** in which such assumptions are presented systematically undermine the philosophy. This approach has given rise to an entire *deconstructionist* movement which is particularly influential in literary studies in the USA. In

this guise, the approach is a 'method' whose only precept is to take nothing for granted – doubt and questioning raised to the level of doctrine. Deconstruction is, then, one of structuralism's logical conclusions. Structuralism sought to challenge the **common sense** assumption that meanings are the result of their author's intentions, or that language is simply a referential nomenclature (an instrument that simply names an already-existing world). Deconstruction takes these notions further, and concerns itself solely with the **signifier** (not the **signified** or the socially 'fixed' **sign**). Applied to the study of literature, deconstruction has produced a characteristic form of criticism in which the verbal virtuosity of the critic is as much in evidence as reflections on the object of study. The object of study (a work of literature, for instance) is in fact given no especially privileged status; it is not a warrant for its own reading. On the contrary, deconstruction is dedicated to teasing out the repressed, marginalized and absent in the chosen discourse.

(3) *Post-structuralism* which is hard in practice to separate from structuralism. It is more alert to **psychoanalytical theories** and the role of **pleasure** in producing and regulating meanings than was the highly rationalist early structuralism. Post-structuralism is also more concerned with the *external* structures (social process, **class, gender** and **ethnic** divisions, historical changes) that make meaning possible than was the early version, which was mostly concerned with *internal* or 'immanent' textual structures. Hence structuralism shifted its focus from the text to the **reader**, but this shouldn't be taken as a radical break – post-structuralism is implicit in structuralism itself.

Structuralism has been seen as a characteristically twentieth-century way of understanding the world. The nineteenth century was notable in many different fields for work which sought causes and origins (Darwinism, Marxism, Freudianism) as the framework of explanation. Structuralism shares with other twentieth-century enterprises – in physics and astronomy especially – attention to relations and systems as the framework for explanation. Instead of treating the world as an aggregate of things with their own intrinsic properties, structuralism and physics respectively seek to account for the social and physical world as a system of relations in which the properties of a 'thing' (be it an atom, a **sign** or an **individual**) derive from its internal and external relations.

JH

See **difference, discourse, postmodernism, semiotics**
Further reading Hawkes (1977); Culler (1983); Norris (1982); Sturrock (ed.) (1979)

style   ⋆ The means by which cultural identity and social location are negotiated and expressed. ⋆   We tend to think initially of styles as classifications of many sorts of *things*; products, **texts**, or artefacts such as clothes, paintings, buildings, cars, and so on. In addition we commonly recognize that styles are related to *how certain things are done*, for example, how music is played, speeches delivered, clothing worn, hair cut or books written. In both senses style is often defined as elusive, an indefinable 'something' that, often implicitly, **signifies** or expresses recognizable **difference** or similarity. Recognizing this is part of making the 'things' or the 'ways of doing things' meaningful. In both cases, we relate particular instances to a wider set of stylistic **paradigms, discourses** or mental 'maps', which serve to organize the **meanings** and **values** we attribute to the specific example.

Styles are recognizable, then, in as much as they combine certain recurrent and patterned elements into a distinctively structured ensemble or **form** which signifies and proposes an identifiable position within wider social and cultural relations. In this sense, even our own identification and interpretation of styles are part of the ways in which we negotiate our cultural identity. The ways in which we make sense of and evaluate their meanings very often says something about our own position in wider social and cultural relations. Styles are therefore an integral part of those sets of **rules, codes** and **conventions** which organize and are contested and expressed in forms of social interaction,

305

communication and identity. As Hebdige (1979) notes: 'Ultimately, if nothing else, they are expressive of "normality" as opposed to "deviance" ' (p. 101).

Analysis or discussion of style might usefully aim, therefore, to bring together and relate two levels of questions. First, what are the identifiable elements of particular styles? How are they combined, encoded and interrelated? What are their **distinctive features**? Second, what do they represent? How do they signify an identity, and articulate a sense of cultural location? Bringing together these types of questions makes it impossible to detach styles from wider historical, social and political processes, and the cultural interplay between dominant, subordinate and oppositional groups in society. Equally it is important not to restrict explanations of the sources of style to the fragmented level of individual personality or originality.

Work on youth **subcultures** has, for example, been concerned to examine the complex interlocks between the often highly visible styles and ensembles adopted by young people, and their subcultural locations and determinants. In this sense styles may be regarded as the **symbolic** property of particular social **groups**, articulating their **orientation** and stance within wider social, **cultural** and stylistic relations.

TO

See **bricolage, culture, genre, lifestyle, subculture**
Further reading Hebdige (1979, 1988); Epstein (1978); Melly (1972).

subconscious ⋆ A psychic structure that represents partial awareness of information which either has left **consciousness** or is usually located within the **unconscious**. ⋆ The subconscious thus represents a transitional twilight state within a psychic system, although it is unclear as to how long specific experiences and **memories** remain within such a **subliminal** and intermediary state of awareness. In **psychoanalytical theory** the term is used synonymously with the concept of unconscious, although Jung has discussed the subconscious in more detail. The prefix *sub* is misleading because it implies a lower level of awareness, which in

Jung's opinion (1969) denies the advanced understanding of some universal, archetypal, and even inherited awareness of humanity.

DS

See **archetype, consciousness, psychoanalytical theory, subliminal, threshold, unconscious**
Further reading Jung (1969)

subculture ⋆ As the prefix implies, *sub*cultures are significant and distinctive negotiations located within wider cultures. These correspond with the particular positions, ambiguities and specific contradictions faced by certain social groups within wider social and historical structures. ⋆ The term and its supporting theory have developed almost exclusively in the study and explanation of youth, notably with regard to **deviance**. Here it has served to displace earlier ideas of a unified and separate 'youth culture' corresponding to *all* young people (for example, Eisenstadt 1956; Parsons 1954) by attempting to synthesize both age and social class as determinants of the differing subcultural identities and activities of young people. In this way the concept hinges on several important assumptions.

First, that western societies are characterized principally by their division into social **classes**, based on inequalities of **power** and wealth, and their consequent relations of dominance and subordination. Second, that these unequal and conflicting divisions and relations are realized and articulated in the form of class **cultures**, themselves sets of complex cultural responses to particular social class positions. Third, within these class cultures (often referred to in this context as 'parent cultures') youth negotiate and advance 'their own' distinctive and especially symbolic *subcultural* responses to the problems posed not only by age or generational status, subordination and control, but also by class position and inequality, particularly as they are experienced and combined in the spheres of education, work and leisure. As Clarke *et al.* (1976) argue:

> Sub-cultures, then, must first be related to the 'parent cultures' of which they are a sub set. But sub-cultures must *also* be

307

analysed in terms of their relation to the dominant culture – the overall disposition of cultural power in the society as a whole. (p. 13)

Within this framework, subcultural analysis has generated and continues to propose an important way of deconstructing and understanding the appearance, behaviour and significance of differing youth groups in the postwar UK. Specific studies (see Brake 1980; Hebdige 1979, for résumé), have concentrated predominantly on working-class youth subcultural groups, emphasizing the ways in which their often 'spectacular' appearances (their **styles** of fashion and dress, for example) and their 'spectacular' activities (especially those defined as deviant and threatening) represent meaningful forms of specific subcultural response and resistance, through specialized subcultural identities and **rituals**. Subcultures thus function to win, or at least contest, 'cultural space' for their members; in so doing they also generate and confirm important modes of both collective and individual identity and **orientation** towards the dominant **values** of the wider social and cultural order.

Subcultural theory has established and now comprises the orthodox approach to the study of youth. However, this orthodoxy is not above criticism, as recent debates and work have suggested. Briefly, there are two particular problems. First, the tendency for subcultures to be interpreted as significant *only* in terms of resistance. This, for example, has produced an unbalanced concentration on those subcultural activities and styles that could be construed as offering resistance, or radical opposition, as opposed to **conformity**, acceptance or incorporation. Second, subcultural accounts of youth have displayed an even more glaring imbalance with regard to **gender** divisions. In their focus on mainly working-class but overwhelmingly male subjects, as McRobbie (1980) suggests, 'Women and the whole question of sexual division have been marginalised' (p. 37).

TO

See **counterculture, culture, style**
Further reading Hall and Jefferson (eds) (1976); Bilton *et al.* (1981); Brake (1980); Middleton and Muncie (1981); Mungham

and Pearson (eds) (1976); Hebdige (1979, 1988). For critical accounts see Clarke (1982); Cohen (1980); McRobbie (1980)

subject/subjectivity ⋆ Subjectivity in recent textual theories has become a major focus of attention. In this context, the term represents all that can be signified by allowing a collision or collusion between three of the established senses of the word 'subject'. ⋆ These are:

(1) *Subject as in political theory* – the citizen as subject of the state or law. This sense implies the subject's lack of freedom of action with respect to the **power** to which s/he is subjected.

(2) *Subject as in idealist philosophy* – the thinking subject; the site of **consciouness**. This sense implies a division between subject and object, between thought and reality, or between self and other. Hence subjectivity in this sense is the representation of that which appears to the self as opposed to that which is taken to exist in fact.

(3) *Subject as in grammar* – the subject of a sentence (as in subject–verb–predicate), and hence the subject of a **discourse** or **text**; that which the action is about or determined by.

The way these three senses can be worked together arises from an attempt to deal with the inadequacies of sense (2) taken alone. In this sense, subjectivity is the site of consciousness but it suggests a free-floating consciousness or unitary identity which then appears as the *source* of action and meaning rather than their product. The implicit **individualism** of this philosophical position fails to account for the role played by social relations and **language** in determining, regulating and producing what any one 'thinking subject' can be.

At this point the other two senses can become active. Sense (1) allows for subjectivity to be understood as a social relation – our subjectivity isn't a property that we own, but on the contrary we are subjects *of* various agencies. Our individual identity, then, is determined, regulated and reproduced as a structure of relationships. For instance, we may be subjects of (subjected to) parental affection/authority; legal protection/compulsion; commercial enterprise/exploitation; national or cultural characteristics/**stereotypes**; and so on. Bringing sense (1) into play, then, encourages a notion of subjectivity that is not 'inherent' in the individual nor unitary – just as we are subjects of and subjected to these various agencies, so our subjectivity is a contradictory mix of confirming and contending 'identities'.

Introducing sense (3) into the discussion allows for the determining, regulating and productive role of language, discourse and sense-making. This is the sense that has preoccupied textual analysts in recent years. The idea is that no matter what a text or discourse is about in referential terms, its subject when it is reproduced in the act of reading or utterance is the reader or speaker. Texts and discourses, then, are the means by which the relationship between the social (sense (1)) and the individual (sense (2)) is communicated. But just as **consciousness** is not a free-floating entity, so texts and discourses are themselves **determined**, regulated and produced in the historical circumstances of time, place and structure. So we can identify with specific discourses – for instance those of **nation** (the **signifiers** for Welshness available at any one time), or of **gender** (what it means to be a man or a woman depends on gendered subject positions within discourses with which we can identify or differentiate ourselves), and so on.

Subjectivity is a way of conceptualizing text/reader relations without reproducing either as fixed unitary categories. At the level of analysis, a lot of work has been done to show how cultural products (especially films and television) employ textual devices and strategies like point-of-view, **mode of address** and **narration** to propose or fix a subject position from which they can be made sense of when read. In fact, in some versions this work suggests that the act of reading is little more than a process of occupying the 'spaces' offered by such texts. Thus there's a tendency in this area for texts to be privileged as the constructors or producers of our subjectivity, and for individuals to be seen as more or less passive 'subjects in **ideology**', constantly reconstituted in the image of whatever discourse they may be inhabiting for the time being.

Actually such a radically determinist position does offer a useful counterbalance to the commonly held notion that our subjectivity is inherently ours, and not a product of social relations and sense-making. Although it seems untenable if taken to its limits, the idea that subjectivity is a product of social relations and discursive resources opens it up to analysis.

JH

See **culture, discourse, ideology, individual**

subliminal ⋆ The product of stimulus presentation that is so rapid that it denies the conscious processing of such information. ⋆ The **individual** may either have awareness of being exposed to something and yet not be exactly able to define what it is, or else be totally unaware. Packard (1970) refers to these as 'sub-threshold effects' within advertising, where very brief exposure to a brand and/or product name may encourage later consumer buying.

Subliminal advertising was first publicized in 1956, when a subliminal ice-cream commercial was inserted into the middle of a cinema feature film. The effectiveness of such exposure continues to be a subject of debate. The hysterical condemnation of subliminal methods as intrusive and clandestine has been criticized by psychologists such as Dixon (1971). It can be argued, for example, that subliminal exposure is only effective when it cues something that we already know about and are predisposed towards. Such exposure cannot implant any **message/attitude** about any issue within our minds.

Many **media channels** are poorly suited to sub-**threshold** effects because presentation remains too slow – this includes the television screen. However, much depends on the state and receptiveness of the **perceiver**, on ambiguity of stimulus content, and on what other stimuli precede and/or proceed the subliminal stimulus. Despite debates over its effectiveness in advertising, subliminal perception has been supported by some **experimental** data. For example, Smith *et al.* (1959) found that judgements of

311

an expressionless face were more pleasant and favourable if volunteers had been subliminally exposed to the word 'happy' as compared with 'angry' before being shown the picture.

DS

See **defence mechanism, moral panic, perception, subconscious, threshold**

Further reading   Packard (1970); Dixon (1971)

symbol   ⋆ Broadly, a sign, object or act that stands for something other than itself, by virtue of agreement among the members of the culture that uses it. ⋆ The word is loosely used and each context should be studied to ascertain its particular use. Its main ones are:

(1)   Shannon and Weaver, Ogden and Richards, and Berlo, tend to use the word in a broad sense as referring to any type of sign. This use should, where possible, be avoided. More precise though sometimes contradictory uses follow.

(2)   Peirce uses the term to refer to a category of **sign** where there is no resemblance between it and its **object**. He contrasts it with his other types of sign – **icon** and **index**. A word is a symbol, so is ♀ meaning female.

(3)   Freud uses it to refer to an object or act that stands in place of something that is taboo or unpleasant to think of. In the Freudian use there is some resemblance between the symbol and what it stands for, even though this resemblance may be indirect or **metaphoric**. A penis is symbolized by a watering can.

(4)   Barthes uses it to refer to an object or act that stands for an abstraction or a **value**. A gold coin can symbolize wealth, a shepherd and lamb can symbolize the relationship of Christ to his followers. Religious practices and social **rituals** are frequently symbolic in this sense, for example, a christening or the exchange of gifts at Christmas.

(5)   There is also a literary and artistic use of the term which is

similar to uses (3) and (4) in so far as it includes a resemblance between symbol and object. In literature and visual art, the symbol demands attention in its own right, sometimes even demands more attention than that which it stands for.

This word is used so variously that it is unwise to use it except in its specifically defined senses such as those of Peirce and Freud.

JF

See **icon, image, index, motivation (of the sign), reference, referent, ritual**

symbolic interactionism ⋆ An approach to social relations that emphasizes the importance of negotiated meanings associated with symbols exchanged in interaction between the self and others. ⋆ Mead (1934) formulated most symbolic interactionist concepts while in the process of constructing **role** theory and while opposing some of the popular **experimentalism** of his day. Human conduct, he claimed, involves more than simply responding to various stimuli from the external environment. Instead actions are reflected upon and the self may be viewed as both subject and object in **social interaction**. In this sense self-consciousness develops out of a continual appraisal of our various outward appearances as witnessed and comprehended by **others**. The acquisition of **language** becomes an essential feature for the development of mind because it allows for more meaningful communication.

By discussing the possibilities of reflection, anticipation and imagination (as with children at play who are constantly developing **norms** and **rules** through negotiation) symbolic interactionism has been criticized by the more hard-line **empiricists**. But as Mead (1934) and Blumer (1969) point out, the analysis of behaviour cannot always be accomplished via the systematic isolation of suspected variables. Instead the **social context** of interaction must be emphasized, together with the inter-dependence of variables in a variety of settings. Thus the

313

'ecological' study of typical, everyday episodes or scenes, as they occur within real-life contexts, has been preferred.

TO

Further reading Cuff and Payne (eds) (1979); Schellenberg (1978); Rosenberg and Turner (1981); Mortensen (ed.) (1979); Bilton *et al.* (1981); Denzin (1992)

synchronic ⋆ One of a pair of terms – the other is **diachronic** – taken from the work of Saussure: they refer in this context to two different, but not mutually exclusive, ways of conducting semiotic/linguistic analysis. Synchronic analysis concentrates on the state of language (**langue**) at one moment. ⋆ *Diachronic analysis* concentrates on the changes in a given language over time.

Saussure was strongly convinced of the need for synchronic analysis – the attempt to take **language** as a structured whole and understand its internal relations. Synchronic analysis is essentially abstract since it is **empirically** impossible to stop a language (much less **langue**) in its tracks and observe its state. But abstraction was just what Saussure favoured, since his argument was that people had become so bogged down in the empirical fact of particular languages and their word-stores (philology) that there was no developed theory of language-in-general from which to make sense of the empirical data.

Synchronic analysis has become the **norm** in much **semiotic** work, where the emphasis has been on isolating the elements (**signs**) and their internal relationships within an abstract system (**codes**) of many different sign systems. Saussure predicted that synchronic analysis would eventually lead on to a more theoretically adequate diachronic analysis, or even to a combination of the two, which he dubbed *panchronic*. This may be the situation now developing in **semiotics**, where more attention is being paid to the historical development of particular media and **institutionalized discourses** than was hitherto the case.

JH

See **diachronic, discourse, langue, paradigm, parole, sign, signification, syntagm**

syntagm ⋆ A combination of units chosen from **paradigms** to make a signifying whole. ⋆ A sentence is a syntagm of words, an advertisement is a syntagm of visual **signs**, a melody is a syntagm of notes. Syntagms can be combinations in space (visual ones), or in time (verbal or musical ones). The units can interact with each other and thus change each other's significance in the syntagm, so that each syntagm is potentially unique with its own set of **meanings**. Imagine two safety posters, each showing a 10-year-old girl about to cross the road: in one she is holding hands with her brother aged 4, in the other with her father. She 'means' something significantly different in each syntagm. Similarly the same word can have quite different meanings in different sentences. So in a syntagm the meaning of a unit is determined by how it *interacts* with the others, whereas in a paradigm it is determined by how it is *distinguished* from the others.

JF

See **choice, metonymy, paradigm**

syntax/syntagmatic ⋆ Linear patterns or relationships in the process of signification: in language, a set of constraints on the organization or combination of words into sentences. ⋆ Words combine into sentences according to basic patterns or rules, referred to as the *syntax* of a *language*. Some orderings of items are permissible within a language; others are not. A sequence such as 'o'clock is news nine the here' does not count as a sentence within English, whereas the following is a perfectly well-formed sequence: 'here is the nine o'clock news'. Some sequences, therefore, are excluded as not conforming to the basic patterns. This may make the linear **rule** system, the syntax, sound somewhat restrictive. What the syntax does, however, is to specify a set of possibilities for sentence construction, the adherence to which guarantees some degree of mutual intelligibility. Indeed, from the basic core patterns of the syntax an unlimited array of sentences can be composed. And as long as sentences conform to these patterns, they will be interpretable even when they are 'one-off' creations or unique events. For example, readers of this definition will have little difficulty interpreting a sentence such as 'Purple was the shade of her lipstick' even though they are unlikely to have encountered it before. It is the underlying rule system – in part accounted for by the syntax – that enables us to compose these novel utterances and make sense of them.

Constraints on what can follow what apply not only to sentences in language. Similar constraints – *syntagmatic relations* – have been traced in other sign systems, the most noticeable of these being film. The way in which shots are edited together to form a sequence in mainstream film conforms for the most part to a recurring set of conventions. These have been treated by analogy as the syntax of film.

MM

See **competence, deep structure, paradigm, transformation**

Further reading   Chomsky (1965); Metz (1974)

T

text/message ⋆ These two terms are frequently used interchangeably, and refer to a signifying structure composed of **signs**
and **codes** which is essential to communication. ⋆ This structure can take a wide variety of forms, such as speech, writing,
film, dress, car styling, gesture, and so on.

Despite their frequent interchangeability, these two terms do
have differences, and maintaining or even extending them is a
worthwhile enterprise. *Text* usually refers to a message that has a
physical existence of its own, independent of its **sender** or
receiver, and thus composed of representational codes. Books,
records, letters, photographs are texts, so too is a recording of a
television show or a transcript of speech. A gesture or facial
expression, however, sends a message, but does not produce a
text. The term *message* tends to be used by those working in the
process school of communication, by sociologists and psychologists and engineers, and is used with the simple definition of 'that
which is transmitted'. Frequently it is seen as problem-free and is
thus taken for granted. *Text*, on the other hand, derives more
from the **semiotic** or linguistic school, and thus implies the
definition 'that which is central to the generation and exchange of
meaning'. A text, then, consists of a network of **codes** working
on a number of levels and is thus capable of producing a variety of
meanings according to the socio–cultural **experience** of the

317

reader. It is thus problematic and demands analysis.

JF

See **message, preferred reading**
Further reading Fiske (1989a)

threshold ⋆ An experienced state bordering on at least two levels of awareness. ⋆ A threshold can apply to that exact point in time where two stimuli (for example, lights) merge to become one, or to the fading of a single stimulus so that it becomes imperceptible. In **subliminal** conditions a threshold has been crossed where full awareness is denied but information may still be assimilated. This is similar to the distinction between **consciousness**, **unconsciousness** and **subconsciousness** as discussed within **psychoanalytical theory**, where thresholds are postulated for transition points between each psychic state.

DS

See **consciousness, homeostasis, perception, subliminal**

transactional ⋆ Communication involving a mutual exchange of information or influence based on negotiation and reciprocity. ⋆ The concept of transaction thus supersedes the more static one-way approaches to **perception** – where the perceiver observes the environment without affecting it in any way. Mortensen (1979) likens the static approach to a falling line of dominoes, where A affects B, B then affects C, and so on. The more dynamic process of transaction suggests that B when affected by A also changes A.

The transactional approach is well suited to the analysis of, for example, **non-verbal communication**. Argyle (1978) identifies a number of body **signals** that are not completed in isolation, but which rely on continuous **feedback** from one to another. Transactional analysis is a more specific concept introduced by Berne (1964) and refers to a process of exposing game-playing elements in social relationships.

DS

See **interaction**
Further reading Mortensen (ed.) (1979); Berne (1964); Burton and Dimbleby (1988)

transformation ⋆ A particular kind of **syntactic rule** which takes one string of syntatic categories or symbols and converts it into another string by processes of addition, deletion or permutation. ⋆ In *transformational-generative grammar* the relation between *deep structure* and *surface structure* is specified by a set of transformational rules. The notion, however, need not be restricted to syntactic rules for sentences. Some accounts of folk-tales and **myths** propose that their diverse heterogeneity is really the result of transformations being worked upon a small number of very simple underlying structures or formulae.

MM

See **deep structure, syntax**
Further reading Chomsky (1965); Lévi-Strauss (1967); Propp (1968)

transitivity ⋆ Transitivity is a way of describing the relationship between participants and processes in the construction of clauses – basically, 'who (or what) does what to whom (or what)'.⋆ Transitivity relations and the roles of participants depend crucially upon the kind of process encoded by the main verb in the clause. For English, four fundamental types of process may be distinguished (for more complete and complex treatments see Fawcett 1980; Halliday 1985):

   (1) *Material* 'John broke the lock'.
   (2) *Mental* 'She understood immediately'.
   (3) *Verbal* 'Michael said he was hungry'.
   (4) *Relational* 'The main course is excellent'.

   (1) Material action processes (realized by verbs such as 'break', 'wipe', 'dig', 'unbolt') are associated with inherent **roles** such as an AGENT (someone or something to perform the action), and

AFFECTED (ENTITY) (someone or something on the receiving end of the action). Thus:

John	broke	the lock
AGENT	PROCESS	AFFECTED

There need, of course, be no necessary correspondence between the participant role AGENT and the syntactic element 'subject'. The passive makes possible one obvious kind of non–congruence, e.g.:

The lock	was broken	by John
AFFECTED	PROCESS	AGENT
Subject	Predicator	

The passive thereby allows the topicalization or thematization of the AFFECTED.

It also allows the deletion or non–statement of the AGENT, e.g.:

The lock	was broken
AFFECTED	PROCESS

(2) Mental processes (realized by verbs such as 'know', 'feel', 'think', 'believe') are associated with inherent roles such as SENSER (the one who performs the act of 'knowing', 'thinking', or 'feeling') and PHENOMENON – that which is experienced by the SENSER. Thus:

James	considered	the problem
SENSER	PROCESS	PHENOMENON

Mary	understood	the message
SENSER	PROCESS	PHENOMENON

The message	amazed	me
PHENOMENON	PROCESS	SENSER

Quite commonly, the PHENOMENON will not be realized in the surface structure of the clause, but there may be some reference to the CIRCUMSTANCES of the action:

The doctor	thought	hard
SENSER	PROCESS	CIRCUMSTANCE

Mary	understood	immediately
SENSER	PROCESS	CIRCUMSTANCE

(3) Verbal processes are processes of saying, though this comes in many forms – e.g. 'suggest', 'promise', 'enquire', 'tell', 'inform'. Typical participant roles are SAYER, VERBIAGE and RECIPIENT. Thus:

I	said	it was time to leave
SAYER	PROCESS	VERBIAGE

I	told	him	it was time to leave
SAYER	PROCESS	RECIPIENT	VERBIAGE

(4) Relational processes in their simplest form involve some entity which is identified by reference to some attribute. The process may be realized by verbs such as 'become', 'seem', 'be', 'have' and typical roles are IDENTIFIER and IDENTIFIED.

The sky	is	blue
IDENTIFIED	PROCESS	IDENTIFIER

Other important roles are those of POSSESSOR and POSSESSED as in:

He	had	no money
POSSESSOR	PROCESS	POSSESSED

Any event or relationship in the 'real world' is filtered through, and given linguistic shape by means of one or other of the types of process outlined above. Transitivity relations, therefore, go to the heart of the linguistic construction and mediation of experience. And the patterning of transitivity choices in any one text can reveal crucial predispositions to construct experience along certain lines rather than others. The analysis of transitivity, therefore, makes available an important tool for exploring the **ideological** dimensions of text.

MM

See   **ideology, semantics, syntax**
Further reading   Halliday (1985); Montgomery (1986)

transposition   ⋆ Act of changing events or relationships so that each takes the place of the other. ⋆   Within communication studies the concept of transposition has proved useful in linguistic analysis where words, phrases or sentences may be relocated; or where parts of any **message** or **text** may literally be swapped over. Meaning will always be affected by transposition. For example, the sentence 'dog bites woman' contrasts dramatically with its transposed (in this case, reversed) version 'woman bites dog' – as every journalist will tell you. This process is also crucial in advertising where elements of the product and the **image** created for it in the advertisement are transposed **metaphorically**. Marlboro cigarettes and the Wild West transpose connotations from one to the other, as do menthol cigarettes and mountain streams.

JF

two–step flow model   ⋆ An early and important recognition of the way in which media messages are mediated through interpersonal relationships. ⋆   As such the two–step flow model implied a move away from earlier direct or '**hypodermic**' views of the mass communicative process which was a 'one-step' flow:

to a more complex conceptualization of the way in which messages are diffused among social groups, a two–step flow:

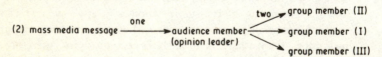

The importance of the model, developed largely through **empirical** analyses of **audience** reception of media coverage of electoral

campaigns (Lazarsfeld *et al.* 1944) and the study of group relations, lies in the challenge it offered to previously held ideas about the audience and the media message. No longer could the audience be seen as a mass of unconnected **individuals**; they were socially related and those relationships influenced the ways they both relayed and received media information. This also meant that the media message itself was not fixed, finite and common to all, but could be interpreted differently by different people. The two–step flow was closely related to the 'rediscovery' of the **primary group** and is strongly associated with the work of Katz and Lazarsfeld (1955).

Multi-step flow model A logical extension of the 'two–step' model, which emphasized further the consequences of communicative and social relationships within the mass media audience. The multi–step model simply extended the former by building more 'breaks' or stages into the processes of audience reception. As such it represented a more comprehensive attempt to measure more accurately the complex networks of 'steps' and influences involved in the transmission of media messages through group relations. It was important in that it indicated a further move away from seeing the audience as unstructured and passive, and from viewing the media message as unidimensional and containing identical meanings for all individuals. It decisively demonstrated a shift from concern about 'what the media do to people' to 'what people do with the media'.

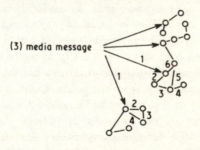

TO

See **effects, hypodermic needle model, opinion leaders**
Further reading McQuail and Windahl (1981); Schramm and Roberts (eds) (1971)

unconscious ★ (1) A descriptive term referring to behaviour about which the actor and/or **audience** is unaware; (2) a process or system involved in relations with other hypothetical psychic structures, and defying **consciousness.** ★ The unconscious was first described by Freud when constructing **psychoanalytical theory**, and was assumed to be the centre of disorganized energy associated with **pleasure** seeking or a desire for revenge. Freud suspected that many of his patients were affected by previous **experiences** that could not actually be remembered verbatim, but would appear within a translated context. Thus dream **images** may acquire especial significance to the dreamer although a full understanding of meaning may be thwarted via **censorship**. Freud demonstrates in *The Psychopathology of Everyday Life* (1904) that the forgetting of a single word or phrase within an otherwise well-remembered context, or even a slip of the tongue, may be very meaningful when **conscious memory** has been repressed.

The unconscious differs from the preconscious in that the latter includes memory of experiences and motives that are available to consciousness but are not immediately present. And to follow Hilgard *et al.*'s (1979) differentiation between the unconscious and subconscious (two terms used synonymously by Freud), the subconscious refers to experience that is located along such an outer perimeter of consciousness and that cannot be closely attended to because it is below some ill-defined **threshold.** In *analytical psychology*, Jung postulates a collective unconscious that is the source of consistent patterns, or **archetypes**, that are common to everybody, and that surface in legends, dreams and literary images.

DS

See **consciousness, image, projection, psychoanalytical theory, subconscious**
Further reading Stafford–Clarke (1967); Jung (1969); Hilgard *et al.* (1979); Corner and Hawthorn (eds) (1989)

uses and gratifications ⋆ That approach to the study of media audiences which proposes that audience members' consumption of media output is motivated and directed towards the gratification of certain individually experienced needs. ⋆ The central suggestion of this approach is that when we watch television and films or read newspapers and books, and so on, we are in fact gratifying and satisfying in varying degrees certain needs. Answering and gratifying a 'need' for specific information by reading a reference book is perhaps the clearest example.

Grounded in American research in the 1940s, directed towards exploring, among other problems, the gratifications sought and obtained by radio 'soap opera' **audiences** (Herzog 1944), the approach has developed and is currently expressed as a theory of audience–media relations. It is particularly associated with the work of Katz *et al.* (eds) (1974) and, as McQuail and Windahl (1981) note in their discussion, 'has seemingly best survived in the United States'.

With its emphasis on the *active* audience, composed of individuals *actively* seeking combinations of gratifications from the range of media output selected and 'used', the approach represented a welcome swing from the passive and static **hypodermic** view of media–audience **effects**. In the much-cited words of Halloran (ed.) (1970) it enabled and encouraged researchers to 'get away from the habit of thinking in terms of *what media do to people*, and substitute for it the idea of *what people do with the media*'.

Working within this tradition McQuail *et al.* (1972) have

constructed a typology of media–person interactions; their study provides a usefully representative way of 'thinking through' the general approach. They suggest that the media in varying ways function to provide gratifications for needs of/for:

(1) *Diversion* The media provide material which is used by people to 'escape' or be diverted from routines – for example, work routines, and a wide variety of problems that confront and constrain them. In so doing the media enable important emotional release and relaxation from these and other constraints, albeit temporarily.

(2) *Personal relationships* Media provide material that gratifies the needs for companionship and sociability. They do this in two ways. First, when we are alone we may use the radio and television to 'keep us company', we may come to 'know' media personalities and characters as if they were personal friends. Second, knowledge and consumption of media programmes and output may often facilitate or serve as a focus for interaction with others.

(3) *Personal identity* Here media contents may be used symbolically to explore, challenge, adjust, or confirm the **individual's** sense of identity and self. This includes the comparison of oneself, one's sense of situation, sets of **values** and outlooks with media situations and scenarios. In this way the media provide ways to 'assess' and 'locate' ourselves, and hence to respond to problems of personal identity management.

(4) *Surveillance* The media provide material which gratifies the need for information about the immediate and more distant social world: information about issues and events that directly and indirectly influence the individual's life.

In summary, the uses and gratifications approach focuses on the social and psychological origins and dynamics of individual 'needs', on the assumption that these lead to differential use of the various media, which in turn results in differential levels of gratifications obtained by the individual audience member. Each medium is perceived as offering a unique combination of contents and attributes, capable of producing different sets and ranges of gratifications (Katz *et al.* 1973). The approach offers a distinctive theory and methodology for coming to terms with the ways in which different members of the media audience may interpret and use media contents in widely different ways. It is, however, important to evaluate it in the context of a number of central criticisms that it has attracted.

First, it has been suggested that the approach contains an over-individualistic and psychologistic emphasis, and as a consequence of this neglects or fails to consider fully the socially structured basis and nature of audience needs and gratifications. This suggestion is usually coupled with a critique of the **functionalism** underlying the notion of media consumption, i.e. fulfilling certain functions whereby individuals' needs are 'balanced' by gratifications. Elliott (1974), for example, in his critical discussion, points to the circularity inherent in the model, and the problems of establishing which come first, 'uses', 'needs' or 'gratifications'. Finally uses and gratifications theorists have been challenged for either taking for granted or neglecting the contents of mass media messages, the ways in which media messages themselves may 'prefer' certain meanings as opposed to others. The suggestion here is that the 'activity' of the audience members is limited not just by their own 'needs' but also by the structure of the media text itself. Morley (1980), Elliott (1974) and McQuail and Windahl (1981) provide useful critical summaries.

TO

See **audience, functionalism, hypodermic needle model, preferred reading**
Further reading Morley (1980); McQuail and Windahl (1981); Katz *et al.* (eds) (1974); Elliott (1974); McQuail (ed.) (1972); Fiske (1982); McQuail (1987); Lull 1990)

V

value ⋆ The judgement of perceived attributes, and of paths to goals, normally associated with an attitude. ⋆ Such evaluations may include goodness, honesty, toughness and other such dimensions and will vary in intensity according to the value judgement.

A distinction should be made between moral values and other values. With moral value the individual prescribes judgement on the basis of, as Brown (1965) calls it, 'moral obligation'. The individual's use of 'ought' or 'should' suggests such obligation, and something that is very different from other statements about values that connote only a sense of desirability; for example, 'I like' or 'I want'. The analysis of value has much relevance to the study of **culture** and communication. Intergroup relations may be based on the operation of differing value systems as a result of different **social** and **cultural** location. Of course the internalization of values depends essentially on communicated information, often through **socialization**.

In the context of linguistics, Saussure (1974) has defined value as the relationship of a word to other related words in the same system, which is established by difference or **distinctive features**. For instance, the value of 'mutton' is that it is not-lamb, not-sheep, not-beef. Linguistic value is a function of differences within the system.

DS

See **attitude, culture, primary group, socialization**

328

Further reading Tajfel and Fraser (eds) (1978); Brown (1965); Fiske (1982); Abrams *et al*. (eds) (1985)

variety ⋆ A systematically distinct way of using a language (say English), determined either by the social–structural position of speakers, or by specific and recurring demands of typical **contexts of situation**. ⋆ In this sense, disc-jockey talk, legal language, truckers' slang, Tynesiders' speech, **creole**, *patois*, and West Country **dialect** all count as *varieties* of English.

It is an important concept for questioning the notion of **language** as a stable, uniform and homogeneous entity. As a concept it provides a perspective from which all language becomes internally differentiated, diverse and heterogeneous through time and social space. It still, however, implies clear-cut boundaries between one variety and another, and in this respect the term takes on some of the difficulties of the notion of 'language' itself. For, ultimately, the boundaries dividing one variety from another defy description in any methodology. What we tend to find is continuous and subtle variation in space (both regional and social), and over time. Current work, therefore, tends to proceed by isolating a *variable feature* or *variant* – such as a vowel, consonant, pause filler, or **discourse** marker – and studies how this variant changes from group to group and from context to context.

MM

See **accent, anti-language, creole, dialect, diglossia, pidgin, standard language**
Further reading Downes (1985); Montgomery (1986)

violence ⋆ The behavioural component of aggression that involves intense and directed action towards an object or person. ⋆ As Tutt (ed.) (1976) emphasizes, violence may be legitimate or illegitimate, with some illegitimate actions of yesterday becoming legitimate today and vice versa. The display of violence can be varied indeed, ranging from obvious physical assault through to verbal argument and even silence or withdrawal. The direction of violence can have similar disparity (see **displacement**). A real 'frustrator' may be directly confronted or a more vulnerable target be selected should the frustrator be too powerful.

Imitation and social learning theory have received particular attention from communication theorists interested in the effects of violent **media** programmes on **audiences**. Although **experimental** studies conducted by Bandura and others have demonstrated that children do behave more violently after viewing a video scene that portrays violence, survey studies reviewed by Hall *et al.* (1978) have concluded that the situation is far more complex. Aggressive individuals may have more of a tendency to view violence, some people may be more susceptible to imitation/impression than others, or other causal factors that are unaccounted for may be confused for media **effects**. And as Gunter (1980) reminds us, media portray altruistic and friendly actions between people which may then interact with and temper any imitation of violent action.

The concept of violence has also been researched for illustrations of **agenda setting**, media orchestration, **moral panic**, and political debate. It has proved to be a popular forum – and a sensational one – for the law and order **frame**. Thus 'violence' becomes the *escalation* of violence leading to a breakdown of control within society leading to demands for increasing resources for police. The underlying themes of fear and chaos have proved to be convenient and popular distractors in political contexts. For example, inner-city riots in London may be described as 'anarchic' and a 'threat to civilization' – which then leads to media debate about more effective policing, equipment and training. Alternative discussions about the *causes* of such violence then take second place, along with strategies which aim to increase the quality of life for inner-city social groups caught in a poverty trap.

DS

See **displacement, prejudice**
Further reading DeFleur and Ball–Rokeach (1975); Corner and Hawthorn (1989); Howitt and Cumberbatch (1975); Fiske (1987); Gunter (1980)

voyeur ★ A person or role who has a privileged view from a hidden or secret location. ★ Voyeurism was originally associated with someone who watches the sexual activities of other people, but without their permission – this is where the concept of a Peeping Tom becomes relevant. More recently the position of voyeur has been argued for **media audiences**, especially those who watch actors on the cinema and television screens (as opposed to listening to radio or reading print: the sight of people's bodies is essential). The position of the spectator can be usefully contrasted with the voyeur in social contexts; the former refers to the open presence of onlookers who see action that is meant to be public, whilst the voyeur gains access to an essentially private world. Such access usually results in dangerous knowledge which if publicized could lead to the downfall of central characters – the most frequent example involving a secret sexual affair between unfaithful partners. The reader should note, however, that other areas fall neatly within the audience's voyeuristic presence – with the spy scene, for example, where the position of voyeur is actually included within the **narrative** structure (the Peeping Tom may be cast as either the **hero** or the villain), and the viewer spies on the spy!

Psychoanalytical interpreters of voyeurism are fascinated by the possibility of recreating an early traumatic scene wherein the infant jealously witnesses sexual intercourse between parents. It may be more meaningful for us to consider Jackson's (1982) reminder about the sexual world of adults as lying beyond locked doors, which inevitably produces deep-seated curiosity about other people's potency and sexuality. Whatever the reasons for the 'appeal' of scenes which so involve the onlooker, at least two implications emerge from voyeuristic gaze: a position of guilt (because the scene is private and you should not be there), and/or a position of **power** (the camera is magical in that it defies the laws of nature and reveals knowledge which could damage central characters if revealed). It is interesting to note that whenever voyeurs are actually included as central characters in scenes, then they are portrayed as extremes – for example as a guilty fool (Polonius in *Hamlet*) or as a superhuman (James Bond).

Voyeurism ultimately implies omnipotence because of the all-seeing property of the camera. Although we rarely think about it whilst watching media productions, the lens is going through walls and windows and homing in on people without fear of being detected (when it is, and the actors are actually surprised by the camera, then it is often a matter for central concern – see Michael Powell's *Peeping Tom*, or for laughter – see Mel Brooks's *High Anxiety!*). Take Dervin's (1985) analysis of Hitchcock's *Psycho*: the camera records a beautiful woman stealing money and having an affair, but to begin with we peep through a window before somehow getting into the bedroom. It does not spoil the credibility of the plot or our concentration on the scene, yet ultimately it gives us secret information about a feminine character who in the film's terms is morally suspect. Perhaps it is because of our past conditioning in media productions, but we now expect her to be punished – leading of course to the infamous shower scene. This awareness takes the concept of voyeur to yet another level, where the viewer has secret information not only about the past, but also about the future. To know, or at least to suspect, what will happen to people is of course a powerful position to be in – and the masterful directors will provide both a feeling of knowing and a twist in the tail to avoid complacency. Through this style of voyeuristic exploration the viewer enjoys guessing but is kept guessing – the secret of mystery, enigma and narrative.

DS

See **audience, psychoanalytical theory, symbolic interactionism**
Further reading Dervin (1985)

worldview ★ A distinctive set of attitudes, beliefs and values that are held to characterize particular individuals or social groups. ★ The term often implies a relationship between the social location or situation of such **individuals** and **groups** and their consequent outlook or view of social reality. This is more systematically achieved via the term **ideology**.

TO

See **discourse, ideology**

REFERENCES

Abrams, M., Gerard, D. and Timms, N. (eds) (1985) *Values and Social Change in Britain*, London, Macmillan.

Adorno, T. W. (1991) *The Culture Industry: Selected Essays on Mass Culture*, edited by J. M. Bernstein, London, Routledge.

Adorno, T. W., Frenkel-Brunswick, E., Levinson, D. J. and Sanford, R. N. (1950) *The Authoritarian Personality*, New York, Harper & Row.

Allport, G. (1980) *The Nature of Prejudice*, Reading, MA, Addison-Wesley.

Allport, G. W. and Postman, L. (1948) *The Psychology of Rumour*, London, Holt.

Althusser, L. (1971) *Lenin and Philosophy and Other Essays*, Harmondsworth, Penguin.

Alvarado, M. and Buscombe, E. (1978) *Hazell: The Making of a TV Series*, London, BFI/Latimer.

Anderson, B. (1983) *Imagined Communities*, London, Verso.

Ang, I. (1991) *Desperately Seeking the Audience*, London and New York, Routledge.

Argyle, M. (1978) *The Psychology of Interpersonal Behaviour*, 2nd edn, Harmondsworth, Penguin.

—— (1987) *The Psychology of Interpersonal Behaviour*, 4th edn, Harmondsworth, Penguin.

—— (1988) *Bodily Communication*, London, Methuen.

Aries, P. (1962) *Centuries of Childhood*, London, Cape.

Aronson, E. (1980) *The Social Animal*, 3rd edn, Reading MA, Freeman.

—— (ed.) (1988) *Readings about the Social Animal*, 5th edn, New York, Freeman.

Aronson, E. and Mills, J. (1959) 'The effects of severity of initiation on liking for a group', *Journal of Abnormal Social Psychology*, 59, 177–81.

Atkinson, J. M. (1984) *Our Masters' Voices*, London, Methuen.

Atkinson, J. M. and Heritage, J. C. (eds) (1984) *Structures of Social Action: Studies in Conversation Analysis*, Cambridge, Cambridge University Press.

Atkinson, P. (1985) *Language, Structure and Reproduction*, London, Methuen.

—— (1990) *The Ethnographic Imagination*, London, Methuen.

Atkinson, R. C. and Shiffrin, R. M. (1971) 'The control of short term memory', *Scientific American*, 225, 82–90.

Austin, J. L. (1962) *How to do Things with Words*, Oxford, Oxford University Press.

Badcock, C. (1980) *Psychoanalysis of Culture*, Oxford, Basil Blackwell.

Baddeley, A. D. (1976) *The Psychology of Memory*, New York, Harper & Row.

Bandura, A. (1973) *Aggression: A Social Learning Analysis*, Englewood Cliffs, NJ, Prentice-Hall.

—— (1978) 'Introduction', in Rosenthal and Zimmerman (1978).

Banton, M. (1965) *Roles*, London, Tavistock.

Barber, P. J. and Legge, D. (1976) *Perception and Information*, London, Methuen.

Barbera-Stein, L. (1979) 'Access negotiations: comments on the sociology of sociologists' knowledge', paper presented at the 74th annual meeting of the American Sociological Association, Boston, August.

Barker, M. (1989) *Comics: Ideology, Power and the Critics*, Manchester, Manchester University Press.

Barthes, R. (1973) *Mythologies*, St Albans, Paladin.

—— (1977) *Image–Music–Text*, London, Fontana.

Bartlett, F. C. (1932) *Remembering*, Cambridge, Cambridge University Press.

Bateson, G., Jackson, D., Haley, J. and Weakland, J. (1956) 'Toward a theory of schizophrenia', *Behavioural Science*, 1, 251–64.

Beattie, J. (1966) *Other Cultures*, London, Cohen & West.

Becker, H. (1963) *Outsiders*, New York, Free Press.

Beechey, V. and Donald, J. (1985) *Subjectivity and Social Relations: A Reader*, Milton Keynes, Open University.

Belsey, C. (1980) *Critical Practice*, London, Methuen.

Bennett, T. (1977) 'The media and social theory: mass society theories and conceptions of class', Unit 3, OU: DE353 *Mass Communication and Society*, Milton Keynes, Open University.

—— (1979) *Formalism and Marxism*, London, Methuen.

Bennett, T., Boyd-Bowman, S., Mercer, C. and Woollacott, J. (eds) (1981a) *Popular Television and Film*, London, BFI/Open University.

Bennett, T., Martin, G., Mercer, C. and Woollacott, J. (eds) (1981b) *Culture, Ideology and Social Process*, London, Batsford.

Berger, A. A. (1992) *Popular Culture Genres*, London and Newbury Park, Sage.

Berger, B. and Berger, P. (1976) *Sociology: Biographical Approach*, Harmondsworth, Penguin.

Berger, P. (1973) *The Social Reality of Religion*, Harmondsworth, Penguin.

Berger, P. and Luckmann, T. (1971) *The Social Construction of Reality*, Harmondsworth, Penguin.

Berlo, D. K. (1960) *The Process of Communication: An Introduction to Theory and Practice*, London, Holt, Rinehart & Winston.

Berne, E. (1964) *Games People Play: The Psychology of Human Relationships*, Harmondsworth, Penguin.

Bernstein, B. (1971) *Class, Codes and Control*, St Albans, Paladin.

Bettelheim, B. and Janowitz, M. (1964) *Social Change and Prejudice, Including Dynamics of Prejudice*, New York, Free Press.

Beynon, J. (1985) *Initial Encounters in the Secondary School: Sussing, Typing and Coping*, London, Falmer.

Biddiss, M. (1977) *The Age of the Masses*, Harmondsworth, Penguin.

Billig, M. (1976) *Social Psychology and Intergroup Relations*, London, Academic Press.

—— (1982) *Ideology and Social Psychology*, Oxford, Basil Blackwell.

Bilton, T., Bonnett, K., Jones, P., Stanworth, M., Shearth, K. and Webster, A. (1981) *Introductory Sociology*, London, Macmillan.

Birdwhistle, R. L. (1970) *Kinesics and Context*, London, Allen Lane.

Blackman, D. (1974) *Operant Conditioning: An Experimental Analysis of Behaviour*, London, Methuen.

Blumer, H. (1969) *Symbolic Interactionism: Perspective and Method*, Englewood Cliffs, NJ, Prentice-Hall.

Bocock, R. (1974) *Ritual in Industrial Society*, London, Allen & Unwin.

—— (1992) 'Consumption and lifestyles', Ch. 3. in R. Bocock and K. Thompson, (eds) *Social and Cultural Forms of Modernity*, Oxford, Polity/Open University Press.

Bogardus, E. S. (1928) *Immigration and Race Attitudes*, Lexington, Heath.

Bonner, F., Goodman, L., Allen, R., Janes, L. and King, K. (eds) (1992) *Imagining Women*, Cambridge, Polity/Open University Press.

Bourdieu, P. (1984) *Distinction: A Social Critique of the Judgement of Taste*, London, Routledge & Kegan Paul.

Bourdieu, P. and Passeron, J. C. (1977) *Reproduction: In Education, Society and Culture*, Beverly Hills, Sage.

Box, S. (1971, new edn 1981) *Deviance, Reality and Society*, London, Holt, Rinehart & Winston.

Boyd-Barrett, O. (1977) 'Media imperialism: towards an international framework for the analysis of media systems', Ch. 5. in Curran *et al.* (eds) (1977).

Brake, M. (1980) *The Sociology of Youth Culture and Youth Subcultures*, London, Routledge & Kegan Paul.

Brittan, A. (1973) *Meanings and Situations*, London, Routledge & Kegan Paul.

Brown, J. A. C. (1972) *Techniques of Persuasion*, Harmondsworth, Penguin.

Brown, R. (1965) *Social Psychology*, New York, Free Press.

—— (1986) *Social Psychology*, 2nd edn, London, Collier Macmillan.

Browne, K. (1992) *An Introduction to Sociology*, Cambridge, Polity.

Brunsdon, C. and Morley, D. (1978) *Everyday Television: 'Nationwide'*, London, British Film Institute.

Burns, T. (1977) *The BBC: Public Institution and Private World*, London, Macmillan.

—— (1992) *Erving Goffman*, London and New York, Routledge.

Burton, G. and Dimbleby, R. (1988) *Between Ourselves: An Introduction to Interpersonal Communication*, London, Edward Arnold.

Campbell, E. Q. (1975) *Socialization: Culture and Personality*, New York, Brown.

Carey, J. W. (1989) *Communication as Culture*, Boston, Unwin Hyman.

Cauthen, N. R. (1971) 'Stereotypes: a review of the literature 1926–68', *Journal of Social Psychology*, 84, 241–53.

Centre for Contemporary Cultural Studies (1982) *The Empire Strikes Back: Race and Racism in 70's Britain*, London, Hutchinson.

Cherry, C. (1957) *On Human Communication*, Cambridge, MA, MIT Press.

Chibnall, S. (1977) *Law and Order News*, London, Tavistock.

Chomsky, N. (1965) *Aspects of the Theory of Syntax*, Cambridge, MA, MIT Press.

—— (1968) *Language and Mind*, New York, Harcourt Brace Jovanovich.

Cicourel, A. (1964) *Method and Measurement in Sociology*, New York, Free Press.

Clarke, G. (1982) *Defending Ski-jumpers: A Critique of Theories of Youth Sub-Cultures*, Stencilled Paper 71, Centre for Contemporary Cultural Studies, Birmingham University.

Clarke, J. (1991) *New Times and Old Enemies*, London, Harper Collins.

Clarke, J., Hall, S., Jefferson, T. and Roberts, B. (1976) *Subcultures, Cultures and Class*, pt 1 of Hall and Jefferson (eds) (1976).

Cohen, P. (1968) *Modern Social Theory*, London, Heinemann.

Cohen, S. (ed.) (1971) *Images of Deviance*, Harmondsworth, Penguin.

—— (1972, new edn 1980) *Folk Devils and Moral Panics*, Oxford, Martin Robertson.

Cohen, S. and Young, J. (eds) (1973, new edn 1981) *The Manufacture of News: Deviance, Social Problems and the Media*, London, Constable.

Cormack, M. (1992) *Ideology*, London, Batsford.

Corner, J. (1991) 'Meaning, genre and context: the problematics of "public knowledge" in the new audience studies', Ch. 13 in J. Curran and M. Gurevitch (eds) *Mass Media and Society*, London, Edward Arnold.

Corner, J. and Hawthorn, J. (eds) (1989) *Communication Studies: an Introductory Reader*, London, Edward Arnold.

Cottle, T. (1978) *Black Testimony*, London, Wildwood House.

Coulthard, M. and Montgomery, M. (eds) (1981) *Studies in Discourse Analysis*, London, Routledge & Kegan Paul.

Coward, R. (1984) *Female Desire: Women's Sexuality Today*, London, Paladin.

Crookall, D. and Saunders, D. (eds) (1989) *Communication and Simulation: From two Fields to one Theme*, Clevedon, Multilingual Matters, London, Sage.

Cuff, E. C. and Payne, G. C. F. (eds) (1979) *Perspectives in Sociology*, London, Allen & Unwin.

Culler, J. (1976) *Saussure*, London, Fontana.

—— (1983) *Barthes*, London, Fontana.

Curran, J., Gurevitch, M. and Woollacott, J. (eds) (1977) *Mass Communication and Society*, London, Open University/Edward Arnold.

Curran, J. and Seaton, J. (1991) *Power without Responsibility*, 2nd edn, London, Routledge.

Curran, J., Smith, A. and Wingate, P. (eds) (1987) *Impacts and Influences: Essays on Media Power in the Twentieth Century*, London, Routledge.

Dahl, R. (1961) *Who Governs?*, New Haven, Yale University Press.

Dance, F. E. (1967) *Human Communication Theory*, New York, Holt, Rinehart & Winston.

Davey, A. (1983) *Learning to be Prejudiced: A Growing up in Multi-ethnic Britain*, London, Edward Arnold.

DeFleur, M. and Ball–Rokeach, S. (1975, 4th edn 1982) *Theories of Mass Communication*, New York, McKay.

DeFleur, M. and Dennis, E. (1981) *Understanding Mass Communication*, Boston, Houghton-Mifflin.

Denzin, N. K. (1992) *Symbolic Interactionism and Cultural Studies*, Oxford, Blackwell.

Dervin, D. (1985) *Through a Freudian Lens Deeply: A Psychoanalysis of Cinema*, Newbury Park, Analytical Press.

de Vaus, D. A. (1986) *Surveys in Social Research*, London, Allen & Unwin.

Dixon, N. F. (1971) *Subliminal Perception: The Nature of a Controversy*, New York, McGraw-Hill.

Dominick, J. and Rauch, G. (1972) 'The image of women in network TV commercials', *Journal of Broadcasting*, 16, 259–65.

Donald, J. (1982) 'Language, literacy and schooling', Unit 29, OU:U203, *Popular Culture*, Milton Keynes, Open University.

Donald, J. and Mercer, C. (1982) 'Reading and realism', Unit 15, OU:U203, *Popular Culture*, Milton Keynes. Open University.

Donald, J. and Rattansi, A. (eds) (1992) *'Race', Culture and Difference*, London, New York and New Delhi, Open University Press/Sage.

Donnelly, M. (1986) *Managing the Mind: A Study of Medical Psychology in Early Nineteenth-Century Britain*, London, Tavistock.

Dorfman, A. and Mattelart, A. (1975) *How to Read Donald Duck*, New York, International General.

Douglas, M. (ed.) (1973) *Rules and Meanings*, Harmondsworth, Penguin.

Douglas, M. (1987) *How Institutions Think*, London, Routledge & Kegan Paul.

Downes, B. (1985) *Language and Society*, Glasgow, Fontana.

Downes, D. and Rock, P. (1982) *Understanding Deviance*, Oxford, Clarendon Press.

Downing, J., Mohammadi, A. and Sreberny-Mohammadi, A. (eds) (1990) *Questioning the Media: A Critical Introduction*, Newbury Park and London, Sage.

Duck, S. (1986) *Human Relationships: An Introduction to Social Psychology*, Newbury Park and London, Sage

Durkheim, E. (1950) *Rules of Sociological Method*, New York, Free Press.

Dyer, G. (1982) *Advertising as Communication*, London, Methuen.

Dyer, R. (1979a) *Stars*, London, BFI.

—— (1979b) 'The role of stereotypes', in J. Cook and M. Lewington (eds) *Images of Alcoholism*, London, BFI.

—— (1987) *Heavenly Bodies: Film Stars and Society*, London, BFI.

Eco, U. (1965) 'Towards a semiotic enquiry into the television message', in Corner and Hawthorn (eds) (1980), pp. 131–50.

—— (1981) *The Role of the Reader*, London, Hutchinson.

Eisenstadt, S. N. (1956) *From Generation to Generation*, New York, Free Press.

Eiser, J. R. (1986) *Social Psychology: Attitudes, Cognition and Social Behaviour*, Cambridge, Cambridge University Press.

Elliott, P. (1972) *The Making of a Television Series: A Case Study in the Sociology of Culture*, London, Constable.

—— (1974) 'Uses and gratifications: a critique and a sociological alternative', Ch. 12 in Katz *et al.* (eds) (1974).

—— (1977) 'Media organisations and occupations: an overview', Ch. 6 in Curran *et al.* (eds) (1977).

—— (1980) 'Press performance as political ritual', in H. Christian (ed.) *The Sociology of Journalism and the Press*, Sociological Review Monographs, no. 29, Keele, University of Keele Press, pp. 141–79.

Ellis, J. (1982) *Visible Fictions*, London, Routledge & Kegan Paul; 2nd edn, 1992.

Enzensberger, H. M. (1970) 'Constituents of a theory of the media', in McQuail (ed.) (1972); see also H. M. Enzensberger (1974) *The Consciousness Industry*, New York, Seabury Press.

Epstein, E. (1978) *Language and Style*, London, Methuen.

Evans, R. R. (ed.) (1969) *Readings in Collective Behaviour*, Skokie, IL, Rand McNally.

Fawcett, R. (1980) *Cognitive Linguistics and Social Interaction*, Heidelberg, Julius Groos Verlag.

Featherstone, M. (1987) 'Lifestyle and consumer culture', *Theory, Culture & Society*, 4, 55–70.

—— M. (ed.) (1988) *Postmodernism*, London, Sage.

—— M. (ed.) (1990) *Global Culture: Nationalism, Globalisation and Modernity*, London, Sage.

Felski, R. (1989) *Beyond Feminist Aesthetics*, Harvard, Harvard University Press.

Ferguson, C. A. (1972) 'Diglossia', in P. P. Giglioli (ed.) *Language and Social Context*, Harmondsworth, Penguin.

Festinger, L. (1957) *A Theory of Cognitive Dissonance*, Stanford, Stanford University Press.

Festinger, L. and Carlsmith J. M. (1959) 'Cognitive consequences of forced compliance', *Journal of Abnormal Social Psychology*, 58, 203–10.

Festinger, L., Riecken, H. W. Jr and Schacter, S. (1956) *When Prophesy Fails*, Minneapolis, University of Minnesota Press.

Fink, A. and Kosecoff, J. (1985) *How to Conduct Surveys: A Step by Step Guide*, Beverly Hills, CA, Sage.

Fiske, J. (1982) *Introduction to Communication Studies*, London, Methuen.

—— (1987) *Television Culture*, London, Methuen.

—— (1989a) *Understanding Popular Culture*, London, Unwin Hyman.

—— (1989b) *Reading the Popular*, London, Unwin Hyman.

Fiske, J. and Hartley, J. (1978) *Reading Television*, London, Methuen.

Forgas, J. (1985) *Interpersonal Behaviour: The Psychology of Social Interaction*, Oxford, Pergamon

Foster, H. (ed.) (1985) *Postmodern Culture*, London, Pluto. (Published in North America as *The Anti-Aesthetic: Essays on Postmodern Culture*, Townsend, WA, Bay Press.)

Foucault, M. (1971) *Madness and Civilisation: A History of Insanity in the Age of Reason*, London, Tavistock.

Foulkes, A. P. (1983) *Literature and Propaganda*, London, Methuen.

Fountain, N. (1988) *Underground*, London, Comedia.

Freedman, J. L., Sears, D. O. and Carlsmith, J. (1981, 1982) *Social Psychology*, Englewood Cliffs, NJ, Prentice-Hall.

French, M. (1986) *Beyond Power: On Women, Men and Morals*, London, Abacus/Sphere.

Freud, S. (1904) *The Psychopathology of Everyday Life*, in the *Standard Edition of the Complete Psychological Works of Sigmund Freud*, vol. 6 (1966), London, Hogarth.

Gallop, J. (1982) *Feminism and Psychoanalysis: The Daughter's Seduction*, London, Macmillan.

Gamson, W. A. (1984) *What's News? – a Game Simulation of TV News*, San Francisco, Collier Macmillan.

Garnham, N. (1986) 'The media and the public sphere', in P. Golding, G. Murdock and P. Schlesinger (eds) *Communicating Politics*, Leicester, Leicester University Press.

Garnham, N. and Williams, R. (1980) 'Pierre Bourdieu and the sociology of culture; an introduction', *Media, Culture and Society*, 2:3, 209–23.

Gerbner, G. (1956) 'Toward a general model of communication', *Audio Visual Communication Review*, IV:3, 171–99.

Gerbner, G. and Gross, P. (1976) 'Living with television: the violence profile', *Journal of Communication*, 26:2, 173–99.

Gerbner, G., Gross, P. and Melody, P. (1973) *Communications Technology and Social Policy: Understanding the New 'Cultural Revolution'*, New York, Wiley.

Giddens, A. (1978) *Durkheim*, London, Fontana.

—— (1982) *Sociology: A Brief but Critical Introduction*, London, Macmillan.

—— (1991) *Modernity and Self Identity*, Oxford, Polity press.

Giddens, A. and Held, D. (eds) (1982) *Classes, Power and Conflict*, London, Macmillan.

Gilroy, P. (1987) *There ain't no Black in the Union Jack: The Cultural Politics of Race and Nation*, London, Hutchinson.

Gitlin, T. (1980) *The Whole World is Watching*, Berkeley, University of California Press.

Glasgow Media Group (1982) *Really Bad News*, London, Writers and Readers Publishing Co-operative.

Goffman, E. (1963) *Behaviour in Public Places*, New York, Free Press.

—— (1967) *Interaction Ritual*, Harmondsworth, Penguin.

—— (1968) *Asylums*, Harmondsworth, Pelican.

—— (1969) *Behaviour in Public Places: Notes on the Social Organization of Gatherings*, New York, Free Press.

—— (1971) *The Presentation of Self in Everyday Life*, Harmondsworth, Penguin.

—— (1974) *Frame Analysis*, Harmondsworth, Penguin.

Golding, P. (1974) *The Mass Media*, London, Longman.

Golding, P. and Middleton, S. (1982) *Images of Welfare*, Oxford, Martin Robertson.

Gordon, A. (1986) 'Thoughts out of season on counter culture', in D. Punter (ed.) *Introduction to Contemporary Cultural Studies*, London, Longman.

Gramsci, A. (1971) *Prison Notebooks*, London, Lawrence & Wishart.

Gray, A. (1987) 'Reading the audience', *Screen*, 28:3, 24–36.

Green, J. and Hicks, C. (1984) *Basic Cognitive Processes*, Milton Keynes, Open University Press.

Greene, J. (1975) *Thinking and Language*, London, Methuen.

Gregg, V. (1975) *Human Memory*, London, Methuen.

—— (1986) *An Introduction to Human Memory*, London, Routledge & Kegan Paul.

Gregory, M. and Carroll, S. (1978) *Language and Situation*, London, Routledge & Kegan Paul.

Gregory, R. L. (1977) *Eye and Brain: The Psychology of Seeing*, 3rd edn, London, Weidenfeld & Nicolson.

—— (1988) *Odd Perceptions*, London, Routledge.

Grice, H. P. (1975) 'Logic and conversation', in P. Cole and J. L. Morgan (eds) *Syntax and Semantics*, vol. 3, New York, Academic Press.

Grossberg, L., Nelson, C. and Treichler, P. (eds) (1992) *Cultural Studies*, London and New York, Routledge.

Guilford, J. P. (1959) 'Traits of creativity', in H. H. Anderson (ed.) *Creativity and its Cultivation*, New York, Harper & Row.

Gunter, B. (1980) 'The cathartic potential of television drama', *Bulletin of the British Psychological Society*, 33, 448–51.

—— (1985) *Dimensions of Television Violence*, London, Gower.

Gurevitch, M., Bennett, T., Curran, J. and Woollacott, J. (eds) (1982) *Culture, Society and the Media*, London, Methuen.

Hall, E. T. (1973) *The Silent Language*, Bishop's Stortford, Anchor.

Hall, G. (1983) *Behaviour, an Introduction to Psychology*, London, Academic Press.

Hall, S. (1977) 'Culture, the media and ideological effect', in Curran *et al.* (eds) (1977).

—— (1982) 'The rediscovery of ideology', in Gurevitch *et al.* (eds) (1982).

Hall, S., Critcher, C., Jefferson, T., Clarke, J. and Roberts, B. (1978) *Policing the Crisis: Mugging, the State and Law and Order*, London, Macmillan.

Hall, S., Hobson, D., Lowe, A. and Willis, P. (eds) (1980) *Culture, Media, Language*, London, Hutchinson.

Hall, S. and Jefferson, T. (eds) (1976) *Resistance Through Rituals*, London, Hutchinson.

Halliday, M. A. K. (1973) *Explorations in the Functions of Language*, London, Edward Arnold.

—— (1978) *Language as Social Semiotic*, London, Edward Arnold.

—— (1985) *Functional Grammar*, London, Edward Arnold.

Halliday, M. A. K. and Hasan, R. (1975) *Cohesion in English*, London, Longman.

Halloran, J. D. (ed.) (1970) *The Effects of Television*, St Albans, Panther.

—— (1977) 'Mass media effects: a sociological approach', Unit 7, OU:DE 353, *Mass Communication and Society*, Milton Keynes, Open University.

Hammersley, M. and Atkinson, P. (1983) *Ethnography: Principles in Practice*, London, Tavistock.

Harding, L. (1985) *Born a Number*, Bloomington, Indiana University Press.

Hardt, H. (1992) *Critical Communication Studies*, London and New York, Routledge

Hare, A. (1985) *Social Interaction as Drama: Applications from Conflict Resolution*, London and Newbury Park, Sage.

Harré, R. (1979) *Social Being: A Theory for Social Psychology*, Oxford, Blackwell.

Harris, M. (1977) *Cows, Pigs, Wars and Witches*, London, Fontana.

Harris, P. (1986) *Designing and Reporting Experiments*, Milton Keynes, Open University Press.

Hartley, J. (1982) *Understanding News*, London, Methuen.

—— (1992) *Tele-ology: Studies in Television*, London, Routledge.

Hartley, J. and Montgomery, M. (1985) 'Representations and relations:

343

ideology and power in TV and press news', in T. Van Dijk (ed.) (1985) *Discourse and Communication*, Berlin and New York, Walter de Gruyter.

Hartmann, P. and Husband, C. (1974) *Racism and the Mass Media*, London, Davis-Poynter.

Harvey, D. (1989) *The Condition of Postmodernity*, Oxford, Blackwell.

Hawkes, T. (1977) *Structuralism and Semiotics*, London, Methuen.

Hearn, J. (1987) *The Gender of Oppression: Men, Masculinity and the Critique of Marxism*, Brighton, Wheatsheaf/Harvester.

Hebdige, D. (1979) *Subculture: the Meaning of Style*, London, Methuen.

—— (1988) *Hiding in the Light: On Images and Things*, London, Routledge.

Held, D. (1980) *Introduction to Critical Theory*, London, Hutchinson.

Henriques, J., Holloway, W., Urwin, C., Venn, C. and Walkerdine, V. (1984) *Changing the Subject: Psychology, Social Regulation and Subjectivity*, London, Methuen.

Herridge, P. (1983) 'Television, the "riots" and research', *Screen*, 24:1, Jan./Feb., 86–92.

Herzog, H. (1944) 'What do we really know about daytime serial listeners?, in P. F. Lazarsfeld and F. N. Stanton (eds) (1944) *Radio Research*, New York, Duell, Sloan & Pearce.

Hewstone, M., Fincham, F. D. and Jaspars, J. (eds) (1988) *An Introduction to Social Psychology: A European Perspective*, Oxford, Blackwell.

Hilgard, E. R., Atkinson, R. L. and Atkinson, R. C. (1979) *Introduction to Psychology*, 7th edn, New York, Harcourt Brace Jovanovich.

Hoggart, R. (1957) *The Uses of Literacy*, Harmondsworth, Penguin.

Hood, S. (1986) 'Broadcasting and the public interest: from consensus to crisis', in P. Golding, G. Murdock, and P. Schlesinger (eds) *Communicating Politics*, Leicester, Leicester University Press.

Howitt, D. (1982) *Mass Media and Social Problems*, Oxford, Pergamon.

Howitt, D. and Cumberbatch, G. (1975) *Mass Media Violence and Society*, London, Elek.

Hughes, A. and Trudgill, P. (1979) *English Accents and Dialects*, London, Edward Arnold.

Hunter, I. M. L. (1964) *Memory*, Harmondsworth, Pelican.

Husband, C. (ed.) (1987) *'Race' in Britain: Continuity and Change*, London, Hutchinson.

Hymes, D. (1971) *On Communicative Competence*, Philadelphia, University of Pennsylvania Press.

Jackson, S. (1982) *Childhood and Sexuality*, Oxford, Blackwell.

Jakobson, R. (1960) 'Concluding statement: linguistics and poetics', in T. Sebeok (ed.) *Style in Language*, Cambridge, MA, MIT Press.

Jaspers, J. M. F. (1978), Chs 10 and 11 in Tajfel and Fraser (eds) (1978).

344

Johnson, T. J. (1972) *Professions and Power*, London, Macmillan.
—— (1973) 'The professions', Ch. 9 in G. Hurd, (ed.) *Human Societies*, London, Routledge & Kegan Paul.
Jones, K. (1985) *Designing your own Simulations*, London, Methuen.
—— (1986) *Graded Simulations*, London, Lingual House.
Joyce, J. (1916) *A Portrait of the Artist as a Young Man*, Harmondsworth, Penguin.
Jung, C. (1969) *Four Archetypes*, London, Routledge & Kegan Paul.
Jung, J. (1971) *The Experimenter's Dilemma*, London, Harper & Row.
Katz, D. and Braly, K. W. (1933) 'Racial stereotypes in one hundred college students', *Journal of Abnormal and Social Psychology*, 28, 280–90.
Katz, E., Blumer, J. G. and Gurevitch, M. (eds) (1974) *The Uses of Mass Communication*, Beverly Hills, Sage.
Katz, E., Gurevitch, M. and Haas, E. (1973) 'On the uses of mass media for important things', *American Sociological Review*, 38, 164–81.
Katz, E. and Lazarsfeld, P. F. (1955) *Personal Influence*, New York, Free Press.
Keenan, E. (1974) 'Conversational competence in children', *Journal of Child Language*, 1:2, 163–83.
Klein, M. (1932) *The Psychoanalysis of Children*, London, Hogarth.
Kumar, K. (1977) 'Holding the middle ground: the BBC, the public and the professional broadcaster', in Curran, Gurevitch and Woollacott (eds) (1977).
Laclau, E. (1977) *Politics and Ideology in Marxist Theory*, London, New Left Books.
Laing, R. D. (1969) *Self and Others*, London, Tavistock.
Langer, J. (1981) 'Television's "Personality system" ', *Media, culture & Society*, 4, 351–65.
Larrain, J. (1979) *The Concept of Ideology*, London, Hutchinson.
Lasswell, H. D. (1948) 'The structure and function of communication in society', in L. Bryson (ed.) (1948) *The Communication of Ideas*, New York, Harper & Row, also in Schramm and Roberts (eds) (1971).
Lawrence, E. (1982) 'In the abundance of water the fool is thirsty: sociology and black "pathology" ', Ch. 3 in Centre for Contemporary Cultural Studies (1982).
Lawson, H. (1985) *Reflexivity: The Post-modern Predicament*, London, Hutchinson.
Lazarsfeld, P. F., Berelson, B. and Gaudet, H. (1944) *The People's Choice*, New York, Columbia University Press.
Lazarsfeld, P. F. and Merton, R.K. (1948) 'Mass communication, popular

taste and organised social action', in Schramm and Roberts (eds) (1971).

Leach, E. (1976) *Culture and Communication*, Cambridge, Cambridge University Press.

—— (1982) *Social Anthropology*, London, Fontana.

Leech, G. (1966) *A Linguistic Guide to English Poetry*, London, Longman.

Leech, G. N. (1983) *Principles of Pragmatics*, London, Longman.

Leiss, W., Kline, S. and Jhally, S. (1986) *Social Communication in Advertising: Persons, Products and Images of Well Being*, London, Methuen.

Leith, D. (1983) *A Social History of English*, London, Routledge.

Lévi-Strauss, C. (1967) *The Structural Study of Myth*, London, Routledge & Kegan Paul

Levinson, S. (1983) *Pragmatics*, Cambridge, Cambridge University Press.

Lewis, L. A. (ed.) (1992) *The Adoring Audience: Fan Culture and Popular Media*, London and New York, Routledge.

Leymore, V. L. (1975) *Hidden Myth: Structure and Symbolism in Advertising*, London, Heinemann.

Lindsay, P. H. and Norman, D. A. (1977) *Human Information Processing*, 2nd edn, New York, Harcourt Brace Jovanovich.

Linton, R. (1963) *The Study of Man*, New York, Appleton-Century-Crofts.

Lippmann, W. (originally published 1922, republished 1965) *Public Opinion*, New York, Free Press.

Lorenz, K. (1966) *On Aggression*, London, Methuen.

Lovell, T. (1981) *Pictures of Reality*, London, BFI.

Lukes, S. (1969) 'Alienation and anomie', in P. Laslett and W. G. Runciman (eds) *Philosophy, Politics and Society*, Oxford, Blackwell.

—— (1974) *Power: A Radical View*, London, Macmillan.

Lull, J. (1990) *Inside Family Viewing*, London, Routledge.

Lyons, J. (1977) *Semantics*, vol. 2, Cambridge, Cambridge University Press.

—— (1981) *Language, Meaning and Context*, Glasgow, Fontana.

McBurney, D. H. and Collings, V. (1977) *Introduction to Sensation/Perception*, Englewood Cliffs, NJ, Prentice-Hall.

MacCabe, C. and Stewart, O. (eds) (1986) *The BBC and Public Service Broadcasting*, Manchester, Manchester University Press.

McCroskey, J. C. and Wheeless, L. R. (1976) *Introduction to Human Communication*, Newton, Allyn & Bacon.

McGuigan, J. (1992) *Cultural Populism*, London, Routledge.

MacKay, D. M. (1972) 'Formal analysis of communicative process', in

Hinde, R. A. (ed.) (1972) *Non Verbal Communication*, Cambridge, Cambridge University Press.

McKeown, N. (1982) *Case Studies in Communication*, London, Methuen.

McLellan, D. (1975) *Marx*, London, Fontana.

McLeod, J. M., Kosicki, G. M. and Pan, Z. (1991) 'On understanding and misunderstanding media effects', Ch. 12 in J. Curran and M. Gurevitch, (eds.) *Mass Media and Society*, London, Edward Arnold.

McLuhan, M. (1962) *The Gutenberg Galaxy*, London, Routledge & Kegan Paul.

—— (1964) *Understanding Media*, London, Routledge & Kegan Paul (Abacus edn, 1973).

Macpherson, C. B. (1962) *The Political Theory of Possessive Individualism: Hobbes to Locke*, Oxford, Oxford University Press.

McQuail, D. (1969) *Towards a Sociology of Mass Communications*, London, Macmillan.

—— (ed.) (1972) *Sociology of Mass Communications*, Harmondsworth, Penguin.

—— (1975) *Communication*, London, Longman.

—— (1977) 'The influence and effects of mass media', Ch. 3 in Curran *et al.* (eds) (1977).

—— (1987) *Mass Communication Theory: An Introduction*, Beverly Hills, Sage.

McQuail, D., Blumler, J. G. and Brown, J. R. (1972) 'The television audience: a revised perspective', Ch. 7 in D. McQuail (ed.) (1972).

McQuail, D. and Siune, K. (eds) (1986) *New Media Policies*, London and New York, Sage.

McQuail, D. and Windahl, S. (1981) *Communication Models*, London, Longman.

McRobbie, A. (1980) 'Settling accounts with subcultures: a feminist critique', *Screen Education*, 34, spring, 24–43.

Mair, L. (1972) *Introduction to Social Anthropology*, Oxford, Oxford University Press.

Manstead, A. S. R. and McCulloch, C. (1981) 'Sex-role stereotyping in British television advertisements', *British Journal of Social Psychology*, 20, 171–80.

Marcuse, H. (1972) *An Essay on Liberation*, Harmondsworth, Penguin.

Marsh, P. *et al.* (1978) *Aggro: The Illusion of Violence*, London, Dent.

Marsh, P., Rosser, E. and Harré, R. (1978) *The Rules of Disorder*, London, Routledge & Kegan Paul.

Marshall, S. and Williams, N. (1986) *Exercises in Teaching Communication*, London, Kogan Page.

347

Martin, L. J. and Heibert, R. (1990) *Current Issues in International Communication*, London and New York, Longman.

Marx, K. (1971) *A Contribution to the Critique of Political Economy*, London, Lawrence & Wishart.

—— (1977) *Karl Marx: Selected Writings* (edited by David McLellan), Oxford, Oxford University Press.

Mattelart, A., Delcourt, X. and Mattelart, M. (1984) *International Image Markets*, London, Comedia.

May, A. and Rowan, K. (eds) (1983) *Inside Information: British Government and the Media*, London, Constable.

Mead, G. H. (1934) *Mind, Self, and Society from the Standpoint of a Social Behaviourist*, Chicago, University of Chicago Press.

Mehrabian, A. (1972) *Non Verbal Communication*, Hawthorne, NY, Aldine Atherton.

Melly, G. (1972) *Revolt into Style*, Harmondsworth, Penguin.

Mercer, C. (1982) 'Pleasure', Unit 17, OU:U203, *Popular Culture*, Milton Keynes, Open University.

Merrill, J. C. and Lowenstein, R. L. (1979) *Media, Messages and Men: New Perspectives in Communication*, London, Longman.

Merton, R. K. (1946) *Mass Persuasion*, New York, Free Press.

—— (1957) *Social Theory and Social Structure*, New York, Free Press.

Mestrovic, S. (1991) *The Coming Fin de Siècle*, London, Routledge.

Metz, C. (1974) *Film Language*, Oxford, Oxford University Press.

Middleton, R. and Muncie, J. (1981) 'Pop culture, pop music and post-war youth: countercultures', Unit 20, OU:U203, *Popular Culture*, Milton Keynes, Open University.

Milgram, S. (1974) *Obedience to Authority*, New York, Harper & Row.

Miller, G. A. (1956) 'The magical number seven, plus or minus two: some limits of our capacity for processing information', *Psychological Review*, 63, 81–97.

—— (1965) 'Some preliminaries in psycholinguistics', *American Psychologist*, 20, 15–20.

—— (1966) *Psychology: The Science of Mental Life*, Harmondsworth, Penguin.

—— (ed.) (1973) *Communication, Language and Meaning*, New York, Basic Books.

Miller, G. A., Galanter, E. and Pribham, K. H. (1960) *Plans and the Structure of Behaviour*, London, Holt, Rinehart & Winston.

Miller, S. (1984) *Experimental Design and Statistics*, London, Methuen.

Mills, J. (1990) *Women and Words*, London, Virago.

Mills, S. (1991) *Discourses of Difference*, London, Routledge.

Milroy, J. and Milroy, L. (1987) *Authority in Language*, London, Routledge.

Minority Press Group (1980) series 1: *Here is the other News*; series 2: *Where is the other News*, London, Comedia.

Mitchell, J. (1974) *Psychoanalysis and Feminism*, Harmondsworth, Penguin.

Monaco, J. (1977) *How to Read a Film*, Oxford, Oxford University Press.

Montgomery, M. (1986) *An Introduction to Language and Society*, London, Methuen.

Moores, S. (1992) 'Texts, readers and contexts of reading', in P. Scannell, P. Schlesinger and C. Sparks (eds) *Culture and Power*, London and Newbury Park, Sage.

Morley, D. (1980) *The 'Nationwide' Audience*, London, BFI.

—— (1981) 'Interpreting television', Unit 12, OU: U203, *Popular Culture*, Milton Keynes, Open University.

—— (1986) *Family Television: Cultural Power and Domestic Leisure*, London, Comedia.

—— (1989) 'Changing paradigms in audience studies', Ch. 1 in E. Seiter *et al.* (eds).

—— (1992) *Television, Audiences and Cultural Studies*, London, Routledge.

Morris, D. (1977) *Manwatching: A Field Guide to Human Behaviour*, London, Cape.

Morris, M. (1988) 'At Henry Parkes Motel', *Cultural Studies*, 2:1–47.

Mortensen, C. D. (ed.) (1979) *Basic Readings in Communication Theory*, 2nd edn, New York, Harper & Row.

Mulhausler, P. (1986) *Pidgin and Creole Linguistics*, Oxford, Blackwell.

Muncie, J. (1981) 'Pop culture, pop music and post-war youth: sub-cultures', Unit 19, OU:U203, *Popular Culture*, Milton Keynes, Open University.

Mungham, G. and Pearson, G. (eds) (1976) *Working Class Youth Cultures*, London, Routledge & Kegan Paul.

Murdock, G. (1977) 'Patterns of ownership; questions of control', Unit 10, OU:DE353, *Mass Communication and Society*, Milton Keynes, Open University.

—— (1980) 'Class, power and the press: problems of conceptualisation and evidence', in H. Christian (ed.) *The Sociology of Journalism and the Press*, Sociological Review Monograph, 29, University of Keele.

—— (1981) 'Political deviance: the press presentation of a militant mass demonstration', in Cohen and Young (eds) (1981) pp. 206–26.

—— (1989) 'Class stratification and cultural consumption: some motifs in the work of Pierre Bourdieu', in F. Coulter (ed.) (1989) *Freedom and Constraint: The Paradoxes of Leisure*, London, Comedia/Routledge.

349

Murdock, G. and Golding, P. (1977) 'Capitalism, communication and class relations', Ch. 1 in Curran *et al.* (eds) (1977).

Murdock, G. and McCron, R. (1976) 'Youth and class: the career of confusion', in Mungham and Pearson (eds) (1976).

Murdock, G. and McCron, R. (1979) 'The television and delinquency debate', *Screen Education*, 30, 51–69.

Murphy, J., John, M. and Brown, H. (1984) *Dialogues and Debates in Social Psychology*, New Jersey, Lawrence Erlbaum Associates.

Myers, G. E. and Myers, M. T. (1976) *The Dynamics of Human Communication: A Laboratory Approach*, New York, McGraw-Hill.

Myers, K. (1986) *Understains . . . the Sense and Seduction of Advertising*, London, Comedia.

Nan Lin (1973) *The Study of Human Communication*, Indianapolis, Bobbs-Merrill.

Nash, J. (1985) *Social Psychology, Society and Self*, St Paul, West.

Negrine, R. (1989) *Politics and the Mass Media in Britain*, London, Routledge.

Neisser, U. (1966) *Cognitive Psychology*, New York, Appleton–Century-Crofts.

—— (1976) *Cognition and Reality: Principles and Implications of Cognitive Psychology*, San Francisco, Freeman.

Newell, A. and Simon, H. A. (1972) *Human Problem Solving*, Englewood Cliffs, NJ, Prentice-Hall.

Noble, G. (1975) *Children in Front of the Small Screen*, London, Constable.

Norris, C. (1982) *Deconstruction: Theory and Practice*, London, Methuen.

Noyce, J. (1976) *Directory of British Alternative Periodicals 1965–74*, Brighton, Harvester.

Ogden, C. and Richards, I. (1923; 2nd edn, 1949) *The Meaning of Meaning*, London, Routledge & Kegan Paul.

Ong, Walter J. (1982) *Orality and Literacy*, London, Methuen.

Open University (1982) *Popular Culture*, OU:U203, Milton Keynes, Open University Press.

Packard, V. (1970) *The Hidden Persuaders*, Harmondsworth, Penguin.

Parkin, F. (1972) *Class Inequality and Political Order*, St Albans, Paladin.

Parsons, T. (1954) 'Age and sex in the social structure of the United States', in *Essays in Sociological Theory*, New York, Free Press, pp. 89–103.

Peirce, C. S. (1931–58) *Collected Papers* (8 vols), Cambridge, MA, Harvard University Press.

Perkins, T. E. (1979) 'Rethinking stereotypes', in M. Barrett, P. Corrigan, A. Kuhn and J. Wolff (1979) *Ideology and Cultural Production*, London, Croom Helm.

Phillips, J. L. Jr (1981) *Piaget's Theory: A Primer*, San Francisco, Freeman.

Philo, G. (1990) *Seeing & Believing: The Influence of Television*, London, Routledge.

Piaget, J. (1959) *The Language and Thought of the Child*, 3rd edn, London, Routledge & Kegan Paul.

—— (1973) *Memory and Intelligence*, London, Routledge & Kegan Paul.

Probyn, E. (1987) 'Bodies and anti-bodies: feminism and the post-modern', *Cultural Studies*, 1:3, 349–60.

Propp, V. (1968) *Morphology of the Folk Tale*, Austin, Texas University Press.

Rank, O. (1924) *The Trauma of Birth*, New York, Harper & Row.

Reppen, J. (ed.) (1985) *Beyond Freud: A Study of Modern Psychoanalytic Theorists*, New Jersey, Lawrence Erlbaum Associates.

Robbins, D. (1991) *The Work of Pierre Bourdieu*, Milton Keynes, Open University Press.

Robinson, M. (1984) *Groups*, New York, Wiley.

Rock, P. (1973) *Deviant Behaviour*, London, Hutchinson.

Rokeach, M. (1960) *The Open and Closed Mind*, New York, Basic Books.

Roloff, M. and Miller, G. (eds) (1980) *Persuasion: New Directions in Theory and Research*, Beverly Hills, Sage.

—— (1987) *International Processes: New Directions in Communication Research*, Beverly Hills, Sage.

Root, J. (1984) *Pictures of Women: Sexuality*, London, Pandora.

Rose, N. (1985) *The Psychological Complex: Psychology, Politics and Society in England 1869–1939*, London, Routledge & Kegan Paul.

Rosenbaum, M. (ed.) (1983) *Compliant Behaviour: Beyond Obedience and Authority*, New York, Human Sciences Press.

Rosenberg, M. and Turner, R. H. (1981) *Social Psychology: Sociological Perspectives*, New York, Basic Books.

Rosenthal, T. and Zimmerman, B. J. (1978) *Social Learning and Cognition*, London, Academic Press.

Roszak, T. (1971) *The Making of a Counterculture*, New York, Doubleday.

Roth, I. and Frisby, J. (1986) *Perception and Representation*, Milton Keynes, Open University Press.

Rowan, J. (1978) *The Structured Crowd*, London, Davis-Poynter.

Royal Commission on the Press (1977) *Periodicals and the Alternative Press*, series 6, London, HMSO.

Rubington, E. and Weinberg, M. S. (eds) (1978) *Deviance, the Interactionist Perspective*, London, Macmillan.

Rycroft, C. (1968) *A Critical Dictionary of Psychoanalysis*, Windsor, Nelson.

Sackville–Troike, M. (1982) *The Ethnography of Communication*, Oxford, Blackwell.

Sahlins, M. (1976) *Cultural and Practical Reason*, Chicago, Chicago University Press.

Said, E. (1978) *Orientalism*, London, Routledge & Kegan Paul.

Samuels, A. (1985) *Jung and the Post-Jungians*, London, Routledge & Kegan Paul.

Saunders, D. and Turner, D. (1987) 'Gambling and leisure: the case of racing', *Journal of Leisure Studies*, 6, 281–99.

Saussure, Ferdinand de (1974) *Course in General Linguistics* (first published 1916), London, Fontana.

Scannell, P. (1989) 'Public service broadcasting and modern public life', *Media, Culture & Society*, 11, 135–66.

—— (1990) 'Public service broadcasting: the history of a concept', in A. Goodwin and G. Whannel (eds) (1990) *Understanding Television*, London, Routledge.

Schellenberg, J. (1978) *Masters of Social Psychology: Freud, Mead, Lewin and Skinner*, Oxford; Oxford University Press.

Schlesinger, P. (1987) *Putting Reality Together*, London, Methuen.

—— (1991) *Media, State and Nation*, London and Newbury Park, Sage.

Schramm, W. and Roberts, D. F. (eds) (1971) *The Processes and Effects of Mass Communication*, Champaign, University of Illinois Press.

Schudson, M. (1991) 'The sociology of news production revisited', Ch. 7 in J. Curran and M. Gurevitch (eds) *Mass Media and Society*, London, Edward Arnold.

Scott, M. B. (1968) *The Racing Game*, Chicago, Aldine.

Searle, J. (1969) *Speech Acts*, Cambridge, Cambridge University Press.

Sedgwick, P. (1982) *Psychopolitics*, London, Pluto.

Seiter, E., Borchers, H., Kreutzner, E. and Warth, E. M. (eds) (1989) *Remote Control: Television Audiences and Cultural Power*, London, Routledge.

Seligman, M. (1975) *Helplessness: On Depression, Development and Death*, San Francisco, Freeman.

Sereno, K. K. and Mortensen, C. D. (1970) *Foundations of Communication Theory*, New York, Harper & Row.

Seymour-Ure, C. (1974) *The Political Impact of Mass Media*, London, Constable.

Shannon, C. and Weaver, W. (1949) *The Mathematical Theory of Communication*, Champaign, University of Illinois Press.

Shibutami, T. (1966) *Improvised News: A Sociological Study of Rumour*, Indianapolis, Bobbs-Merrill.

Shimanoff, S. B. (1980) *Communication Rules: Theory and Research*, Beverly Hills, Sage.

Shirts, G. (1971) *Starpower*, La Jolla, CA, Simile II.

Skinner, B. F. (1953) *Science and Human Behaviour*, New York, Free Press.

—— (1957) *Verbal Behaviour*, New York, Appleton-Century-Crofts.

—— (1974) *About Behaviourism*, New York, Knopf.

Smith, A. (1980) *The Geopolitics of Information*, London, Faber.

Smith, G. J. W., Spence, D. P. and Klein, G. S. (1959) 'Subliminal effects of verbal stimuli', *Journal of Abnormal Social Psychology*, 59, 167–76.

Spender, D. (1985) *Man Made Language*, London, Routledge & Kegan Paul.

Sreberny-Mohammadi, A. (1991) 'The global and the local in international communications', in J. Curran and M. Gurevitch (eds) *Mass Media and Society*, London, Edward Arnold.

Stafford-Clarke, D. (1967) *What Freud Really Said*, Harmondsworth, Penguin.

Stempel, G. H. and Westley, B. H. (eds) (1981) *Research Methods in Mass Communication*, Eaglewood Cliffs, NJ, Prentice-Hall.

Storr, A. (ed.) (1983) *Jung: Selected Works*, London, Fontana.

Sturrock, J. (ed.) (1979) *Structuralism and Since*, Oxford, Opus.

Swingewood, A. (1977) *The Myth of Mass Culture*, London, Macmillan.

Tajfel, H. (1963) 'Stereotypes', *Race*, 2, pp. 179–87.

—— (1981) *Human Groups and Social Categories,* Cambridge, Cambridge University Press.

Tajfel, H. and Fraser, C. (eds) (1978) *Introducing Social Psychology*, Harmondsworth, Penguin.

Taylor, L., Cohen, S. and Taylor, I. (eds) (1973) *Violence*, London, Sociopack.

Thompson, K. (1982) *Emile Durkheim*, London, Tavistock.

Thomson, G. (1977) *Capitalism and After*, London, China Policy Study Group.

Todd, L. (1984) *Modern Englishes: Pidgins and Creoles*, Oxford, Blackwell.

Tomlinson, A. (ed.) (1990) *Consumption, Identity and Style*, London, Comedia/Routledge.

Tomlinson, J. (1991) *Cultural Imperialism*, London, Pinter Publishers.

Tracey, M. (1977) *The Production of Political Television*, London, Routledge & Kegan Paul.

Tuchman, G. (1978) *Making the News: A Study in the Construction of Reality*, New York, Free Press.

Tudor, A. (1974) *Image and Influence: Studies in the Sociology of Film*, London, Allen & Unwin.

353

Tulving, E. (1972) 'Episodic semantic memory', in E. Tulving and W. Donaldson (eds) *Organisation of Memory*, London, Academic Press, pp. 381–403.

Tumber, H. (1982) *Television and the Riots*, London, BFI.

Tunstall, J. (1970) *Journalist at Work*, London, Constable.

—— (1977) *The Media are American*, London, Constable.

Turner, G. (1990) *British Cultural Studies*, Boston, Unwin Hyman.

Turner, V. W. (1974) *The Ritual Process*, Harmondsworth, Penguin.

Tutt, N. (ed.) (1976) *Violence*, London, HMSO.

UNESCO (1980) *Many Voices One World* (Final Report of the McBride Commission), London, Kogan Page; New York, Unipub; Paris, UNESCO.

Van den Berghe, P. L. (1967) *Race and Racism: A Comparative Perspective*, 2nd edn, New York, Wiley.

Van Dijk, T. A. (1991) *Racism and the Press*, London and New York, Routledge.

Van Gennep, A. (originally published 1909; translated 1960; 1977) *Rites de Passage*, London, Routledge & Kegan Paul.

van Ments, M. (1983) *The Effective Use of Role Play: A Handbook for Teachers and Trainers*, London, Kogan Page.

Vernon, P. E. (ed.) (1970) *Creativity*, Harmondsworth, Penguin.

Volosinov, V. (1973) *Marxism and the Philosophy of Language*, New York, Seminar Press.

Vygotsky, L. (1964) *Thought and Language*, Cambridge, MA, MIT Press.

Walker, S. (1975) *Learning and Reinforcement*, London, Methuen.

Warren, N. and Jahoda, M. (1976) *Attitudes*, 2nd edn, Harmondsworth, Penguin.

Weeks, J. (1989) *Sexuality*, London, Routledge

Wells, J. C. (1982) *Accents of English* vols 1–3, Cambridge, Cambridge University Press.

White, D. M. (1950) 'The Gatekeeper: a case study in the selection of news', *Journalism Quarterly*, 27, 383–90.

White, G. (1977) *Socialisation*, London, Longman.

White, G. and Mufti, R. (eds) (1979) *Understanding socialisation*, Understanding Social Science Series 1, Nafferton, Nafferton Books.

Whorf, B. L. (1940) 'Linguistics as an exact science', *Technological Review*, 43, reprinted in Whorf (1956).

—— (1956) *Language, Thought and Reality*, Cambridge, MA, MIT Press.

Wilkins, L. T. (1964) *Social Deviance*, London, Tavistock.

Williams, R. (1958) *Culture and Society*, Harmondsworth, Penguin.

—— (1974) *Television: Technology and Cultural Form*, London, Fontana.

—— (1976a) *Keywords*, London, Fontana.

—— (1976b) *Communications*, 3rd edn, Harmondsworth, Penguin.

—— (1977) *Marxism and Literature*, Oxford, Oxford University Press.

—— (1981) *Culture*, London, Fontana.

Willis, J. and Wollen, T. (eds) (1990) *The Neglected Audience*, London, BFI.

Willis, P. E. (1978) *Profane Culture*, London, Routledge & Kegan Paul.

Wilmot, W. W. (1975) *Dyadic Communication: A Transactional Perspective*, Reading, MA., Addison–Wesley.

Wolff, J. (1981) *The Social Production of Art*, London, Macmillan.

Wollen, P. (1972) *Signs and Meaning in the Cinema*, London, BFI.

Woollacott, J. (1982) 'Class, sex and the family in situation comedy', Unit 23, OU:U203, *Popular Culture*, Milton Keynes, Open University.

Worsley, P. (1957) *The Trumpet Shall Sound*, London, MacGibbon & Kee (Paladin, 1970).

—— (ed.) (1977) *Introducing Sociology*, Harmondsworth, Penguin.

—— (1982) *Marx and Marxism*, London, Tavistock.

Wright, C. R. (1975) *Mass Communications: A Sociological Approach*, New York, Random House.

Wrong, D. (1961) 'The oversocialised conception of man in modern society', *American Sociological Review*, 26, 184–93.

Young, J. (1971) *The Drugtakers*, St Albans, Paladin.

—— (1981) 'The myth of drugtakers in the mass media', in Cohen and Young (eds) (1981).

INDEX

The method of alphabetization used is word-by-word. Page numbers in **bold** give the location of items in the text as headwords.

agencies 134; social institutions 144 *see also* Reithian

balance *see* impartiality
bardic function 5, **25–6** *see also* accessing; binary opposition; hegemony; meaning systems; ritual condensation
base **26–7**, 142, 182, 244, 262 *see also* alienation
behaviourism **28–9**, 46, 52, 156, 214, 222
bias 28, **29–30**, 188, 209, 254 *see also* attitude
binary opposition 26, **30–3**, 44, 136, 151 *see also* choice; gender; ritual condensation
body language *see* non-verbal communication
bricolage **33**
broadcasting **33–4**, 70, 183, 201, 245, 298; autonomy 24; impartiality 145; language 3, 91 *see also* public service broadcasting; Reithian

campaign 10, **35–6** *see also* effects
case study **36**, 109
catharsis **37** *see also* escapism
censorship **37–8**, 79, 224, 290, 324
channel 20, **38–9**, 259, 266; communication 51, 126, 151, 226, 311; television/radio 82, 184, 251 *see also* noise
choice **39**, 167 *see also* distinctive feature(s); syntagm
class/social class **39–42** *see also* alienation; counterculture; cultural capital; elaborated and restricted codes; Frankfurt

school; popular; production/ consumption; race; socialization; stratification
closure 22, **42–3**, 273 *see also* aberrant decoding; absence; actuality; anchorage; genre; multi-accentuality; multi-discursive; naturalizing; negotiation
code **43–5** *see also* aesthetics; analogue; channel; communication theory; dialect; diglossia; foregrounding; frame; language; langue; medium; news values; non-verbal communication; norm; parole; preferred reading; rules; signification
cognition/cognitive **45–7**, 185, 280, 282, 300; attitude 18, 48, 136; and perception 79, 152 *see also* rumour
cognitive dissonance **47–8**
collocation **48–9**, 279
common sense 29, **49–50**, 57, 172, 173, 300
communication **50–1**, 82, 106, 138, 140, 283 *see also* communication theory
communication theory 38, **51–2**, 116, 203 *see also* channel; information processing; noise
commutation test 2, **52–3** *see also* absence
competence **53–4** *see also* syntax
compliance *see* conformity
concentration **54–5** *see also* alternative media
condensation **55–6** *see also* archetype; metaphor
conformity 19, **56–7**, 154, 270, 308

deviance **83–5**; anomie 14; control agency 242; stereotype 300; 'them and us' 31 *see also* anti-language; conformity; power

diachronic **85**, 302 *see also* creole; language

dialect **86–7**, 228 *see also* diglossia; variety

dialogic **87**, 189

diegesis **88–9**, 187

difference **89–91**, 167, 212, 232, 305; patriarchy 220; racism 256 *see also* choice

diglossia **91–2** *see also* variety

discourse **92–5** *see also* aberrant decoding; audience; bias; code; conversation analysis; cultural capital; culture; difference; experience; institutions; language; linguistic relativity; pragmatics; preferred reading; ritual condensation; semantics; speech act; structuralism; subject; synchronic, worldview

displacement **95–6** *see also* prejudice; psychoanalytical theory; violence

distinctive feature(s) **96–7**, 187, 198, 300, 306, 328

dramaturgy 19, **97–8** *see also* interpersonal communication; model; performance; simulation

dyad **98–9**, 213, 248, *see also* interaction

effects/effects tradition 35, **100–2**, 113, 325, 330 *see also* mass society; narcotization; opinion leaders; two-step flow model

elaborated and restricted codes **102–3** *see also* redundancy

elite 55, 61, **103–4**, 171, 230, 251;

control of media 224; ethnic groups 108; high culture 70, 71, 190; minority 182; news values 203 *see also* Reithian empiricism 46, 62, 81, **104**, 142, 153; criticism of 73; effects 101, language 163; symbolic interactionism 313 *see also* experiment

encoder *see* sender/receiver

encounter 19, **104–5**, 122, 223, 283, 294 *see also* interaction

entailment **105**, 279

entertainment **105–6**, 148, 173, 200, 229, 251

entropy 7, **106** *see also* communication theory

escapism **106–7**

ethnic **107–8**, 109, 190, 196, 233, 304; language 229, 295; prejudice 241

ethnography **109–10** *see also* dramaturgy

ex-nomination **110–11**, 140 *see also* absence

experience 18, 20, 25, **112–13**, 156, 317; language 152; socialization 292; unconscious 324 *see also* common sense; simulation

experiment 28, **113–14**, 148, 219, 266, 330; conditions 104; defence mechanism 79; and role theory 313; subliminal 311 *see also* simulation

facework **115–16** *see also* dyad; interaction; performance

false consciousness *see* ideology

fantasy *see* escapism

feedback **116–17**, 151, 204, 318 *see also* communication theory; noise

profession; race; rules; status; status conferral

pragmatics **236–8** *see also* deixis; implicature; sense

preferred reading 23, 156, **238–40**, 282, 284 *see also* aberrant decoding; absence; analogue; anchorage; audience; frame; orientation; text; uses and gratifications

prejudice 29, 154, 171, 224, **240–2**, 258 *see also* ethnic; violence

primary code *see* code

primary definers **242–3** *see also* amplification of deviance

primary group **243**; 323 *see also* other; value

production/consumption 19, 81, 117, 144, 148, **243–4**; globalization 130 *see also* primary group

profession/professionalism/ professionalization 4, 25, **244–6**, 264; *see also* minority; production/consumption

projection **246** *see also* hero/heroine; unconscious

propaganda 173, **246–8** *see also* censorship

proxemics 12, **248–9**

psychoanalytical theory 72, 96, 139, **249–50**, 304, 318; escapism 106; methodology 181; semiotics 282 *see also* censorship; condensation; model

public and private spheres **250–1**

public service broadcasting **251–2**, 264

questionnaire 109, **253–4**, 266

race 16, 18, 111, 196, **255–7**; racism 106, 108, 112, 203, 224, 302

reader *see* sender/receiver

realism 111, 181, 197, **257–9**, 277 *see also* actuality; convention

reality **259**, 262 *see also* culture

receiver *see* sender/receiver

recency *see* memory

redundancy 65, 102, **259–61** *see also* communication theory; entropy; information theory; noise

reference **261–2**, 277, 285 *see also* deixis; symbol

referent 51, 69, **262**, 277, 286 *see also* interpretant; object; symbol

reflection theory (mirror metaphor) 4, 142, **262–3**, 277

register **263–4** *see also* speech event; standard language

Reithian 184, **264–5** *see also* public service broadcasting

relative autonomy *see* autonomy

representation 5, 15, 26, 144, 256, **265–6**; art 277; bias 29; naturalism 198; realism 258; reality 262 *see also* alternative media; concentration

response 11, 137, 156, 247, **266**

restricted code *see* elaborated and restricted codes

rhetoric 25, 43, 120–1, 211, **266–7**, 287; authorship 21, 23; and diegesis 88; political 49, 258, 266

ritual 31, 156, 192, 223, **267–9**; subculture 72, 308 *see also* dramaturgy; encounter; symbol

ritual condensation **269–70**

role/roles 68, 84, 207, 244, **270–1**, **313** *see also* interpersonal communication; minority; simulation; status